gourmet *gifts*

Sugar Pumpkin Chutney

1 yd. + large scrap

1½ yds

dicent Valence pattern or 1 yd scrap

1⅔ yds x 54"

1 x 1½ yds + 2 panels 3 yds long

Antique Linen Sheet almost 4 yds x 3⅓ yds (more ornate)

gourmet *gifts*

100 delicious recipes for every occasion

to make yourself & wrap with style

dinah corley

PHOTOGRAPHS BY ALISON SHAW

The Harvard Common Press · Boston, Massachusetts

The Harvard Common Press
535 Albany Street
Boston, Massachusetts 02118
www.harvardcommonpress.com

Printed in China
Printed on acid-free paper

Library of Congress Cataloging-in-Publication Data
Corley, Dinah.
 Gourmet gifts : 100 delicious recipes for every occasion to make yourself
and wrap with style / Dinah Corley.
 p. cm.
 Includes index.
 ISBN 978-1-55832-435-0 (alk. paper)
1. Cooking. 2. Gifts. 3. Cookbooks. I. Title.
 TX652.C7474 2011
 641.5--dc23
                    2011012156

Special bulk-order discounts are available on this and other Harvard
Common Press books. Companies and organizations may purchase books
for premiums or resale, or may arrange a custom edition, by contacting
the Marketing Director at the address above.

PHOTOGRAPHY by Alison Shaw

10 9 8 7 6 5 4 3 2 1

for jackson

contents

introduction

Creativity and generosity are admirable qualities shared by most good cooks. We find real gratification in sharing what we cook with others, and creating food that delights the eye as well as the palate is an integral and enjoyable part of that process. Making gifts of the foods we cook is an expression of our generosity. Making these gifts beautiful provides an outlet for our creativity.

Food gifts in themselves are certainly nothing new. Our culture has a long history of giving food as a token of esteem, a gesture of concern, or an expression of affection. An apple for the teacher, homemade soup for an ailing friend, and chocolates for a sweetheart are just a few iconic examples.

I hope you will find that the gifts in this book are delicious and attractive and that they have been designed to meet the same high standards that make any gift truly successful.

The way a gift is wrapped immediately conveys our joy in giving and our affection for the recipient. The presentation should tangibly reflect the time and attention lavished on the contents. That means no flimsy paper plates covered with plastic wrap and no disposable aluminum pans. And because a gift by its very definition has no conditions and incurs no obligations, the beautiful wrapping must be part of the gift. After all, no one enjoys washing and returning dishes.

A successful gift also should provide instant gratification for the recipient. It should lack nothing that is necessary for its immediate enjoyment. Therefore, the gifts in this book are designed to share all the pleasures of the table but none of the workload. You will not find in these pages any jars of muffin mix or baskets of raw ingredients with recipes attached. Those are not gifts; they are chores. I certainly cannot imagine giving a friend yarn and needles instead of a handmade sweater, and by the same token I would not give them muffin mix instead of muffins.

I hope, too, that you will find that the gifts I've created here suit the way we live today. Nowadays, everyone is overburdened and overwhelmed by all their possessions. "Things" and their maintenance encroach upon an ever-diminishing amount of personal space and time. So a gift that can be consumed instead of kept, one that is intended to be savored rather than saved, is ideal. After all, the only way food can be enjoyed is by eating it. There is nothing left to store, or dust, or move.

Most of us feel the pinch of a purchase more sharply these days. The costliest and most luxurious gifts of homemade foods are still far less expensive than any comparably luxurious purchased gift. We save money when we make our own food gifts. Moreover, we control the environmental footprint of the gifts we make, which cannot be said of the gifts we buy. When we make our own food gifts there's less manufacturing and shipping, and fewer packaging materials involved.

I created this book to illuminate the possibilities for creating delicious food and presenting it with uncommon attention to detail. Each of the gifts in this book is complete and portable, attractive as well as delicious. The recipes and their wrappings are designed specifically for giving. I am confident that you will agree with me when I say they taste fabulous, look amazing, and travel well.

A GOURMET GIFTS PANTRY

Creating gifts in the kitchen is a way of sharing the pleasure we find in cooking and baking, and when we enjoy the process it shines through in the end results. A well-stocked pantry and the proper equipment make cooking easier, and therefore more enjoyable, simply because when you have the right ingredients and the proper tools things tend to go smoothly. Here is an annotated list of some key ingredients that are used frequently throughout the book. Most of these items can be found around town if you live in or near any large or medium-size city; for the few items that may be harder to find, there is a Resources section (page 290) at the back of the book that can help you out.

Salt: Sea salt, which many of these recipes use, has a cleaner and sharper taste than iodized table salt. It comes either in fine or coarse granules. Kosher salt is a viable substitution. Flaked sea salt, such as Maldon, has a powerfully salty taste. I love using it as a garnish for savory items and for salty-sweet treats like nuts and caramels.

Flour: Unbleached all-purpose flour has been used in the testing of all the recipes in the book. Cake flour is bleached and made from soft wheat; it is used alone or in conjunction with unbleached all-purpose flour. Semolina is a fine, light wheat flour that gives a crumbly, earthy texture to baked goods; white cornmeal is a satisfactory substitute.

Sugar: Confectioners' sugar or powdered sugar should be kept very dry and should be sifted or whisked before you use it in any recipe. Turbinado sugar or "raw" sugar has a slightly coarser grain than granulated sugar and a light brown color. Turbinado can be used as a prebaking garnish to give cookies and cakes a rustic glitter. I use it in pastry recipes when I want to achieve a coarser, more interesting texture. Sanding sugar or caster sugar is a superfine garnishing sugar that gives a cool and subtle sheen to baked goods. Coarse sugar is at the opposite end of the garnishing sugar spectrum. The large crystals give a very sparkly and crunchy finish to sweets of almost any type. Pearl sugar, with its large, opaque, white grains, is one of my favorite "secret ingredients" for baking, because it really changes the texture and taste as well as the appearance of cakes, sweet breads, and cookies but it can be difficult to find. Substitute crushed sugar cubes or order it online (see Resources, page 290).

Almond paste keeps forever, so try to keep a tube or two on hand.

Crème fraîche is richer and thicker than heavy cream, with a longer refrigerated shelf life. Crème fraîche can be used in place of heavy cream, but do not substitute heavy or sour cream for crème fraîche. You can make your own using the recipe on page 46, or you can buy it at well-stocked supermarkets.

Dried fruit is easy to keep on hand in airtight containers or in the freezer. Raisins both dark and golden, chopped dates, dried figs, apricots, and currants are the basics. Dried cherries, cranberries, blueberries, and banana chips are expensive but nice to have.

Extra-virgin olive oil is probably something you already have on hand, but the importance of quality cannot be overemphasized. The cost per ounce for fine olive oil can be prohibitive, however. There are several companies that sell and ship gallon cardboard dispenser boxes of excellent organic extra-virgin olive oil made in California for a fraction of the retail price per ounce .

Fresh herbs add more color and flavor than the dried variety, and they are readily available in most supermarkets. If you must substitute dried herbs for fresh ones, I suggest that you use about ⅔ of the quantity specified for fresh herbs and add a tablespoon or two of fresh parsley to intensify the color.

Nuts and seeds can be expensive at supermarkets. Buy these items where they are sold in bulk for better prices; they tend to be fresher that way, too. If you are purchasing at least one pound of a given nut or seed, the best prices are often found online. Nuts and seeds generally freeze very well.

Pure natural flavor extracts and oils are specified throughout the book. Artificial flavorings have higher water content, not to mention inferior taste, which can alter the recipe results.

Strained or Greek-style yogurt has a less acidic flavor and much thicker consistency than other commercial yogurts; it is available in the dairy section of most large supermarkets.

SOME NOTES ABOUT KITCHEN EQUIPMENT

Airtight containers are essential for storing and giving many of the items in this book, and for a very good reason. All your hard work may be for naught if the finished product is not stored and packaged properly. Air and moisture can very quickly do irrevocable damage to many perishable items.

Baking rack and **cooling rack** are interchangeable terms for any elevated rack. You can improvise a large cooling rack by positioning an oven rack over four heavy cans or inverted coffee mugs.

Cake boards, whether homemade or store-bought, are used by bakers because these sheets of white corrugated cardboard (page 9), cut to suitable shapes and sizes, give cakes and tarts a finished look and a base sturdy enough for gift-wrapping and delivery.

Candy thermometers are the only type of thermometer you can use when boiling sugar. Most models will register both a degree and a stage (hard ball, soft crack, etc.). Their price is usually less than that of one ruined batch of candy.

Cheesecloth is, of course, essential for making cheese (and crème fraîche). It is equally useful for lining mesh strainers and funnels before decanting syrups, brines, and other liquids, so they will be clearer and stay fresh longer.

Cupcake and muffin pans come in several sizes, starting with "mini" and ending with "king"-sized or "giant" muffin pans. You can certainly get by with a couple of standard cupcake pans.

Silicone baking cups also come in several sizes and shapes and can be used as substitutes for cupcake and muffin pans. Set them on a baking sheet before placing them in the oven.

Disposable paper and wooden bakeware is more expensive but also more attractive than disposable aluminum pans. Like its aluminum counterpart, this bakeware can save substantial preparation, cleanup, and wrapping time when you are doing a lot of baking. The paper and wooden versions make a huge difference in the final appearance of gifts, and I consider them well worth the price. Several different styles are available at upscale gourmet and kitchen boutiques, but the prices are better and the assortment larger online (see Resources, page 290).

Electric mixers, whether heavy-duty stand mixers or portable handheld models, are essential to some recipes. Each recipe will specify which mixer (if any) is needed. In most cases, determination, elbow grease, and a sturdy whisk or wooden spoon can be substituted for either model of mixer.

Food processors vary in their power and capacity, as do **blenders**. For some recipes a food processor is essential. Process ingredients in batches if your food processor is a smaller model. A good blender can often, but not always, be used in place of a processor.

Heatproof or heat-tempered containers are able to withstand the temperatures of boiling brines and syrups. Both canning jars and microwave-safe containers are heat-tempered. Regular glass and plastic can shatter or melt if the contents are extremely hot.

Instant-read thermometers are inexpensive and almost indispensable, especially for less-experienced cooks. They eliminate all the guesswork from tasks like proofing yeast or determining the doneness of breads.

Large pastry bags and plain tips are not essential to any recipe in the book. But if you feel comfortable using a pastry bag, you can pipe neat rows of evenly sized cookies and macaroons very quickly. You can use a pastry bag to fill small or narrow containers with cake batter and efficiently fill sandwich cookies.

Microplane graters work faster and better than any other type of grater.

Paper baking cups or cupcake liners are not just for cupcakes. Use them for baking cookies, pastries, and sweet breads and for molding candies to give them an entirely different look. Using baking cups will enable you to bake very consistently sized items for prettier gifts that require less additional packaging.

Parchment paper performs more tasks more consistently than silicone pan liners, in my opinion. But the two are often interchangeable.

Sheet pan and baking sheet are different terms for the same very shallow pan that measures approximately 11 × 17 inches. Cookie sheets have no sides, making it easy to transfer items to a baking rack to cool.

Swivel-bladed vegetable peelers do far more than peel vegetables. Use them to remove the zest from citrus, peel soft fruits for poaching, and make paper-thin slices of hard cheese and cold butter.

WRAPPING IT UP THE RIGHT WAY

Remarkable gifts of food are both delicious and beautiful. But even the most beautiful wrappings lose a good deal of their charm if they are impractical or ill suited for the contents. Well-wrapped food gifts arrive intact—not in pieces—because they are designed to travel halfway around the block or the globe. A winning presentation of food is tantalizing and totally self-contained, designed to make the gift hassle-free for the recipient.

containers

A container is not always essential to a gift of food. In fact, many of the food gifts in these pages do not call for a container. For the ones that do, the right container can make a gift seem more significant and add another layer to a present for someone special. An attractive container can actually save you a lot of time in wrapping and embellishment.

The trick is in finding just the right container, one that is appropriate, integral to the gift, and affordable. Remember, successful gifts have no strings attached, so the container must be something the recipient can keep. Believe me, no one enjoys washing and returning dishes.

I keep on hand a cache of containers that includes recycled or repurposed items like attractive gift boxes, cookie and biscuit tins, nicely shaped jars and bottles, and large aluminum cans. And I plead guilty to occasionally buying something only because I covet its container (and if you start doing this, you'll know you've become a true "gourmet gifter"). I try to keep an eye out for great containers at the right price wherever I happen to be shopping. Here are some good places to look for inexpensive and appropriate containers if you want to start a gift-container cache of your own:

Consignment and resale shops, flea markets, and tag sales are undoubtedly the most fun and frequently have the lowest prices on many items—often in brand-new condition—from kitchen-storage containers to ceramic bakeware. But the best finds are the vintage pottery, ceramic, china, and glass items. You can also occasionally come across great old picnic baskets, retro coolers, pretty hatboxes, and vintage tins.

Container stores are an obvious shopping spot, but head directly to the least obvious departments for the real bargains. Paper or plastic closet storage boxes for shoes, hats, and accessories are easily transformed into chic containers. Pick up ornament-storage boxes (good for cookies, cupcakes, and crackers) and wreath-storage boxes (perfect for cakes and pies) on post-holiday clearance aisles. Look for seasonal markdowns, too, on thermal totes, thermos bottles, and lunchboxes.

Hardware stores and large home-improvement centers are full of affordable items you can use for fun containers. Paint cans, metal bins and scoops, storage boxes, and canvas totes are just a few examples. The outdoor or gardening departments of home-improvement stores have plenty of affordable terra cotta or plastic flower pots and planters as well as inexpensive cachepots. Flat-bottomed hanging wire plant baskets, trowels, metal watering cans, and buckets all have potential.

Home-design or bed-and-bath outlet stores are a wonderful source for a wide variety of upscale yet affordable containers. There are usually lots of glass, pottery, wicker, and wire containers on the clearance aisles. Bed-and-bath outlets are my "go to" source for inexpensive quilted place mats and coordinating napkins, which I use for totes, cozies, basket liners, and fabric wraps.

The Internet is the most reliable and time-efficient shopping resource for very specific containers. If it exists, you will find it for sale out there in cyberspace. A little hunting and pecking is much better than a lot of driving and parking. The Web is an excellent source when you are making a large number of gifts that require identical containers, or when you are seeking unique, one-of-a-kind containers for luxury gifts. With perseverance and some comparison shopping, you will unearth serious bargains and maybe even avoid annoying shipping fees. Sign up for e-mail alerts from favorite sources, so you won't miss out on the best sales and special offers.

Large import stores and smaller ethnic markets are well worth exploring. You can find covered rice bowls, teapots, Bento boxes, sushi mats and trays, dabbas, tiffins, spice boxes, and tagines at unbeatable prices. You may also be able to stock up on seasonings and exotic ingredients while you're there.

Office-supply stores are a bargain resource for smaller containers. Peruse the organization and desk-accessory sections for small airtight tins and inexpensive wire bins or trays.

Party-supply stores and craft stores are the best resource for the largest selection of low-priced favor boxes and other smaller novelty containers, paper lanterns, goodie bags, and take-away boxes.

Don't overlook your own storage closets as a resource for potential containers. Start saving attractive bottles and jars, vases from the florist, cookie tins, nice gift boxes, and baskets for starters.

Supermarkets may be more than happy to give you large empty cans from the deli, crates from the produce department, or boxes and bags from the bakery. You can buy wax paper sandwich bags, small craft-paper lunch sacks, and inexpensive metal bakeware there as well.

wrapping materials and supplies

The most appropriate and appealing look for edible presents is one that is practical, clean, and simple. Food just doesn't look right when it is wrapped in overly fussy—or fuzzy—materials. The following list details the simple materials used in the wrapping projects in this book. They can all be found at your local craft store. Office-supply stores and supermarkets carry many of the same items. Feel free, too, to improvise with the materials you have on hand or to substitute materials that reflect your taste and style.

Adhesive-backed labels come in many shapes and sizes and have multiple uses. I use labels as cover-ups on the insides of boxes that have been punched through to hold ribbon or embellishments in place. They also hold twine or cord in place on the outsides of boxes or other packages. Uncut 8½ × 11-inch sheets of printer labels with adhesive backing can be embellished with downloaded images or text from online sources and then peeled, cut, or punched out into various shapes and sizes for inexpensive, customized gift labels.

Adhesive-backed hook-and-loop tape (a.k.a. Velcro) is a quick and easy solution for fastening and attaching embellishments to fabric, metal, wood, and paper containers.

Beads, buttons, and bows are just starters on an impossibly long list of potential embellishments. Use anything that appeals to you, but always opt for something simple. Never use sparkly or glittered embellishments, as the sparkles invariably commingle with the food. Tiny embellishments usually don't look as good as larger versions with a bolder scale and simpler silhouette. Consider introducing natural elements like nuts, acorns, and leaf skeletons into some of your wraps.

Card stock comes in very handy. Printer-weight card stock makes a lot of details easier, assuming you have a computer and printer. You can download text or images to create labels, tags, and recipes in beautiful fonts and colors, and you can print directly onto the card stock. Regular-weight card stock works for tags and labels with cut or punched embellishments, and for constructing small boxes or containers by hand.

Cellophane is indispensable for gift-wrapping food. An "over-wrap" of cellophane makes a gift more compact and protects it. Using cellophane expands your choice of containers, since no lid is needed. Cellophane immediately makes any gift look special and sophisticated without being fussy.

Corrugated cardboard can be used as a sturdy base for gift-wrapping many items in lieu of a container. You can recycle good (and clean) corrugated cardboard and cut it to size, or you can buy precut white squares, rectangles, and circles (called cake boards).

Craft paint is usually nontoxic and child-safe, but always read labels carefully before applying any paint or finish to items that will come in direct contact with food.

Craft paper, both brown and white, is inexpensive, easy to work with, and highly versatile. Write labels and gift messages directly on craft-paper–wrapped gifts instead of adding tags or cards. Or stamp, emboss, and embellish this ideal surface to your heart's content.

Decoupage medium dries quickly to a matte or high-gloss finish. It makes thin paper and fabric adhere to just about any surface and simultaneously gives the project a protective seal.

Double-face tape in various widths and strengths is an essential for neat, attractive wrapping, and it is used often in this book. "Red line tape" has become a generic term for very-heavy-duty double-face tapes.

Gift-wrapping tissue for lining containers and wrapping jars or bottles can also be stacked and machine-stitched into charming and inexpensive drawstring pouches for jars or odd-shaped gifts. While it may be harder to find (see Resources, page 290), waxed tissue is indispensable. Designed for food service applications, it is nonabsorbent and sturdier than gift-wrapping tissue.

Heat-fusible seam or hem tape is essential (if you don't own a sewing machine) to construct fabric bags or container linings.

Indelible waterproof markers are the best choice for labels and gift cards. If you want to do any stamping, choose inks that are indelible and waterproof as well.

Medium-weight pasteboard is suitable for constructing medium-sized boxes and similar containers.

Metal brads, plain or fancy, can be used instead of glue or staples for constructing small paper, pasteboard, or wire-mesh containers. They give any presentation a very streamlined and contemporary look when you use them as closures, embellishments, or both.

Paper baking cups or cupcake liners in all variations prove as useful in the craft room as they are in the kitchen. Neat rows of cookies, candy, and crackers stacked in baking cups or liners look so much nicer in tins or boxes than the usual jumbled mass, which can shift and crumble. Large baking cups can be used as containers for small gifts, as cover-ups for disposable tartlet pans, and, inverted, will dress up a jar lid.

Parchment, vellum, and glassine papers have that crisp, fresh look that is so appropriate for food, and they all work well for lining, wrapping, and labeling.

Ribbon, string, and cord choices are a matter of taste. Generally speaking, thin cotton twill tape, bias hem tape, waxed string, plain cotton twine, and thin, smooth hemp cording, along with raffia and thin paper ribbon, lend themselves well to craft-paper and fabric wraps. Wired ribbon in flat, smooth weaves and narrower widths is useful for some food wraps.

Sandpaper or sanding sponges in medium to very fine grit are necessary for any painting or decoupage project. Sanding between coats makes for a flawless finish.

Shipping tags can be attached to just about anything with just about anything, and they always look just right. You can make your own out of card stock or pasteboard, or you can pick them up very inexpensively at an office-supply store.

Spray adhesive or "dry mount" is the best adhesive for quickly applying paper or fabric to containers or heavy pasteboard.

Super-tacky craft glue is a particularly strong, thick, and sticky craft glue that's repositionable. It dries quickly and clear.

Tack cloths, pieces of slightly sticky material, are best for removing every speck of dust from projects between coats of paint or decoupage medium.

Thick cotton canvas and burlap are both very inexpensive, and both can be used for a lot of projects. I hoard inexpensive new and vintage cotton placemats, napkins, and tea towels. The placemats are for stitching into totes and "cozies" or for lining crates and boxes. The napkins are for breads and cakes bundled in a "hobo" style or for lining wire containers and baskets. The tea towels are wrapped around cakes, bottles, and breads.

Thin fabrics like chintz and gingham can be used to wrap boxes, bottles, and jars. These fabrics can also be glued over paper gift boxes and decoupaged to any surface. Sew gift bags, jar-lid covers, or bottle totes from this type of fabric. Stitch it over leak-proof plastic bags for snack pouches.

Wire, in several varieties, is an important material for crafting and packaging. Craft wire is very easy to bend, fold, curl, and crinkle into fantastic embellishments. It is a quick and attractive way to add tags or embellishments to gifts, and it's strong enough to attach spoons and spreaders to jars and trays. The prettiest floral wire is wrapped in shades of green or brown thread. Use it to create tendrils of vine, twigs, or nests for simple natural embellishments. Wire twist ties (or small coated elastic bands) are the best choice to tightly bundle and tie-off cellophane over-wraps.

CRAFT TOOLS

The following tools will make a wide variety of projects easier. There are so many fabulous gadgets and tools for crafting that you may find it impossible to stop collecting them once you get started. All of these items are available at craft stores. Things like fancy paper punches, decorative border cutters, beautiful stamps, and embossers are all great additions to this list, but they're not essential.

An awl or small ice pick will safely punch holes in thin wood, papier-mâché, and cardboard.

A bone folder makes crisp and precise folds and creases. Use a paper knife or credit card if you don't have a bone folder.

An assortment of long carpet or upholstery needles with large eyes will accommodate waxed string and twine. You can use these needles to sew boxes and other simple containers or to sew gift cards and labels to gift boxes and paper containers. Regular tapestry needles and embroidery floss are nice for sewing up simple bags and for attaching embellishments.

A cloth measuring tape will enable you to accurately measure the diameter of jars and oddly shaped items.

A computer can be a tremendously useful tool for reproducing and scaling images and templates, efficiently and attractively printing out large numbers of labels and gift tags, and countless other jobs, depending on your expertise. The Internet provides an inexhaustible free source for ideas, tutorials, patterns, and advice, and for downloadable images, labels, and tags. Online shopping can save you substantial amounts of money and time, too.

A craft squeegee eliminates air bubbles from decoupage medium or adhesive papers. Use a small metal or plastic straightedge or ruler as a substitute.

Glue guns come plain or fancy and are priced accordingly. A variable-heat gun works with both high-temp and low-temp glue sticks as well as with sealing-wax glue sticks.

A heavy-duty stapler that works in both the "lay-out" and upright positions is helpful when you are constructing simple containers. Use it for tightly covering corrugated cardboard with fabric or paper.

A long-reach hole punch is a fantastic invention. Use it for making neat holes in card-stock tags and labels and creating simple decorative borders on paper and card stock. With a hole punch, brads, and paste board, you can quickly and easily make a simple box. Small needle-nosed craft pliers give you a little extra pulling power when punching or sewing thick materials like papier-mâché and cardboard with twine or wire. Use them as well for stringing embellishments and coiling or twisting floral wire and crafting wire.

A handheld power craft drill with interchangeable bits is a great investment for any serious crafter. Manually operated craft drills are slower but less expensive. Either type will work for drilling nuts, small wood turnings, and other embellishments so they can be strung on gift ties or attached to gift containers.

An assortment of scissors that includes a good pair of heavy-duty craft scissors, a pair of small, pointed detail scissors, and some inexpensive pinking shears will be sufficient for every craft project in this book.

A sewing machine is essential for a few projects in this book, but in most cases you can substitute heat-fusible seam tape or good-quality fabric glue.

A small single-blade detail cutter, such as an X-Acto Knife, is the safest tool for cutting in places too small for scissors.

Metal or thick plastic straightedges are useful for accurately measuring flat surfaces as well as marking and cutting straight lines.

RUNNING (AROUND WITH) HOT AND COLD

Almost all of the recipes in this book are designed to be enjoyed at room temperature and will remain stable at room temperature for extended periods. Thermal tote bags and small insulated coolers will help keep a hot dish hot and a cold dish cold just in case. A few recipes in this book may need additional "cold support" if the time in transit is lengthy or the ambient temperature is exceptionally warm. Ice packs can come in very handy. You can purchase ice packs, or save money and make your own using the following "recipes": For solid ice packs, fill leak-proof plastic storage bags with water, lay them flat on a cookie sheet, and freeze them solid in the freezer. For flexible ice packs, use the same technique but fill them with a mixture of 6 parts water and 1 part 80 proof vodka instead of plain water. For large, solid ice packs, recycle plastic water bottles: Fill the empty bottles with water, allowing an inch or two for expansion as the water freezes, and place the bottles in the freezer.

GETTING THE MOST FROM THIS BOOK

I am confident that you will find in these pages doable recipes for fabulous food and unique ways to give it to others, regardless of your cooking experience, crafting skills, or budget. At the beginning of each project there is some basic guidance about how long each project takes, how easy or challenging it is to make, and how expensive it is likely to be. This "database" will also tell you if something freezes and ships well, and how long it will keep. Many projects are fast, easy, and inexpensive, but I have included a few challenging recipes and more time-consuming projects because I think they are very special as well as fun to make and give. The results make these projects well worth the effort involved. I encourage you to stretch a little and try some things that might seem very challenging. I think you will be pleasantly surprised by what you can do. Besides, that is part of the fun in both cooking and crafting—not to mention the only way to improve your skills. Above all, I hope this book will serve as a platform and departure point from which your own ideas, skills, and interpretations will soar.

If you are a well-seasoned cook, rethink and adapt your own favorite recipes into gifts using the packaging and crafting ideas you find here. If you are an avid baker or candy maker, or a wizard at canning and preserving, share those talents with others in packages worthy of your creations.

Conversely, you may be an experienced crafter in search of an appropriate recipe to complete a beautiful package you have made. Look for a recipe that suits your creation and your style and wrap it in your handiwork. Or apply the crafting techniques you love to augment or modify the projects I have designed. If you like, change the projects entirely to showcase your talent, perhaps by making a box in lieu of a bag, decoupaging a container instead of painting it, sewing instead of pasting, stamping instead of printing, or drawing instead of tracing. I urge you to take as much creative license as possible with everything you discover in this book. My goal is to make cooking and creating gifts as enjoyable and gratifying for you as it has always been for me.

GETTING STARTED

Begin by scanning the chapter titles and reading the short chapter introductions to find the type of gift you would like to create. The division of the projects into chapters is intended to match recipes and presentations to the time and money you have available and to the circumstances for giving. So whether you want to make one small hostess gift or a large number of identical gifts, stay on a budget or blow it sky high, create something special in a jiffy or lavish lots of time on a one-of-a-kind present, the chapters will help you pinpoint what you are searching for.

Once you have decided on a chapter that best describes the type of gift you want, look over the recipe names to find something that you think will be fun to make and welcomed by your recipient(s). As a second step, go to the "Wrapping It Up" heading, which follows the recipe proper. Read the brief overview of the wrapping style and look over the suggested supplies list and directions for making the wrap. Do remember that you should feel free to mix and match the recipes and the wraps in this book— just one of the ways you can put your individual stamp on the gifts you create.

You are ready to start, but before you begin a specific recipe in earnest, please take the time to read both the ingredient list and the directions carefully. This way you can assemble the ingredients and tools needed before you begin cooking, making the project easier and much more fun. This advice applies to the "Wrapping It Up" portion of the project as well.

Delicious and beautiful gifts of food are as rewarding to make as they are to receive. I hope you enjoy both the process and the wonderful results, and I wish you many years of happy gourmet gifting!

small tokens

Creating a successful gift is always a balancing act. There are occasions when a big gift might be inappropriate, but no gift at all would be even more so. Small tokens are thoughtful rather than grand gestures, gifts intended to charm instead of overwhelm the recipient.

For me, the most thoughtful and appreciated gifts are ones given for no particular reason, special day, or social obligation. The small tokens in this chapter are perfect for this kind of gift giving. They are appropriate for hostess gifts, too, and they are a wonderful way to acknowledge the people who make our lives easier and more pleasant on a regular basis. Several of the items in this chapter can double as thoughtful invitations, announcements, or place cards. You will find ideas and inspirations for creating little presents to delight old friends (and potential new friends). Each of the gifts is distinct not only in content and appearance, but in the time, money, and skill required to make them. But they all share a careful attention to detail, which makes each small token worthy of any occasion—or, better yet, of no occasion whatsoever. I like to think of small tokens as useful luxuries—things like distinctive cocktail treats, unusual garnishes, or intriguing condiments. These are the sorts of things that we would all like to have on hand but seldom do; small tokens make us feel special and pampered.

Small tokens should have a tasteful contrast between container and contents. Wrap simpler gifts more elaborately, but when the gift itself is more elaborate, keep the wrapping simple.

"Small" is the key word. These gifts are small enough to be given casually and somewhat discreetly, creating no fuss and requiring no thanks in return.

hazelnut brittle in a faux bundle of letters

Write a thank you note, invitation, or simple hello on this small, embellished box, fold it up, and put a very sophisticated sweet like this golden brittle of hazelnuts inside. This is an irresistible little gift. Do use caution as you make the brittle: Boiling sugar isn't just hot, it is positively molten. Use heavy oven mitts once you begin to heat the sugar and nuts.

¼ cup (½ stick) unsalted butter

1 cup chopped hazelnuts (you can substitute pecans or almonds)

1 cup superfine sugar

½ cup light corn syrup

½ teaspoon sea salt

1 teaspoon cognac

1 teaspoon baking soda

1. Using 3 tablespoons of the butter, heavily coat the bottom of a standard sheet pan (11 × 17 inches) and set it aside.

2. Combine the nuts, sugar, corn syrup, and salt in a microwave-safe bowl. Microwave the mixture on High for 3 minutes, pause the oven to stir the mixture well, and microwave on High for 3 minutes more. Pause the oven again, stir the mixture once more, and microwave on High for another minute.

3. Add the remaining 1 tablespoon butter to the brittle mixture without stirring and microwave on High for 2½ minutes more. Remove the bowl from the microwave and gently stir in the cognac and baking soda, taking care because the boiling mixture may foam and sputter when you add these ingredients. Quickly pour the hot brittle onto the buttered sheet pan. Working very quickly, pick up the sheet pan

overall prep time: 1¼ hours

active prep time: 15 minutes

easy

moderately expensive

do not freeze

ships well

do not double

shelf life: 1 week in an airtight container at room temperature

makes: 20 pieces

with oven mitts and tilt the pan back and forth and side to side to spread the molten brittle into as thin a layer as possible over the sheet pan before it cools and hardens.

4 Cool the pan on a rack for at least 1 hour. Break the brittle by hand into generous bite-sized pieces. Store in an airtight container until the pillow box wrapping is completed and you are ready to assemble the gift.

wrapping it up

Images of beautiful vintage letters, postcards, and other antique paper ephemera can be downloaded to your computer or printer from several free sources (see Resources, page 290). Use printer-weight card stock when reproducing the images. You can also clip images from magazines or old books and dry-mount them onto card stock to achieve a similar effect. The embellished card stock can be mounted on a commercially produced cardboard pillow box (or you can make your own using a purchased box as a template).

suggested supplies

dry-mount spray adhesive

lightweight cardstock with printed or dry-mounted images of antique letters, postcards, or other ephemera

1 cardboard pillow box (purchased or homemade), folded size approximately 5 x 9 inches

waxed tissue paper

thin ribbon or twill tape

sealing wax or hot glue gun sealing wax, with stamp

how to put it in a letter

Use the dry-mount adhesive to attach the embellished card stock to the outside of the pillow box before folding it into shape. Small scissors or a craft knife can be used to trim around all the outside edges of the pillow box so the attached images are the exact same size as the pillow box. To make sure the images are well attached with no gaps, wrinkles, or bubbles, place the embellished box under a stack of heavy books for a few hours.

Wrap the brittle in waxed tissue and place it in the box. Wind the ribbon or twill tape around the box and knot it tightly. Apply a small circle of real or glue-gun sealing wax to the ends of the ribbon and impress it with a stamp.

like an *avocado* only *butter*

Here is a whimsical presentation, with a whimsical name, of a seriously good compound butter that is delicious on everything from crackers and sandwiches to grilled chicken or baked salmon.

1 ripe Hass avocado

1 tablespoon fresh lemon juice

½ cup (1 stick) unsalted butter, cool but not cold

¼ teaspoon ground coriander

¼ teaspoon sea salt

pinch of ground white pepper

1 Carefully halve the avocado with a sharp knife, and remove and set aside the pit. Using a soup spoon, carefully remove all the pulp without tearing the peels. Set the peels aside with the reserved pit.

2 Place the avocado pulp and the lemon juice in the work bowl of a food processor. Pulse the processor on and off a few times to roughly chop the pulp. Process the chopped mixture until it is a smooth puree. Add the butter and the seasonings to the avocado puree, and process until the mixture is perfectly smooth and completely blended.

3 Fill each half of the peel with the soft avocado butter and level it off with a small icing spatula so the filling is flush with the edges of the peel. Return the pit to one of the filled avocado halves and press it firmly into the center of the avocado butter. Smooth out the surface around the pit with the spatula and refrigerate both filled halves, covered with plastic wrap, for 20 minutes.

recipe continues

overall prep time: 1½ hours

active prep time: 15 minutes

easy

inexpensive

freezes well without avocado shell

do not ship

can be doubled or tripled

shelf life: 4 days tightly wrapped in the freezer

makes: 1½ cups

4 Join the two halves of the avocado and press them firmly together. Scrape away the avocado butter that oozes out when the halves are firmly joined. Wipe the avocado with a clean, damp cloth, and wrap it tightly in plastic wrap. Freeze the avocado for at least 1 hour (and up to 2 hours), until it is very firm and you are ready to assemble and deliver the gift.

wrapping it up

"Crate" the avocado to resemble fresh-shipped premium produce.

suggested supplies

waxed green tissue paper (the type used by florists and produce markets) or unwaxed dark-green tissue paper

excelsior or shredded cellophane

1 small balsa wood box (available at craft stores and online)

food-safe indelible marking pen

1 small wooden spreader

1 square (10 inches) clear cellophane

stickers or adhesive tape

natural-colored raffia

1 plain shipping tag

how to crate an avocado

Remove the plastic wrap from the frozen avocado and wrap the avocado tightly in a small sheet of the green tissue. Surround it with some excelsior. Snugly pack the wrapped and cushioned avocado in the balsa "crate." Use the marking pen to write "Fresh Avocado Butter" on the wooden spreader and set it aside to dry completely before adding it to the crate. Wrap the box in cellophane, taping or stickering the edges to the bottom of the box. Tie the package with a raffia bow, stringing the raffia through the shipping-tag gift card.

simply marvelous
macaroons

These classic almond macaroons are wrapped and ready to go in about an hour, and they're made with ingredients you may very well have on hand. They are simple to prepare and marvelous to eat.

1½ cups almond paste, cut into small pieces, plus up to ¼ cup additional almond paste, as needed

1½ cups granulated sugar

3 egg whites, plus 1 additional egg white as needed

pinch of salt

1 teaspoon pure almond extract

½ teaspoon pure vanilla extract

1 Preheat the oven to 325°F. Place the almond-paste pieces and the sugar in the work bowl of a food processor. Process the mixture with a series of rapid pulses until it resembles brown sugar.

2 In a small bowl, whisk egg whites and salt, and add the mixture to the food processor. Pulse rapidly again until the mixture is completely smooth. Add the almond and vanilla extracts and pulse the machine two or three times. Check the consistency of the batter; it should drop lazily from a spoon. If the batter is too moist, add additional almond paste; if it is too dry, add another egg white. Process the batter briefly again before rechecking the consistency.

3 Line a large baking sheet with parchment paper. Fit a large pastry bag with a ½-inch plain tip and fill it with the macaroon batter. Pipe rounds of batter about 2 inches in diameter onto the prepared baking sheet, spacing the rounds 1 inch apart.

recipe continues

overall prep time: 45 to 50 minutes

active prep time: 10 to 20 minutes

easy

inexpensive

do not freeze

ships well in an airtight container

can be doubled

shelf life: 4 days in an airtight container

makes: 20 to 22

4 Bake the macaroons on the middle rack of the oven for 30 minutes. Turn off the oven, prop the door slightly ajar with a wooden spoon, and allow the macaroons to rest for 10 minutes. Place the baking sheet on a rack to cool completely before peeling the macaroons off the parchment. Store them in an airtight container until you are ready to assemble the gift.

wrapping it up

This is your chance to use some attractive containers—such as a glass vase, a cachepot, or a pretty tin—that you probably have on hand already. To keep the macaroons dry and to protect them from breaking, wrap them in pairs.

suggested supplies

20 to 22 paper cupcake liners, 2 for each pair of cookies

10 or 11 squares (7 inches each) clear cellophane, 1 for each pair of cookies

20 to 22 wire twist ties, 2 for each pair of cookies

thin ribbon

how to wrap pairs of macaroons

Place 2 macaroons back to back, and place them in a cupcake liner. Invert a second liner on top of the macaroons. Repeat with remaining macaroons. Twist each pair of cookies in a square of cellophane, like hard candy in a wrapper. Secure each twisted end of the wrapper with a wire twist tie. Cover the wire twist ties with thin ribbon, which can be knotted or finished with small bows. The wrapped macaroons can be packed into various types of containers, including simple cachepots, small woven or wire baskets, and cellophane bags.

salt-glazed *almonds*

As ubiquitous in Spanish *tabernas* as salted peanuts in American bars, salt-glazed almonds are probably taken for granted by the natives. The almonds appear polished with a shiny glaze that gives them an incomparable crackly bite and shine. They have a hint of bay leaf behind just the right amount of salt. A gift of salt-glazed almonds will definitely not be taken for granted!

If you cannot find whole blanched almonds in your supermarket, look for them in health-food stores. You can also blanch them yourself.

overall prep time: 4¼ hours

active prep time: 15 minutes

easy

moderately expensive

do not freeze

ships well

can be doubled or tripled

shelf life: 6 months in an airtight container

makes: 12 ounces

---

1 large egg white, lightly beaten

½ teaspoon water

12 ounces whole blanched almonds

2 teaspoons sea salt flakes, such as Maldon Sea Salt

6 or 7 fresh bay leaves

---

1 Preheat the oven to 150°F. Line a sheet pan with parchment paper.

2 Pour the egg white through a fine-mesh strainer into a small bowl, using the back of a wooden spoon to press it through the strainer. Beat the strained egg white with ½ teaspoon water until it is frothy and loose. Pour the egg white into a large shallow baking dish and add the almonds. Using your hands, toss the almonds until they are completely and evenly coated and there is no egg white left in the bottom of the baking dish. Transfer the almonds to the lined pan and spread them out in a single layer. Crumble the sea salt flakes over the almonds, tossing the almonds once or twice by hand to distribute the salt evenly. Strew the bay leaves among the almonds.

recipe continues

3 Put the sheet pan on the middle rack of the oven. Prop the door of the oven open with the handle of a wooden spoon. Dry the almonds in the oven for 4 hours, or until they are hard, shiny, and completely dry.

4 Set the pan on a baking rack until the almonds are completely cool before packing them, along with the bay leaves, in an airtight container until you are ready to assemble the gift.

wrapping it up

A lidded papier-mâché box is a great gift container for dried nuts because it is attractive enough for serving the nuts and sturdy enough for storing them. A length of sewing-notions elastic attached to the box will hold the lid tightly in place while still allowing it to open easily.

suggested supplies

1 small lidded cardboard gift box or papier-mâché box

1 length (4 to 6 inches) black or white elastic

stapler

super-tacky craft glue or low-temp glue stick and glue gun

1 adhesive-backed sticker

1 small flat embellishment, such as a grosgrain bow, a large button, or a flat bead

parchment paper or tissue paper

how to make a box with an elastic strap

Find and mark the center of the box lid. Cut two small slots or punch two holes no more than 2 inches apart on either side of the center mark (and equidistant from the center mark) that are slightly smaller than the width of the elastic. Tightly stretch the elastic around the covered box, mark the end, and cut the elastic on the mark. (You want to use enough elastic to hold the lid snugly in place but leave sufficient "give" so the box can be opened.) Thread the elastic from the top of the box lid down through the first slot to the underside of the lid and up through the second hole. Slide the elastic through the slots so that the ends meet at the center of the box bottom. Staple the ends together and glue them to the bottom of the box. Glue a small card or press a small adhesive label over the stapled raw edges of the elastic to cover them. Use the glue to affix a button, bow, or other embellishment over the slots or holes in the box lid. Slip a gift card under the elastic and line the box with parchment or tissue paper before adding the dried almonds and the bay leaves to the box.

seville *orange slices* in caramelized sugar

These slices of orange look and even feel like amber-tinted rounds of stained glass. Amateur baristas and bartenders will love adding these stunning slices to their garnishing repertoire. A caramelized orange slice is a pretty way to sweeten espressos and lattes, and crushed slices can be used in classic cocktails like Whiskey Sours, Old Fashioneds, and Manhattans. A whole slice floated in a coupe of Champagne makes a beautiful, orange-infused version of the Champagne Cocktail.

This recipe is best made on a very dry day; on a humid day, the sugar may not harden completely and instead will be sticky. You will need some version of a mandoline slicer to cut the orange slices thin enough.

....

2 small Seville oranges	1 cup granulated sugar

....

1 Preheat the oven to 500°F. Using a mandoline or other handheld mechanical slicer, cut the oranges crosswise into even slices no more than ⅛ inch thick.

2 Cover an 11 × 17-inch sheet pan with heavy-duty foil. Place a sheet of parchment paper over the foil and spread half of the sugar evenly over the entire surface. Carefully arrange the orange slices on top of the sugar, allowing ½ inch of space between the slices. Sprinkle the remaining sugar over the slices, trying to coat them evenly and completely.

recipe continues

overall prep time: 2 hours

active prep time: 30 minutes

easy

inexpensive

do not freeze

ships well

can be doubled

shelf life: 3 or 4 weeks in an airtight container stored in a cool, dry place

makes: about 24, enough to fill two 4-inch round tins

3 Place the sheet pan on the middle rack of the oven. Cook, watching the pan constantly and rotating it every 2 or 3 minutes to make sure the sugar browns evenly. It will take 6 to 8 minutes for the sugar to melt and turn a deep amber color. Carefully remove the baking sheet from the oven and cool it on a rack for 1 hour. (It is almost inevitable that some orange slices will brown more than others, but they are all pretty.)

4 Gently pull the orange slices off the parchment and store them in an airtight container until you are ready to assemble the gift.

wrapping it up

The orange slices must be kept perfectly dry, or they will get very sticky. Four-inch round tins with screw tops are ideal airtight containers. Some versions of these little tins even have "windows" in the center of the lid that show off the pretty slices inside. Tins of this type are available at kitchen shops, home stores, and office-supply stores. Line the containers with parchment paper or waxed tissue paper and stack the orange slices inside. Tie the tin up with a tiny silken ribbon and attach a pretty gift tag with serving suggestions.

iced *fennel* wrapped in *prosciutto*

This recipe epitomizes the elegance of simplicity. It can be served as a first course, a side dish, or an hors d'oeuvre. I serve and give this often.

overall prep time: about 3 hours

active prep time: 20 minutes

easy

moderately expensive

do not freeze or ship

can be doubled or tripled

shelf life: holds well for 1 to 2 hours

serves: 4 as a first course, 6 for hors d'oeuvres

1 rimmed plastic or metal plant saucer, 8 or 9 inches in diameter and about 2 inches deep

1 large bulb fresh fennel (1 to 1¼ pounds)

6 ounces sliced prosciutto

1 large, flat piece (3 to 4 ounces) Parmigiano Reggiano or other good-quality Parmesan-type cheese

coarsely ground white pepper to taste

1 Fill the plant saucer halfway with water and place it in the freezer until the water is frozen solid.

2 Trim the green leafy tops from the fennel bulb and refrigerate them for garnishing the final dish. Slice off the bottom of the fennel bulb, peel away any tough or bruised outer stalks, and wash the bulb. Cut the fennel in half vertically and cut each half in thick vertical slices about 1½ inches wide. Cut each of these slices again vertically two or three times, so you have long, finger-like pieces of fennel. Cut each slice of prosciutto lengthwise into 3 strips and wind a strip of prosciutto around each finger of fennel. Arrange the wrapped fennel pieces on a tray or cookie sheet, cover them loosely with plastic wrap, and refrigerate until you are ready to assemble the gift.

3 When the water in the plant saucer has frozen solid, cover it with a circle of parchment paper and cover the parchment with the reserved fennel tops. Tightly arrange the wrapped fennel pieces in an overlapping spiral pattern over the leafy lined parchment. Use a cheese shaver or a swivel-bladed vegetable peeler to shave large thin pieces from the chunk of Parmesan cheese; tuck the cheese pieces between the fennel pieces and strew them liberally over the top. Grind a generous amount of coarse white pepper over everything. The gift must be assembled and delivered immediately.

wrapping it up

This beautiful dish should be accompanied by a small vial or cruet of extra-virgin olive oil. I repurpose the glass vials from spices and vanilla beans, but any container with a leak-proof stopper that will fit in the saucer will do.

suggested supplies

1 square (24 inches) clear cellophane

⅓ cup extra-virgin olive oil in a small vial or cruet

1 rectangle (20 × 40 inches) clear cellophane

1 wire twist tie

pale pink or rose-colored paper ribbon or twill tape

how to wrap an iced saucer

Center the iced fennel on the cellophane square and nestle the vial or cruet of olive oil among the fennel pieces. Tightly twist and crumple the rectangle of cellophane and wrap it tightly around the edge of the fennel saucer twice, pressing it tightly to the edge of the tray. Gather the square of cellophane very tightly up over the gift and twist the ends together very tightly. Secure the twist of cellophane with the wire twist tie and cover the twist tie with several wraps of ribbon or twill. Trim both the ribbon ends and the twisted top of the cellophane. The gift is ready to deliver; it will stay cold for 2 hours in a cool ambient temperature.

cool cucumber *vodka*

overall prep time: about 2 days

active prep time: 10 minutes

easy

moderately expensive

vodka never freezes solid but can be stored in the freezer almost indefinitely

do not ship

can be doubled or tripled

shelf life: 1 year in the freezer

makes: 1 fifth

Give someone the essential ingredient for the most astounding summer cocktails! Cucumber vodka has a beautiful color to go along with a fantastic flavor that reminds me of fresh borage flowers. This is so easy to make it would be a shame to start one more summer without it.

2 organic gherkins or small organic pickling cucumbers, scrubbed and sliced thickly crosswise

3 stalks lemon grass, gently crushed

1 fifth imported vodka

1 In a large ceramic or glass container, combine the sliced cucumbers and crushed lemon grass with the vodka and cover the container tightly with plastic wrap or a heavy plate. Put the covered container in a dark, cool, dry place for 2 days to infuse the vodka with the cucumber flavor.

2 Pour the vodka mixture into a large pitcher, straining it through a large strainer lined with several layers of cheesecloth. Cover the strainer and pitcher with a tea towel and allow the cucumbers to drain all their color and juices into the vodka, which should take about an hour.

3 Discard the cucumbers and lemon grass, and pour the vodka through a cheesecloth-lined funnel into either the original vodka bottle or a different one of similar size.

wrapping it up

If you want to use the original vodka bottle for decanting the cucumber vodka, be sure to buy a brand of vodka with a paper label. There is no earthly way (that I have found, anyway) to remove the type of label that's printed directly on glass bottles. A simple tendril of silk or paper leaves looped around the neck and cascading down the bottle front looks like summer.

suggested supplies

2 lengths (18 to 20 inches each) green floral wire

small paper or silk leaves

super-tacky craft glue or low-temp glue stick and glue gun

how to make a bottle neck tendril of leaves

Twist the wires together from end to end. Form a loop to go around the neck of the bottle, and bend and shape the remaining wire so it cascades down the bottle front. Dab the backs of the leaves with glue and attach them to the floral wire. You can gently untwist the bottom of the wire and wind each piece around a pencil or small dowel to form curly ends for the tendril.

butter button *cookies*

overall prep time: 3 hours

active prep time:
30 minutes

easy

inexpensive

both dough and cookies freeze well

ships well

can be doubled or tripled

shelf life: 1 week in an airtight container

makes: 4 to 5 dozen

Cuter than buttons and far better tasting, these fat little French butter cookies are rich and tender. The round button box is a charming and amusing container.

. . . .

1 cup (2 sticks) cold unsalted butter cut in small pieces

¼ cup light brown sugar

½ cup superfine sugar

2 cups unbleached all-purpose flour

¾ cup cake flour

½ teaspoon vanilla extract

. . . .

1 Place the butter and the two sugars in the work bowl of a food processor. Pulse the machine on and off for 30 to 40 seconds or until the butter and sugar are creamed. Add the all-purpose flour, ½ cup of the cake flour, and the vanilla. Process for 45 seconds with a rapid succession of short pulses. The mixture will be crumbly and moist, and it will not form a solid mass of dough.

2 Turn the mixture out onto an 11 × 17-inch sheet of parchment paper. Dust your hands with some of the remaining cake flour, then pat and shape the dough into a solid mass. Flatten the dough into a rectangle, cover the dough with another 11 × 17-inch sheet of parchment paper, and use a heavy rolling pin to roll the dough out evenly between the sheets of parchment, rolling it all the way to the edges of the paper. Slide the dough with the parchment sheets onto a large baking sheet and refrigerate it for at least 2 hours.

3 When you're ready to bake the cookies, preheat the oven to 300°F. Peel off the top sheet of parchment and set it aside. Dip a small round cookie cutter or a small glass into the remaining cake flour and cut round "buttons" in the dough 1 inch apart. Peel away the extra dough, flatten it on the reserved parchment, and refrigerate it.

4 Using the blunt end of a wooden skewer, pierce each cookie with four "thread holes." Bake the cookies on the middle rack of the oven for 12 minutes. Rotate the pan and bake for another 8 to 10 minutes, or until the cookies are slightly resistant to the touch and are a very pale golden color. Set the baking sheet on a rack to cool. Do not remove the cookies until they have cooled. Repeat steps 3 and 4 with the refrigerated scraps of dough, rerolling as needed. Store the cookies in an airtight container until you are ready to assemble the gift.

wrapping it up

A small round box with a few ingenious embellishments can look like a very big button.

suggested supplies

1 round pasteboard box or papier-mâché box with lid

black marking pen

waxed twine or embroidery floss

upholstery needle

card stock

super-tacky craft glue

parchment paper or tissue paper

1 gift card

how to box up the buttons

Imagine the box top is a big button. Trace 4 small circles onto the box top to represent the thread holes in a button. Fill in the tracings with the black marker. Thread the waxed twine or embroidery floss onto the upholstery needle. Starting on the underside of the box lid, "sew" the twine from hole to hole in a crisscross fashion several times. Finish with the threaded needle on top of the lid so you can use it to attach a gift card. Cut a circle of card stock that will fit inside the box lid and glue it in place. Line the box with tissue or parchment and fill it with button cookies. Close the box and run the threaded needle through the gift card, cut the needle free, and make a knot with the twine.

mango and tomatillo *salsa*

overall prep time: 35 to 40 minutes

easy

moderately expensive

do not freeze

can be shipped

can be doubled or tripled

shelf life: 1 week refrigerated

makes: 2 quarts

The tomatillo is a smaller and less acidic relative of the tomato. The combination of the firm, green tomatillo with silky, bright-orange mango makes a mild and fruity salsa that is exceptionally pretty.

3 ripe mangoes, peeled, pitted, and finely diced

2 cups finely diced tomatillos (6 to 8 tomatillos)

1 sweet red chile pepper, seeded and sliced into thin rings

juice and zest of 2 large limes

3 tablespoons champagne vinegar

6 scallions, thinly sliced

½ cup chopped fresh cilantro

3 tablespoons roughly chopped fresh basil

¼ cup olive oil

2 tablespoon crushed green peppercorns

salt and freshly ground white pepper to taste

1 Combine all of the ingredients in a ceramic or glass mixing bowl.

2 Pack the salsa into jars, cover the jars tightly, and wipe them down with a damp cloth. Refrigerate the jars of salsa until you are ready to assemble and deliver the gift.

wrapping it up

The intricate designs of *papel picado*, the lacy tissue banners seen at Mexican festivals and in Mexican restaurants, can only be created by skilled artisans. But a much simpler version of this traditional Mexican folk art is almost as easy to make as cutting paper dolls or snowflakes. The perforated tissue wrap gives the recipient a glimpse of all those amazing colors in the salsa.

suggested supplies for each jar

2 sheets colored tissue paper	double-face tape
2 large sheets freezer paper	colored twine or waxed string

how to make faux "papel picado"

Stack two sheets of colored tissue paper and cut them 2 or 3 inches wider than the height of the salsa jar and 2 or 3 inches longer than the jar's diameter. Carefully crease the tissue into 8 narrow accordion folds (as if you are going to cut some really skinny paper dolls). Press the folded paper with a dry iron on the lowest setting. Use scissors or punches to cut out a simple design, being careful not to cut into the folded edges so the sheets remain intact when unfolded. Cut a scalloped or zigzag design at the top and bottom edges of the folded tissue. Unfold the paper, smooth it out between sheets of freezer paper, and press it flat with the dry iron. Apply a strip of double-face tape around the center of the salsa jar and wrap the freshly ironed paper around the jar, making sure the bottom edge

of the tissue is flush with the bottom of the jar; press the tissue into the tape to secure it. Wrap the twine around the tissue at the neck of the jar and knot it tightly. Gently separate the two layers of tissue above the tie, turning one inward over the jar top and the other outward to form a lacy ruffle.

fromage blanc

overall prep time: 24 to 36 hours

active prep time: 30 to 45 minutes

slightly challenging

inexpensive

do not freeze or ship

can be doubled after practice with a single recipe

shelf life: 1 week refrigerated

makes: one 6-inch log

I am never sure whether people are more impressed with the flavor of this delicious cheese or the fact that it is homemade. For me, cheesemaking is a fascinating and rewarding process. It seems more like alchemy than cooking. Making your own simple soft cheeses is fairly easy, requiring no special equipment or esoteric ingredients, just a little time and patience. This cheese has a wonderful texture and a fresh creamy taste. You can enhance the flavor by rolling the finished cheese in various kinds of crushed peppercorns, crumbled dry herbs, blends of ground spices, or fresh herb leaves. I have found that organic dairy products produce the best cheeses in the shortest amount of time.

3 cups whole milk	1 cup sour cream	1 teaspoon coarse sea salt
1 cup buttermilk	3 tablespoons sherry vinegar	8 to 10 fresh bay leaves

1 Combine the milk, buttermilk, and sour cream in a heavy saucepan. Place over low heat and bring to a rolling boil, stirring occasionally. Remove the pan from the heat momentarily and stir in the sherry vinegar. Return the pan to the heat and slowly bring the mixture back to a simmer, stirring occasionally, until the milk just begins to curdle. Immediately remove the pan from the heat and set it aside for 10 minutes.

2 Line a fine-mesh strainer with a double thickness of damp cheesecloth and set it over a deep, narrow bowl. Gently pour the contents of the saucepan into the lined

strainer, and cover the strainer with plastic wrap. Set the covered strainer and bowl aside in a cool place for at least 12 and up to 24 hours.

3 Gather the cheesecloth around the cheese curds that have collected in the strainer. Holding the cheesecloth, lift the cheese out of the strainer and, keeping it over the bowl, slowly twist the cloth around the curds as tightly as possible to extract as much whey as you can. Tie the twisted top of the cheesecloth bundle with a length of kitchen twine.

4 Discard the liquid whey in the bowl and suspend the bundle of curds over the bowl by tying the twine to the handle of a wooden spoon that spans the bowl. Cover the bowl with plastic wrap and set it aside in a cool place for 12 more hours.

5 Carefully unwrap the cheese, flatten it with your hands into a 4- to 5-inch circle, and pat it dry with paper towels. Shape the cheese into a log approximately 6 inches long.

6 Sprinkle the log with the sea salt, and lay 8 to 10 fresh bay leaves in an overlapping pattern down the center of the cheese, gently pressing the leaves into the cheese. Wrap the log tightly in plastic wrap. Store the cheese up to 1 week in the refrigerator until you are ready to assemble and deliver the gift.

wrapping it up

Remove the plastic wrap and roll up the cheese in a square of wax paper or deli paper before rolling it up diagonally in a small square of parchment paper. Fold and tuck the open ends of the parchment paper under the cheese package and hold them in place with a criss-cross winding of twine or waxed string knotted tightly over the top of the package. You can cover the ends of the twine with a dab of sealing wax or an adhesive label.

armenian *apricots*

When apricots are in season, usually in June and July where I live, making several jars of these apricots goes to the top of my to-do list. The layers of saturated color fill a jar superbly. The sweet poached apricots and crunchy pistachios are wonderful on their own or accompanying a plain sponge cake or pound cake. Traditionally, they are served with strained yogurt.

overall prep time: about 3½ hours

active prep time: 30 to 40 minutes

easy

inexpensive when apricots are in season

do not freeze

ships well

can be doubled or tripled

shelf life: 10 days refrigerated

makes: 3 to 4 cups

....

2 pounds ripe and uniformly sized fresh apricots

½ cup granulated sugar

½ cup freshly squeezed orange juice (blood oranges are best)

8 whole coriander seeds, slightly crushed

1 cup shelled unsalted pistachio nuts

....

1 Bring a large pot of water to a boil. Have ready a large bowl of ice and water. Blanch the apricots, a few at a time, in the boiling water for 45 to 60 seconds, and immediately plunge them into the bowl of ice and water. Slip the peel from each apricot and halve the apricots along the cleft in the fruit. Remove the stones and arrange the apricot halves, cut side up, in shallow nonreactive dish or pan.

2 Spoon the orange juice over the apricot halves, then sprinkle the sugar over them. Cover the dish with plastic wrap and set it aside to macerate for 3 hours. The apricots will give off a generous amount of thin syrup.

3 Place the apricot halves, cut side down, in a deep sauté pan; pour the accumulated syrup over them. Place the pan over medium heat and cook until the syrup begins to simmer. Reduce the heat to low and add the coriander seeds. Cover the pan and gently simmer the apricots for about 5 minutes, until they are tender enough to pierce with the tip of a paring knife.

4 Transfer the apricots from the syrup with a slotted spoon to a shallow dish and cover the dish with plastic wrap. Increase the heat under the pan of syrup to bring it to a gentle simmer; cook until it is reduced by half, about 20 minutes. Strain the syrup into a heatproof pitcher or bowl and set it aside while preparing the pistachio nuts and sterilizing the jar.

5 Blanch the pistachio nuts in a small pan of boiling water for 3 to 4 minutes. Drain the nuts and spread them on a tea towel. Fold the towel over the nuts. Use the palms of your hands to roll the nuts back and forth in the towel to remove the skins from the pistachios. Discard the papery skins and chop the nuts coarsely. Put the chopped pistachios on a plate lined with paper towels and set them aside.

6 Sterilize a 3- to 4-cup glass jar and lid by washing them in hot soapy water and drying them in a 190°F oven.

7 Pack the warm jar with alternating layers of apricots and chopped nuts. Gently compress each layer with a wooden spoon before adding the next. Fill the jar to within ½ inch of the jar rim. Slowly fill the jar with the reserved apricot syrup all the way to the rim. Use a wooden skewer to eliminate any air bubbles in the jar, adding more syrup if needed. Cover the jar tightly and wipe with a clean, damp cloth. Refrigerate the jar until you are ready to assemble and deliver the gift; the apricots should be consumed within 10 days.

wrapping it up

Here is a way you can make the jar lid as pretty as the layered fruit and nuts.

suggested supplies

indelible marker

1 large paper cupcake liner

double-face tape

coated elastic band (such as a hair elastic)

1 length (16 inches) thin silky ribbon

how to dress up a jar lid

Use the marker to write a gift message or a label for the apricots on the bottom of the cupcake liner. Apply a strip of double-face tape to the lid of the apricot jar, then press the baking cup, written side up, over the jar lid and press it firmly onto the tape. Slip the coated elastic band around the jar so that it fits snugly into the ridge where the lid meets the jar; the band should ruffle the edges of the baking cup. Cover the elastic with the ribbon and tie the ribbon in a simple bow.

olive bar selections, dressed and accessorized

overall prep time: about 12 to 24 hours

active prep time: 5 to 10 minutes

easy

moderately expensive

do not freeze or ship

can be doubled or tripled

shelf life: 4 weeks refrigerated

makes: about 3 cups

Just about every supermarket has an olive bar nowadays, and some markets have very good olive bars. Fresh herbs and citrus, along with excellent extra-virgin olive, can easily transform even a mediocre selection of these olives into something special enough for a gift, especially when the gift is wrapped with a wooden olive spoon.

2½ cups mixed cured olives (such as Niçoise, Picholine, Manzanilla, and Ligurian)

1 lemon

½ cup extra-virgin olive oil

1 small dried red chile pepper

3 sprigs fresh thyme

4 fresh or 8 dried bay leaves

1 tablespoon cracked white peppercorns

1 Drain the olives in a large colander and rinse them under tepid running water for a couple of minutes. Blot the olives dry with paper towels and put them in a medium heatproof bowl.

2 Use a zester to remove long thin strips of zest from the lemon. Juice the lemon. In a nonreactive saucepan, combine the zest and juice, the olive oil, chile pepper, and herbs. Warm the mixture over low heat for 10 minutes, stirring occasionally. Remove the pan from the heat and pour the mixture oil over the olives. Add the peppercorns, cover the bowl with plastic wrap, and set it aside to marinate for 12 to 24 hours at room temperature.

3 Transfer the olives with a slotted spoon to a wide-mouthed jar, then fill the jar with the marinade. Refrigerate the jar until you are ready to assemble the gift.

wrapping it up

Wooden olive spoons with their pierced bowls are useful little items. They can be found at almost all import and kitchen stores. If you can't find one, use a handheld power craft drill and make your own from any small wooden spoon.

suggested supplies

glassine paper

waxed string

1 olive spoon

1 small gift card

how to wrap olives with a spoon

Wrap the jar in a wide band of glassine paper and wind the waxed string around the jar to hold the paper in place. Hold the spoon against the jar and wind the string around the jar and spoon several more times, and finish with a double knot over the center of the spoon handle. Slip a small gift card under the string.

tuscan *melon* filled with raspberries and red wine syrup

overall prep time:
30 minutes

active prep time: 15 minutes

easy

expensive

do not freeze or ship

can be increased to any number

shelf life: 2 to 3 days
refrigerated

makes: 1

A Tuscan melon looks like a cantaloupe with especially deep green-veined channels. This sumptuous gift resembles something out of a sixteenth-century French still life, and it tastes like summer evenings somewhere near heaven.

¼ cup granulated sugar

½ cup red wine

1½ to 2 cups fresh raspberries, rinsed and dried

1 small, ripe Tuscan melon

1 In a large measuring cup, combine the sugar and the wine, and stir until the sugar is dissolved. Place the raspberries in a shallow bowl, and pour the wine mixture over them. Cover the berries loosely with plastic wrap and set them aside to macerate at room temperature while you carve the melon.

2 Prepare the melon just as you would a jack-o'-lantern, making a lid and gently scooping out the seeds. Place the lid in the refrigerator. Invert the melon onto a plate lined with paper towels and refrigerate it until you are ready to assemble and deliver this gift. Refrigerate the raspberries and wine as well.

3 When you are ready to assemble the gift, drain the raspberries (reserve the wine syrup for another use) and fill the melon cavity with them. Fit the lid on the melon.

recipe continues

wrapping it up

This is a very pretty gift that needs a bit of stabilizing before it can be wrapped and delivered. I tried a good many things for keeping the melon upright without spoiling its looks. I finally found the perfect solution at the hardware store: a clear plastic disk for placing under furniture legs!

suggested supplies

1 square (10 inches) cellophane

1 clear plastic furniture glide or "cup"

3 or 4 large fig or ivy leaves

1 wire twist tie

1 or 2 wooden cocktail picks or skewers

raffia

how to wrap a melon

Spread the cellophane on the work surface and put the glide in the center of sheet. Cover the glide with the leaves. Set the bottom of the melon on top and make sure it rests level and secure in the leaf-lined glide. Gather the cellophane around the top of the melon and tightly twist the cellophane so that it tautly covers the melon and presses it to the glide. Secure the twisted cellophane top with a wire twist tie. Use one or two skewers to pierce the cellophane and secure the lid to the melon. Tie the raffia around the wire twist tie and knot it tightly; finish with a simple bow.

foolproof *crème fraîche* in a box of berries

Commercially made crème fraîche literally pales by comparison to this homemade version, which is the color of beeswax. It is about 10 times richer and thicker than any packaged crème fraîche on this side of the Atlantic. I make this crème fraîche regularly, and it is the only one I use. It is very easy to make once you get the hang of it. This crème fraîche surrounded by fresh berries makes the most wonderful gift for any cooking enthusiast; attaching the recipe to the gift makes it an even better one.

overall prep time: about 10 hours

active prep time: 15 minutes

easy

inexpensive

do not freeze or ship

do not double

shelf life: 2 weeks refrigerated

makes: 3 cups

1 cup sour cream
½ cup cultured buttermilk

2 cups heavy cream (organic cream is best)

1 pint fresh berries, for garnishing the wrapped gift

1 Wash a 3- to 4-cup–capacity glass jar (a French canning jar with a wire clamp lid is ideal) with a tight-fitting lid and invert it on the rack of a 190°F oven to dry.

2 Combine all of the ingredients (except the berries) in a heavy nonreactive saucepan and place it over low heat. Whisk the ingredients until they are perfectly smooth, and warm the mixture slowly, stirring it occasionally, until it is a little hotter than lukewarm (between 100° and 105°F on an instant-read thermometer). Immediately pour the mixture into the warm jar and seal it tightly. Wrap a thick towel snugly around the jar and store it in a warm, draft-free place overnight.

3 Line a fine-mesh strainer with a double thickness of damp cheesecloth and place it over a deep, narrow bowl. Gently ladle the crème into the strainer. Set it aside to drain for 1 hour. Wash and dry the glass jar.

4 Gently ladle the thickened crème fraîche into the jar. (Discard any liquid that has collected in the bowl.) Seal the jar tightly and store it in the refrigerator until you are ready to assemble and deliver the gift.

wrapping it up

Any small basket or a simple poplar berry box lined with fresh leaves will make a great-looking gift container for the crème fraîche surrounded by seasonal berries.

suggested supplies

1 small basket or a poplar wood berry box (see Resources, page 290)

fresh leaves, such as fig, galax, or lime

1 square (25 inches) cellophane

1 wire twist tie

ribbon or cord

how to make a crème fraîche berry box

If the gift needs to be held at room temperature for 2 hours or more while you transport it, put a small icepack in the bottom of the box or basket before assembling the gift. Line the basket or box with the leaves. Put the jar of crème fraîche in the center. Fill in all the space around the jar with the fresh berries. Place the filled basket or box in the center of the sheet of cellophane. Gather the cellophane tightly up around the gift, twist it tightly to hold everything in place, and secure it with the wire twist tie. Cover the wire twist tie with a ribbon or cord and tie a bow.

crackers, italian style

A nice box of very good crackers is a useful thing to have on hand. Rest assured, this will be an appreciated gift: These crackers are very good indeed and go well with soups or salads. The crackers are made with generous amounts of three excellent Italian cheeses, so they need no dip or spread at cocktail time.

overall prep time: 2½ hours

active prep time:
20 minutes

easy

inexpensive

dough can be frozen for 3 to 4 months before slicing and baking

ships well

do not double

shelf life: 1 week in airtight packaging

makes: 35 to 40

½ cup finely grated Romano cheese

½ cup finely grated Parmesan cheese

½ cup finely grated Asiago cheese

¾ cup all-purpose flour

2 teaspoons dried marjoram

½ teaspoon coarsely ground black pepper

½ teaspoon coarsely ground white pepper

¼ cup (½ stick) unsalted butter, cut in very thin slices

1½ tablespoons ice water

1 teaspoon white wine vinegar

1 Place the cheeses, flour, marjoram, peppers, and butter in the work bowl of a food processor. Pulse the processor on and off 6 or 7 times or until the ingredients resemble brown sugar in consistency.

2 Turn the processor on and add the ice water and vinegar while the machine is running. Process until the mixture forms a ball in the machine.

3 Roll and pat the dough into a compact log about 13 inches long on a lightly floured work surface. Wrap the log tightly in plastic wrap, then flatten the log on four sides to make it square. Place the squared dough in the freezer for an hour or so, until it is firm enough to slice.

4 Preheat the oven to 375°F and line 2 cookie sheets with parchment paper. Cut the chilled dough into ⅓-inch-thick slices and place them 1 inch apart on the prepared cookie sheets. Bake the crackers for 8 minutes on the middle two racks of the oven. Rotate and switch the pans and bake for another 5 to 8 minutes, or until the crackers are resistant to the touch and golden brown around the edges.

5 Place the cookie sheets on racks to cool for 1 hour. Store the crackers in an airtight container until you are ready to assemble and deliver the gift.

wrapping it up

A small metal tin will keep the crackers fresh longer, but you can repurpose any small box for them. It looks attractive when you wrap the stacks of crackers in glassine or parchment paper and fit them snugly in the container you use. Instead of a standard bow, use a wide band of card stock to embellish the box and serve as a gift card.

suggested supplies

glassine or parchment paper	double-face tape
1 appropriately sized box or tin	paper punch
1 strip card stock, about 3 inches wide and long enough to wrap around the box with a small overlap	

how to band instead of bow

Make stacks of crackers and wrap them with the glassine or parchment in a size that fits well in your box. Write a gift message on the band of card stock. If you have decorative paper punches they can be used to create a lacy border on the edges of the card stock band. Starting under the box, wrap it with the band of paper and attach the ends with double-face tape.

cantaloupe *agua fresca*

Agua fresca, Spanish for "fresh water," is lighter and more refreshing than fruit juice. The translucent fruit water is traditionally sweetened with granulated sugar, but a lime-infused simple syrup sets the color and keeps the *fresca* that way for a longer time. *Agua fresca* is served over crushed ice or on the rocks; mixed with tequila or vodka, it makes a great hot-weather cocktail.

overall prep time: 1 hour

active prep time:
30 minutes

easy

inexpensive

do not freeze or ship

can be doubled or tripled

shelf life: 3 days refrigerated in a tightly sealed glass bottle

makes: about 1 quart

FOR THE LIME SYRUP:

1 cup water

1 cup granulated sugar

2 limes cut in small chunks and bundled in a square of cheesecloth

FOR THE AGUA FRESCA:

2 ripe cantaloupes, peeled, seeded, and cut in small chunks

3½ cups distilled water

⅓ cup fresh lime juice

1 To make the lime syrup, combine the water and sugar in a saucepan and stir until the sugar is dissolved. Cover the pan and place it over medium heat. When the syrup boils, remove the cover, add the lime bundle, and continue to boil gently for 7 minutes. Remove the pan from the heat and replace the cover. Allow the syrup to cool completely before removing the lime bundle and discarding it. Pour the cooled syrup into a bottle and refrigerate it. You will have 1½ to 2 cups of syrup, which will keep for up to 2 months in the refrigerator.

2 To make the agua fresca, puree the cantaloupes and the distilled water in a blender. Stir in the lime juice and ladle the puree, one cup at time, into a fine-mesh strainer set over a pitcher or deep bowl. Do not force the puree through the strainer, which

will make the rendered fruit water cloudy and more perishable. Empty the strainer and rinse it before adding another cup to drain. (The pureed fruit that is left behind in the strainer is excellent for making quick refrigerator jellies and jams.)

3 Add the lime syrup to the *agua fresca* a little at a time, to avoid oversweetening. If you use ripe, sweet melons, it shouldn't require more than ¼ cup of syrup. Pour the sweetened *agua fresca* through a cheesecloth-lined funnel into a 1-liter bottle, seal the bottle tightly, and store it in the refrigerator until you are ready to assemble and deliver the gift.

wrapping it up

To protect the *agua fresca* from light, wrap the bottle tightly in a band of glassine paper before adding the crimped wire bottle tag, which will hold separate rounds of cardstock with storage instructions and serving suggestions.

suggested supplies

1 length (18 to 20 inches) thick-gauge craft wire

waterproof marking pens

4 rounds (2 to 2½ inches each) card stock

how to make a crimped wire bottle tag

First un-kink the coiled craft wire by firmly running it back and forth over a smooth, rounded surface like a counter edge or a thick post. Tightly bend the straightened wire back and forth on itself, like accordion folds of paper, starting with a small bend and gradually increasing the length of each bend until a little over half the wire is tightly bent into folds.

Wrap the straight portion of the wire around the neck of the bottle until it is secure. Gently expand the folded wire until it looks a little like a bolt of lightning. Use the markers to write separate bits of information on each round of card stock; a gift message on one, storage instructions on another, serving suggestions on one or two others (see the introduction to this recipe for serving suggestions). Slip each cardstock round between folds of the wire to hold them in place, up and down the bottle front.

sublime *key lime* curd

overall prep time: 1 hour

active prep time: 25 to 30 minutes

slightly challenging

moderately expensive

do not freeze or ship

do not double

shelf life: 3 to 4 days refrigerated

makes: about 2 cups

Everything about this gift is luscious. It would be easy to devour the entire jar with nothing more than the attached spoon. For those with more restraint, the curd can be held in reserve for pound cake, ladyfingers, and best of all, I think, fresh blueberries. Make this only when Key limes are in season; ordinary limes are not an acceptable substitute.

½ cup fresh Key lime juice

2 tablespoons grated Key lime zest

1½ cups granulated sugar

4 large eggs, lightly beaten

2 tablespoons cold unsalted butter, plus 10 tablespoons unsalted butter at room temperature

4 or 5 thin slices Key lime, for garnish

1 In the top of a double boiler, combine the lime juice and zest with the sugar and eggs; whisk them together. Cook the mixture over barely simmering water, stirring almost constantly with a rubber spatula, for 20 minutes, or until it thickens to the consistency of heavy cream.

2 Remove the curd from the heat and add the 2 tablespoons of cold butter to stop the cooking process. Whisk until the butter has melted. With the back of a large spoon, press the curd through a fine-mesh strainer into a bowl, and set it aside to cool until the curd reaches room temperature. Add the room-temperature butter and vigorously beat the curd with a wooden spoon until it is smooth and silky.

3 Flatten the lime slices against the interior of a clean glass jar and carefully fill the jar with the curd. Seal the jar tightly, wipe it down with a clean, damp cloth, and refrigerate the jar until you are ready to assemble and deliver the gift.

wrapping it up

A round jar-top label with a wooden spoon attached to it allows an unobstructed view of the Key lime curd.

suggested supplies

card stock

indelible marker

1 length (8 inches) wired ribbon

1 disposable bamboo spoon (available at gourmet markets and import stores, or online; see Resources, page 290)

double-face tape

how to make a jar-top label with a bow and a spoon

Trace and cut a card-stock circle to fit the top of the jar and punch two small holes side by side in the center of the circle. Write a gift message and label the contents around the cardstock circle. Thread the wired-ribbon ends through the holes from underneath the cardstock circle and then secure the cardstock to the lid of the jar with double-face tape. Place the spoon between the strands of ribbon and tie it down tightly with a double knot and a bow.

rose petal *vinegar*

overall prep time: 2 to 4 days

active prep time: 10 to 20 minutes

easy

moderately expensive

do not freeze or ship

can be doubled or tripled

shelf life: 2 to 3 months in a tightly corked bottle

makes: about 10 ounces

Rose petals impart a delicate and slightly peppery taste, not to mention a superb shade of pink, to a soft and fruity white balsamic vinegar. Rose petal vinegar is wonderful over white peaches or ripe cantaloupe (especially if they are sprinkled with a little turbinado sugar and crushed pink peppercorns). Rose petal vinegar and a light olive oil make one of the best dressings for delicate baby greens. I love the vinegar in sparkling water with lots of ice on a hot day.

Be sure to use rose petals free of pesticides in this recipe. Because modern hybrid roses have little fragrance, "old" rose varieties make the best petal vinegar.

| 1 quart loosely packed fresh rose petals | 10 dried cherries | 10 ounces white or golden balsamic vinegar |

1 Spread the petals in a single layer on a parchment-lined baking sheet and set them in a well-ventilated space to dry for 24 to 36 hours. The petals should be shriveled but still retain their color and feel soft to the touch. Place the dry petals and the dried cherries in a heat-resistant, nonreactive bowl or jar.

2 Gently heat the balsamic vinegar in a nonreactive saucepan just until steam starts to rise from the pan. Pour the heated vinegar over the petals and cover the container tightly with a lid or a plate. Set the covered container in a cool dark place for one or two days, until the vinegar is a beautiful rosy pink.

recipe continues

3 Sterilize an attractive 10- to 12-ounce long-necked bottle with a tight-fitting stopper by washing it in hot soapy water and drying it completely in a 190°F oven. Slowly ladle the vinegar through a funnel lined with a double thickness of cheesecloth into the hot bottle. Allow the juices from the petals and cherries to drain through the funnel, but do not squeeze or press the petals and cherries to extract more juice, which will cloud the vinegar with sediment and cause it to discolor. Discard the cherries and petals. When the bottle is cool to the touch, seal it tightly.

wrapping it up

Decorate the bottle neck with colors like pale peach, warm yellow, or vibrant pink to complement the color of the vinegar.

suggested supplies

double-face tape

1 length (2 yards) double-ply polished cotton embroidery floss

1 card-stock gift tag

how to cover a bottle neck in silky thread

Apply several strips of double-face tape around the bottle neck, starting under the lip of the bottle and continuing to the point where the neck flares into the body of the bottle.

Starting under the lip of the bottle, tightly wind the floss around the bottle neck, trying not to leave any spaces or gaps between the strands of floss. Stop winding the floss at the point where the tape stops. Separate the plies of the remaining floss and wind them twice around the base of the bottle neck in opposite directions. Join and tie the floss ends in a double knot. Punch a hole in the card stock and use the ends of the floss to attach the card to the bottle neck.

dark chocolate *pâté*

It would be hard to find a richer or more decadent chocolate dessert and nearly impossible to find an easier recipe for making one. This chocolate concoction is denser than a mousse but much lighter than fudge, and it bears absolutely no resemblance to cake, so I added pistachio nuts and christened it a pâté.

½ cup (1 stick) unsalted butter

¾ cup shelled, unsalted pistachio nuts

1 can (14 ounces) sweetened condensed milk

1 vanilla bean, split lengthwise

1 package (12 ounces) premium-quality semisweet chocolate chips

1 Prepare two 3 × 8-inch loaf pans by coating them lightly with baking spray. Place a strip of parchment in the pan lengthwise and overlap it with a second strip running crosswise, so that all four sides and the bottom of each pan are lined with parchment. Allow about 3 inches of overhang on all sides.

2 Blanch the pistachio nuts in a small pan of boiling water for 3 to 4 minutes. Drain the nuts and spread them on a tea towel. Fold the towel over the nuts. Use the palms of your hands to roll the nuts back and forth in the towel to remove the skins from the pistachios. Discard the papery skins and chop the nuts coarsely. Put the chopped pistachios on a plate lined with paper towels and set them aside.

3 Melt the butter in the top of a double boiler over medium heat. Add the condensed milk and the vanilla bean. Bring the mixture to a slow boil. Remove the vanilla bean and gently squeeze all the tiny black seeds from the pod back into the mixture. (You can dry and reserve the empty pod for another use, such

recipe continues

overall prep time: 2½ hours

active prep time: 30 minutes

easy

moderately expensive

freezes well

do not ship

can be doubled

shelf life: 2 weeks refrigerated; months in the freezer

makes: 2 loaves

as flavoring sugar.) Add the chocolate chips to the mixture and reduce the heat to low. Continue heating, stirring the mixture every few minutes, until all the chocolate has melted and the mixture is smooth and glossy, 5 to 8 minutes. Stir the pistachios into the chocolate mixture.

4 Using a rubber spatula or metal offset spatula, spread the chocolate mixture carefully into the prepared loaf pans. Set the pans aside for 30 minutes to cool.

5 Fold the overhanging ends of the parchment liners over the tops of the pâtés and then cover each pan tightly with plastic wrap. Gently press the tops of the covered loaf pans to compress the pate and eliminate any pockets of air. Freeze the pâtés for a least 2 hours or until they are frozen solid.

6 Invert the frozen pâtés on a plate to unmold them and peel away the parchment strips. If the parchment has made wrinkles on the surface of the pâté, you can "erase" them with a heated icing spatula. (Return the pâté to the freezer briefly to firm up the surface again.) Transfer each pâté to a small rectangle of cake board or corrugated cardboard and tightly cover it with plastic wrap. Store the wrapped pâtés in the freezer until you are ready to assemble and deliver the gift.

wrapping it up

Frozen pâtés can be gift wrapped and delivered without ice packs. The recipient can either refrigerate or freeze the gift.

suggested supplies

fine-gauge wire craft mesh   **glass or plastic beads**

colored craft wire

how to wrap a chocolate pâté

Wrap the pâté in a sheet of wire mesh and press the mesh to fit the contours of the pâté, taping the raw edges of the mesh to the bottom of the cardboard support. Wind the package with the craft wire in a random pattern and twist the ends of the wire around one another to close them over the top of mesh package. String a few beads onto the ends of each wire and use needle-nose pliers to crimp the end of each wire to hold the beads in place.

white chocolate mandarin *truffles*

Something this sinfully rich and sweet epitomizes how deeply indulgent a small token can be. These truffles rival the finest handmade chocolates in taste and appearance, although few commercially produced truffles are this large or this good. This is a truly useful recipe to add to your repertoire of gifts because you can flavor and embellish the basic white truffle recipe with any natural flavor or ingredient to alter them to your taste.

FOR THE TRUFFLES:

11 ounces premium-quality white chocolate chips

⅓ cup plus 2 tablespoons heavy cream or crème fraîche

8 drops pure mandarin oil or tangerine oil

½ cup confectioners' sugar

FOR THE COATING:

11 ounces premium-quality white chocolate chips

2 teaspoons vegetable shortening

overall prep time: 24 to 48 hours

active prep time: under 2 hours

moderately easy

inexpensive

freezes well before dipping

do not ship

can be doubled or divided

shelf life: several days at cooler room temperature

makes: 12 extra-large truffles

1 To make the truffles, place the 11 ounces of white chocolate in a heatproof bowl and set the bowl in a very low oven to soften while you heat the cream. Combine the cream and mandarin oil in a small saucepan over medium heat and bring it to a boil. Remove the softened chocolate from the oven and pour the boiling cream over it. Set the bowl aside for 5 minutes.

2 Beat the chocolate and cream with a hand mixer at moderately high speed until the mixture forms a smooth and glossy ganache. Increase the mixer speed to high and continue beating the ganache for 8 minutes, or until it becomes fluffy and opaque.

recipe continues

Place a sheet of plastic wrap directly onto the surface of the ganache and refrigerate it in the bowl for 2 to 3 hours, until it is slightly firm to the touch.

3 Scoop the chilled ganache into 12 equal portions and place on a parchment-lined tray; refrigerate for 30 minutes. Meanwhile, sift the confectioners' sugar into a pie plate or other shallow dish and line a tray or cookie sheet with wax paper.

4 Liberally dust your hands with confectioners' sugar and quickly roll the chilled scoops of ganache into perfectly round balls. Arrange the rolled truffles 1 inch apart on the paper-lined tray and set them in a dark, cool place to harden overnight. (An unheated electric oven is ideal.)

5 To make the coating, place the remaining 11 ounces of white chocolate chips and the vegetable shortening in the top of a double boiler; heat over medium-high heat until the chocolate has melted. Stir the coating until it is smooth, remove it from the heat, and set it aside to cool slightly. (Leave the lower portion of the double boiler on the stove and keep the water slowly simmering in case you need to reheat the coating at any point during the dipping process.)

6 The coating chocolate is ready when you can just comfortably place your hand on the outside of the pan; the coating will be warm and thick at this point. Put a chilled truffle on a fork, dip it in the melted chocolate two or three times, and return it to the paper-lined tray. Repeat with remaining truffles. Allow the truffles to harden in the same dark, cool place for at least 12 hours. Put each finished truffle in a paper candy cup or cupcake liner. Store the truffles in an airtight container in a cool place until you are ready to assemble and deliver the gift.

wrapping it up

Making this two-tiered truffle tray is as easy as stringing beads.

suggested supplies

1 disposable bamboo luncheon plate, 6 to 7 inches in diameter

1 disposable bamboo saucer or dessert plate, 4 to 5 inches in diameter

1 length (2 to 3 yards) paper ribbon or thin cord

5 to 7 large wooden beads

12 circles (1½ to 2 inches) card stock

low-temp hot glue

1 wire twist tie

cellophane, in the same color as the ribbon or cord

how to make a small two-tiered tray

Find and mark the center of each of the two plates. Punch two holes side by side in the larger plate near the center. Punch one hole in the center of the smaller plate. Starting on the top side of the larger plate, thread the ribbon or cord down through one hole and back up through the second hole. Slide the ribbon or cord through the two holes until the ends are even. Thread both ends of the ribbon or cord through a large wooden bead and dot both ends of the bead with low-temperature hot glue. Pull the bead tightly to the surface of the plate and hold it in place until the glue sets. Repeat the stringing and gluing with two or three more beads, making sure they are tightly aligned and perfectly stacked. When the beads are strung and the glue has set, they will form the pedestal for the second tier of the tray.

Put both ends of the ribbon or cord through the hole in the bottom of the smaller plate and knot the ends tightly together over the hole in the top plate. String and glue two or three more wooden beads in place. Double-knot the cord ends and finish with a large looped bow.

Glue one card-stock circle to the bottom of the tiered tray, covering the ribbon and holes. Glue the rest of the circles in an overlapping pattern around the bead columns on both tiers. Arrange the truffles on the tiered tray and set it in the center of a large square of cellophane. Gather the cellophane tightly up and over the tray, twisting the ends tightly just under the looped-bow tray topper. Use the wire twist tie to secure the cellophane tightly under the bow. Cover the twist tie with matching ribbon or cord. You can carry the tray by the looped bow to its final destination.

big batches

When the situation calls for a number of identical gifts, your own kitchen may be the most logical place to start. If you enjoy cooking and crafting, your time and budget will probably be better spent preparing and wrapping homemade gifts than searching and shopping for store-bought presents.

The recipes and gift-wraps in this chapter have been especially created to produce multiple and identical gifts efficiently for every conceivable occasion. When you make the gifts and create their packaging, "identical" is no longer synonymous with "impersonal."

Almost every recipe in this chapter can be doubled, making it easy to create any number of gifts. Many of the recipes freeze well, which enables you to get a head start on large projects. The distinctive wrappings and presentations are relatively streamlined in design compared with some of other projects in this book, to facilitate working on multiple gifts at the same time. You have a wide range of recipes and gift-wrapping ideas to choose from.

things to keep in mind

Organization is the key to making big batches of gifts. It is a good idea to make a small test run of a recipe and its packaging before plunging head-first into a full-blown project involving a large number of gifts. This will save you a lot of time and money in the end.

Working "backwards" is often advisable when you are preparing a large number of identical gifts. In other words, it is a very good idea to gather and assemble as much of the packaging as possible before you begin the cooking.

Scale your ambitions to the number of gifts that are needed. If you have a very large number of gifts to make, choose recipes that either freeze well or have a long shelf life so you can prepare them over a longer period of time, and make sure the wraps are fairly simple. Opt for more complicated recipes and elaborate presentations when you have more time available and fewer gifts to prepare.

100 cookies to pinch and press or slice and bake

This big batch of dough makes a lot of cookies. It is an ideal project for cookie exchanges, holiday gift-giving, and bake sales. The basic recipe is followed by several variations for shaping and baking the cookies as well as flavoring them; you can also use the basic dough as a blank canvas for your own improvisations. The cookie bags rival the cookies in versatility and potential variations.

7 cups sifted all-purpose flour	2 cups (4 sticks) butter, at room temperature	1½ tablespoons vanilla extract
5 teaspoons baking powder	3 cups granulated sugar	
1 teaspoon salt	4 large eggs	

1 Sift the flour, baking powder, and salt together in a large bowl and set aside.

2 Place the butter, sugar, eggs, and vanilla in the bowl of a stand mixer. Beat at medium speed for 3 minutes. Add the sifted dry ingredients, 1 cup at a time, to the butter mixture while beating at medium speed.

3 Scrape the dough onto a tray or baking sheet lined with plastic wrap, tightly cover the dough, and seal the edges of the wrap. Refrigerate the wrapped dough for at least 1 hour.

recipe continues

overall prep time: varies, depending on type of cookie

active prep time for dough: 15 minutes

easy

inexpensive

uncooked dough can be frozen for up to 1 month

ships well in an airtight container

do not double

shelf life: 10 days in an airtight container

makes: 8 to 11 dozen, depending on type of cookie

to make pinch-and-press sugar cookies

1 Arrange the oven racks close to the middle of the oven and preheat the oven to 350°F.

2 Pinch off walnut-sized portions of dough and roll them into balls. Place the dough balls 2 inches apart on parchment-lined baking or cookie sheets. Butter the bottom of a drinking glass and dip it in sugar. Press each ball of dough with the glass to flatten; each cookie should be about ⅓ inch thick. Reapply butter and sugar to the bottom of the glass as needed.

3 Bake the sugar cookies 10 to 12 minutes, or until the edges are golden. Set the pans on racks until the cookies are cool enough to handle. Transfer the cookies to racks to cool completely before storing them in airtight containers until you are ready to assemble and deliver the gifts.

PINCH-AND-PRESS FLAVOR VARIATIONS

You can substitute various extracts or flavorings, such as almond extract or espresso powder, for the vanilla while preparing the dough; you can also add cocoa powder or finely grated citrus zest. But you will be able to create a much wider variety of cookies from one batch of dough if you embellish the tops of the cookies with different flavoring elements. Here are two examples:

- *sugar-sanded pecan cookies:* Place a pecan half on the top of each ball of cookie dough, press with a glass as directed for the basic sugar cookie, and top with white sanding sugar. Bake and cool according to the basic directions.

- *cardamom-date cookies:* Place 3 or 4 pieces of chopped date on the top of each ball of cookie dough, press with a glass as directed for the basic sugar cookie, and sprinkle with ground cardamom. Bake and cool according to the basic directions.

to make slice-and-bake cookies

1 Divide the dough into 4 equal parts and knead the flavoring components (see the specific variations below) into the dough. Place each portion of dough on a sheet of wax paper or parchment paper and shape the dough into rolls about 1½ inches in diameter and 18 inches long. Place the rolls in the freezer for at least 2 hours.

2 Flatten the wrapped rolls on four sides with a heavy rolling pin to form neat oblongs 1½ inches square and about 18 inches long. Rewrap the oblongs tightly in fresh paper and return to the freezer for at least another 2 hours.

3 Arrange the oven racks close to the middle of the oven and preheat the oven to 350°F. Use a sharp serrated knife to cut the dough into even slices about ⅓ inch thick, and place the slices 1 inch apart on parchment-lined cookie sheets.

4 Bake the cookies for 8 to 9 minutes, or until the cookies are set and yield only slightly to the touch. The edges and bottoms of the cookies should be golden brown. Set the pans on racks until the cookies are cool enough to handle. Transfer the cookies to racks to cool

completely before storing them in airtight containers until you are ready to assemble and deliver the gifts.

SLICE-AND-BAKE FLAVOR VARIATIONS

You can add nuts, dried fruits, or spices to the basic dough when you are preparing slice-and-bake cookies. Here are two examples that will give you guidelines for the quantities of add-ins to use for one log or oblong of dough (that is, for one-quarter batch of the basic dough):

- *coconut-ginger slice-and-bake cookies:* To one-fourth of the basic cookie dough add ½ cup large-flake coconut (look for this in the frozen-food section of a large market; you can substitute shredded coconut in a pinch) and 1½ tablespoons chopped preserved ginger. Shape the dough into a round log. Wrap, freeze, slice, and bake the cookies as described in the directions for Slice-and-Bake Cookies.

- *dried blueberry–cinnamon slice-and-bake cookies:* To one-fourth of the basic cookie dough add ⅔ cup dried blueberries, the grated zest of 1 lemon, and 1 tablespoon ground cinnamon. Shape into an 18-inch squared-off oblong as described in the directions for Slice-and-Bake Cookies. Wrap, freeze, slice, and bake as described in the directions.

wrapping it up

When you give cookies, give them in a bag, never on a flimsy paper plate. Bags are the most versatile, inexpensive, and practical cookie gift containers around. See the photo on page 3 and DinahsGourmetGifts.com for ideas for bag embellishments and designs.

Simple white paper bags punched with patterns can be lighted from within using novelty-store or toy-store "glow sticks." These cookie bag luminarias can be hung on front doors. They are attractive and surprisingly easy to make.

suggested supplies for each luminaria bag

1 white paper bag, 4 or 5 inches wide and 8 or 9 inches tall	additional yellow cellophane for wrapping the cookies
1 rectangle (10 × 22 inches) yellow cellophane, plus	1 length (40 inches) ½-inch-wide white grosgrain ribbon
	1 glow stick

how to make a luminaria cookie bag

Leave the bag folded flat and punch a row of holes along each side and across the top of the bag. If you slide the punch over the edges of the bag as far as it will reach, your holes will form straight rows without your having to measure. Open the bag and line the inside with the rectangle of yellow cellophane. Wrap individual varieties of cookies in yellow cellophane and fill the lined bag about three-quarters full.

Cut the grosgrain ribbon in half and insert one half through the outermost punched holes at both ends of the bag top. Slide the ribbons through the holes until they are even and tie all four ribbon ends together in a double knot. Break and shake the glow stick according to its directions and place it in the cookie bag just before you hang it over the recipient's front doorknob.

whole preserved *lemons*

overall prep time: about 2 weeks (for curing lemons)

active prep time: 1 hour

easy

moderately expensive

do not freeze or ship

can be doubled or tripled

shelf life: 6 months

makes: 12

A gift of a pretty jar holding a preserved lemon should thrill any experienced or adventurous cook. Salt-cured whole lemons preserved in extra-virgin olive oil are a staple in almost all Mediterranean cuisines. They are used to season slow-cooked dishes like tagines, and diced preserved lemon and its oil can be used to marinate or garnish grilled meats and seafood as well as feta and other dry cheeses. In Greek tavernas small wedges of preserved lemon are served with drinks, along with slivers of dry, aged sheep's milk cheeses, olives, and flatbreads. The oil alone is a perfect addition to marinades and vinaigrettes. Whole cardamom pods and fenugreek seeds can be found in South Asian markets, natural-foods stores, and online (see Resources, page 290). Preserved lemons improve with age and should stay good for about six months. It is essential to cover the lemons by at least a half an inch of olive oil in order to store the jar safely at room temperature.

12 small, firm organic lemons

5 tablespoons coarse sea salt

12 fresh bay leaves

4 cinnamon sticks, each broken into 3 pieces

12 small dried red chile pods

2 tablespoons white peppercorns

2 tablespoons cardamom pods

2 tablespoons fenugreek seeds

2 tablespoons mustard seeds

about 4 cups extra-virgin olive oil

recipe continues

1. Scrub the lemons and cut each one into 8 wedges from the blossom end to, but not through, the stem end, so that the wedges remain attached at the stem end. Arrange the lemons in a glass or ceramic casserole dish. Gently spread the wedges apart and heavily sprinkle each lemon with sea salt. Tightly cover the dish with plastic wrap. Set the salted lemons aside in a cool place for 24 hours.

2. Meanwhile, prepare the jars: You will need 12 small wide-mouthed jars (½-pint canning jars are fine). Wash the jars and lids in hot, soapy water, rinse them, and dry them in a 190°F oven. Keep the jars and lids warm until you are ready to fill them.

3. Drain off and discard any accumulated juices in the casserole of lemons. Put one lemon in each jar along with a bay leaf, a piece of cinnamon, a chile pod, and a small portion of the other seasonings. Fill the jars with olive oil, using about ⅓ cup for each jar, making sure the lemons are covered by at least a half an inch of oil. Use a chopstick or the handle of a wooden spoon to dislodge any air bubbles. Wipe the jar rims with clean paper towels and cover the jars.

4. Store the jars in a cool, dark pantry or closet for 2 weeks, or until the lemons are soft and you are ready to assemble and deliver the gifts.

wrapping it up

The lemons, spices, and rich green olive oil provide about all the good looks any small gift needs. But a great-looking label and a few recipes would complete this gift very nicely. If you have good computer skills, you might consider creating a booklet of recipes (you can search online or in any Mediterranean or Middle Eastern cookbook) to accompany the lemons. You should include a note with storage instructions, too: The lemons can be stored at room temperature, but as they are used, the jar should be replenished with olive oil to keep the remaining lemons covered and fresh. See Resources (page 290) for information on free downloadable labels.

simca's *orange essence wine* from bramafam

As a young cook, for several years I was fortunate enough to spend part of each year with my mentor, Simone Beck, and her husband, Jean Fischbacher, at Bramafam, their country home in the south of France. My yearly pilgrimages coincided with the time Simca set aside to make dozens and dozens of bottles of this fortified white wine, which is very common in southern France. She called her recipe the Bramafam apéritif. My recipe here is very similar. It is pure joy to make and give this splendid gift.

Simca used marc, a strong, clear eau de vie available in the U.S., in her version of this wine. But any good-quality cognac will work fine.

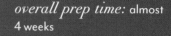

overall prep time: almost 4 weeks

active prep time: 3 hours

easy

expensive

do not freeze or ship

can be doubled or tripled

shelf life: 1 year in a properly sealed bottle stored in a dark, cool place

makes: twelve 750-milliliter bottles

24 juice oranges

12 bottles good-quality Chablis

8 whole cloves

3 cinnamon sticks

¾ cup superfine sugar

⅓ cup good-quality cognac

1 Carefully peel the oranges, removing the peel in long spirals and picking up as little white pith as possible. (Reserve the oranges for another use, such as Sunshine in a Jar, page 243). Using an upholstery or tapestry needle, thread the spirals onto a length of cotton twine, much as you would to make a popcorn or cranberry string for a Christmas tree. Dry the orange peels by suspending the string across a sunny window for at least 5 days, or until the peel is completely dry and brittle to the touch. Remove the twine and put the peels in a very large (3- to 4-gallon) glass or crockery container.

recipe continues

2 Add the wine to the container along with the cloves and cinnamon. Save the bottles and corks, remove the labels, and wash and dry them for rebottling the wine. Cover the container with plastic wrap, then top with a large plate. Store the covered container in a cool closet or cellar for 2 weeks.

3 After 2 weeks, remove the spirals of orange peel from the wine and discard them. Place 4 cups of the wine and the sugar in a large nonreactive saucepan and stir until the sugar has dissolved. Bring the sweetened wine to a simmer over low heat for 8 minutes, add the cognac to the warm wine, and pour the mixture back into the large container of wine. Cover the container again and return it to the storage area for at least 1 week and up to 3 weeks more.

4 Decant the wine into the original bottles, pouring it through a cheesecloth-lined funnel. You'll find yourself with about ½ liter extra—feel free to keep it for yourself! Tightly cork the bottles and store them in a cool, dark place until you are ready to assemble and deliver the gifts.

wrapping it up

The possibilities are virtually endless for decorating and labeling wine bottles. Because I often give this apéritif as a holiday offering, I have become partial to bright orange and red color schemes for embellishing it.

You can make a label that looks like a spiral of orange peel twisting around the bottle from top to bottom by using wide, orange wired moiré ribbon or medium-weight orange card stock. A more classic, and perhaps more elegant, embellishment would be a neat and simple bow at the bottle neck made from deep-orange wired moiré ribbon. Rich-looking accents like red glass beads or small Christmas ornaments can be added to the bow. A colorful "antique" label can be downloaded from any number of websites with free graphics, or you can make your own labels of any design. Whatever style of decoration you choose, be sure to overwrap each bottle in clear or red cellophane to make the gift even more festive.

suggested supplies

1 large sheet (approximately 22 × 28 inches) thin orange pasteboard or card stock, or 12 lengths (16 inches each) orange wired moiré ribbon

dark-orange or burgundy marking pen (if you are using ribbon, make sure the marking pen works on fabric)

double-face tape

clear cellophane

12 wire twist ties

additional wired moiré or coordinating wired organza ribbon for finishing the package

12 gift cards

how to label orange wine aperitif bottles

For card-stock or pasteboard "peeling spirals," use a straightedge as a guide and tear the paper diagonally into long strips about 1¼ inches wide and 16 to 22 inches long. Use the marking pen to label the contents and provide storage and serving suggestions by writing them down the full length of each strip of paper or ribbon.

Back each strip with double-face tape. Starting just under the cork, attach the label strip or ribbon in a spiral around the neck and down the body of the bottle. Roll the bottles in cellophane and hold the cellophane in place with double-face tape on the bottom of each bottle. Tightly twist the cellophane over the top of each bottle and secure it first with a wire twist tie and then a simple ribbon bow.

Be sure to date the bottles. A good way to word the storage and serving suggestions would be: "Once opened, the wine should be refrigerated and will keep for up to 2 months. Serve on the rocks with a fresh slice of orange."

ten country *pâtés*

I must have made hundreds of these country pâtés over the years; they are often my "big batch" gift for the holidays. Because so many cookies are on the Christmas gift circuit, my friends are thrilled to have a little pâté on hand to serve when others drop by to deliver cookies. Even if you have never attempted a pâté, fear not! Think of it as a meatloaf (with a different fat-to-lean ratio) that is weighted after baking to make the texture denser, so that the cold pâté will slice perfectly.

overall prep time: 3 to 4 days

active prep time: 3 to 4 hours

challenging

moderately expensive

do not freeze or ship

can be doubled or tripled

shelf life: 7 to 10 days well wrapped and refrigerated

makes: 10 mini-loaves, approximately 3 × 6 inches each

FOR THE PÂTÉ:

7 tablespoons unsalted butter

7 small yellow onions, finely chopped

8 garlic cloves, finely minced

2 pounds fresh ground pork (a fattier grind is best)

2 pounds ground turkey

1 pound ground veal

3 large eggs

8 tablespoons cognac

2 teaspoons coarsely ground white pepper

1½ teaspoons sea salt

1 teaspoon ground allspice

3 tablespoons fresh thyme leaves

FOR GARNISHING AND LINING THE PÂTÉS:

10 sprigs fresh thyme

20 bay leaves

3 to 4 pounds bacon (about 50 thin slices), preferably a lightly smoked variety

1 To make the pâté, melt the butter over low heat in a large, heavy sauté pan and add the onions. Cook the onions until they are translucent and limp but not brown, 8 to 10 minutes, and transfer them to a very large mixing bowl.

2 Add the garlic, pork, turkey, veal, eggs, cognac, and seasonings to the sautéed onions. Once the onions have cooled, use your hands to blend this mixture well. Cover the bowl tightly with plastic wrap and refrigerate it for at least 2 hours or as long as overnight.

recipe continues

3   Preheat the oven to 350°F, and bring to a simmer a large kettle of water. Prepare ten 3 × 6-inch mini-loaf pans: Place a sprig of thyme and 2 bay leaves in the bottom of each pan. Carefully place 4 or 5 slices of bacon side by side crosswise in the bottom of each pan. Press the bacon slices to the contours of the pan so they line the bottoms and long sides of the pans. Allow the ends of each slice to drape over the sides of the pans.

4   Tightly pack the meat mixture into each lined pan, firmly pressing it into the pans. Bring the overlapping ends of the bacon slices over the top of each pâté and press them into the pâté mixture. Cover each pan with aluminum foil, tightly sealing the edges. Arrange the pâtés side by side in a shallow roasting pan and put them on the middle rack of the preheated oven.

5   Carefully add very hot water to the roasting pan, filling it to a depth of 2 to 3 inches. Bake the pâtés for about 1¼ hours, or until the juices from the pâtés run clear and yellow, not pink. Insert an instant-read thermometer in the center of each pâté to make sure it has reached an internal temperature of 170°F.

6   Carefully remove the roasting pan from the oven. When the water has cooled, take the pâtés out of the pan and empty the water. Discard the foil covers and cover the surface of each cooled pâté with a small sheet of wax paper or parchment paper and put them back in the empty roasting pan.

7   Place a heavy weight (a heavy can, pie weights, etc.) on top of each paper-covered pâté, making sure the weight is resting on the pâté, not the edges of the pan. Set the roasting pan aside until the weighted pâtés pates have cooled to room temperature. Refrigerate the roasting pan with the weighted pâtés for 2 days.

8   Invert and unmold each pâté, revealing the bacon and the herb garnish. Wrap each pâté tightly in plastic wrap and refrigerate until you are ready to assemble and deliver the gifts.

wrapping it up

If you can find them, sleeves of paper-thin birch bark or faux birch-bark paper (see Resources, page 290) suit these country pâtés, but plain white craft paper secured with thick kitchen twine works very nicely, too.

suggested supplies

10 rectangles (5 × 11 inches each) craft paper   **raffia, twine, or natural paper ribbon**

heavy-duty adhesive tape

how to make pâté sleeves

Wrap each pâté (still in its plastic wrap) in a rectangle of paper, making sure the edges of the paper are on the bottom of the pâté; tape the edges tightly to the bottom of each pâté. Double-wrap each pâté lengthwise with raffia, twine, or ribbon, finishing with a tight double knot. Trim the ends of the knot to a desired length and knot them again.

pistachio *sugarplums*

There are countless recipes for sugarplums, and understandably so, for they have been around since the Middle Ages. This version is loaded with spices and dried fruit, shaped to resemble frosty little plums with clove "stems."

I don't know how the Victorians managed to make sugarplums, but I think a food processor is definitely a must for modern-day sugarplum projects. Depending on the size of the processor, it may be necessary to grind the sugarplum mixture in separate batches.

4 cups (about 16 ounces) chopped pitted dates

2⅓ cups coarsely chopped pistachio nuts

1 cup coarsely chopped dried apricots

1 cup coarsely chopped dried figs

⅓ cup brandy

4 tablespoons apricot preserves

3 tablespoons dried orange peel

2 teaspoons ground ginger

1 teaspoon ground cloves

2 teaspoons ground mace

1½ teaspoons ground cinnamon

100 whole cloves (about 2 cups) for the "stems"

1½ cups sanding sugar

overall prep time: slightly more than 24 hours

active prep time: 2 to 3 hours

easy

moderately expensive

can be frozen

ships well

can be doubled or tripled

shelf life: 2 weeks in an airtight container

makes: almost 100

1 Place all the ingredients except the whole cloves and the sanding sugar in a food processor and rapidly pulse the machine on and off for 1 to 2 minutes, or until the mixture is evenly ground into a doughy paste and begins to pull away from the sides of the work bowl. Empty the mixture onto a clean work surface and knead it by hand for 2 minutes to completely blend all the ingredients. Wrap the sugarplum mixture tightly in plastic wrap and refrigerate it for 2 hours or overnight.

recipe continues

2 Place teaspoon-sized scoops of the chilled sugarplum mixture between your palms. Roll the scoops into smooth ovoid shapes (to resemble small plums). Use a wooden skewer or the back of a dinner knife to impress a cleft along the length of each plum shape. Roll the plums in the sanding sugar and insert a whole clove into the fatter end of each sugarplum for a "stem."

3 Lay the sugarplums out on a baking sheet lined with parchment and allow them to firm up in a cool, dry place overnight. Store the sugarplums in single layers in airtight containers at room temperature until you are ready to assemble and deliver the gifts.

wrapping it up

Before the Victorian era, sweet meats or sugarplums were such an expensive treat, they were presented and kept in small, luxurious boxes or coffers. By the mid-nineteenth century, spices, sugar, and dried fruits were less exotic, making sugarplums a far more common confection. They were sold in bulk and packaged in little cones of paper. You can embellish small paper gift boxes and line them with parchment before adding the sugarplums. Small paper cones are available in hundreds of versions, or you can make your own. I favor this simple pyramid-style box, which is adaptable to hanging or standing on its own, for sugarplum gifts. For coffer boxes, I simply embellish small gift boxes I have on hand. The sugarplums should be put in paper candy cups before packaging them in the gift containers.

suggested supplies

store-bought pyramid favor boxes, or, for making your own boxes, heavy paper or lightweight card stock

thin ribbon

ruffled paper candy cups

how to box sugarplum pyramids

A slender pyramid favor box is perfect for sugarplums and other small treats. Stringing a ribbon through the base of the pyramid makes them ideal for decorating a Christmas tree. A ribbon looped through the apex of the pyramid is perfect for holding a gift tag. You can buy pyramid favor boxes at craft stores. You can also make your own pyramid boxes, either by tracing from a store-bought pyramid or downloading a template from any one of several websites that offer free patterns (see Resources, page 290).

Alternatively, you can make a coffer box by embellishing small repurposed gift boxes with paint, paper, stamps, ribbon, or trim. Small wooden beads can be added as feet for the box bottom or knobs for the box lid.

Place individual sugarplums in ruffled paper candy cups. You can then stack the cups in the pyramid or coffer boxes.

round jars of *tomato marmalade* with leafy lids

overall prep time: 24 hours

active prep time: 3 hours

moderately easy

inexpensive

do not freeze

ships well if carefully packed

can be doubled or tripled

shelf life: 6 months refrigerated

makes: sixteen 1-cup jars

Tomato marmalade is good with so many things; corn muffins, toasted sourdough bread, cold chicken, and grilled cheese sandwiches are just a few examples. The marmalade is an excellent garnish for grilled pork chops or salmon. If you don't have a garden or know someone who does, visit your local farmers' market for the best tomatoes at the best price.

8 pounds ripe tomatoes

6 lemons, peels on, scrubbed, seeded, and diced

3 blood oranges, peels on, scrubbed, seeded, and diced

12 cups superfine sugar

½ cup chopped fresh tarragon

2 cups Lillet Blanc or light dry sherry

1 Bring a large pot of water to a boil. Blanch the tomatoes a few at a time in the briskly boiling water and then plunge them into a large basin of ice water until they are cool. The peels will slip off easily. Remove the stem ends from the peeled tomatoes and cut the tomatoes in half. Gently squeeze the halves to extract the seeds (discard the seeds). Dice the seeded tomatoes and measure them (you should have about 12 cups).

2 Combine all the ingredients in a large, nonreactive stockpot, cover the pot, and set it aside in a cool place for 12 hours or overnight.

3 Bring the ingredients in the stockpot to a boil over medium heat, stirring the mixture often so the bottom of the pot does not scorch. Reduce the heat to medium-low and cook the mixture for 1½ to 2 hours, continuing to stir frequently, until it is very thick. (Test the consistency by spooning a small amount of hot marmalade onto a saucer and letting it cool; once it is cool it shows the consistency of the finished marmalade.) If it is still too thin after 2 hours, reduce the heat to low and cook the marmalade, stirring frequently, for another ½ hour.

4 While the marmalade is cooking, sterilize 16 jelly jars (1-cup capacity) and lids in boiling water and invert them on a baking sheet. Keep the jars warm in a 150°F oven.

5 Use a ladle to fill the warm jars with the hot marmalade and let the jars cool for 5 minutes before covering them tightly. Let cool completely, then refrigerate the jars until you are ready to assemble and deliver the gifts.

wrapping it up

Such a large batch of gorgeous marmalade justifies buying the perfect jar in bulk. Squat, round 8-ounce jelly jars with lids are sold online inexpensively (see Resources, page 290). Round jars like these, topped with leaf-covered lids, look just like fat, ripe tomatoes.

suggested supplies for each 8-ounce round jar

double-face tape

5 or 6 large silk or paper leaves

1 length (16 to 20 inches) thin-gauge green floral or craft wire

1 gift card or label

how to make leafy lids

Apply several pieces of double-face tape in a spoke-like fashion to the jar lids. Press the leaves onto the tape in an overlapping pattern radiating from the center of the jar lid and hanging well over the edge. Wrap the wire once around the rim of the jar just under the lid. Wrap the wire around a second time, capturing all but 2 or 3 of the overhanging leaves. Tighten and then twist the wire to hold it in place. Curl the wire ends around a thin dowel or pencil to create tiny tendrils of vine. Punch a hole in the gift card or label and thread it onto one of the curly tendrils.

toffee lady *apples* with pink sea salt

overall prep time: 9 hours

active prep time: 1 hour

slightly challenging

expensive

do not freeze or ship

do not double

shelf life: 2 days carefully wrapped and stored in a cool, dry place

makes: 24 to 26 toffee apples

Lady apples are very small green apples with a red blush that are available at most supermarkets starting in late October or early November. Enrobing these tiny apples in buttery toffee and haloing them with pink sea salt transforms a trick-or-treat favorite into a decidedly adult sweet. I have used these toffee apples for party favors, holiday gifts, and even place cards. Whether a single apple or an entire tray of 25 or so, this makes a wonderful autumn or holiday gift.

24 to 26 Lady apples

24 to 26 bamboo cocktail picks or small craft sticks

2 to 3 tablespoons unsalted butter, softened

24 to 26 small white paper cupcake liners

1 tablespoon pink sea salt (available at gourmet shops and well-stocked grocery stores)

½ cup (1 stick) unsalted butter, cold, thickly sliced

2 cups firmly packed light brown sugar

1 cup light corn syrup

1 can (14 ounces) sweetened condensed milk

1 teaspoon vanilla extract

1 Wash and dry the apples and carefully remove their stems. Insert a bamboo pick or small craft stick into the stem end of each apple, pushing the sticks three-quarters of the way into the centers of the apples. Set the apples aside on a tray.

2 Smear a tiny amount of the softened butter in the bottom of each paper cupcake liner and sprinkle the butter with a little pink sea salt. Arrange the prepared cupcake liners on a heavy-duty tray or baking sheet.

3 Combine the ½ cup cold butter, brown sugar, corn syrup, and sweetened condensed milk in a large heavy-bottomed saucepan. Cook the mixture over medium heat, stirring constantly, until it reaches a boil.

4 Attach a candy thermometer to the inside of the pan and reduce the heat to low. Continue cooking the toffee, stirring very frequently, until it registers 245°F on the candy thermometer. Remove the pan from the heat and stir in the vanilla.

5 Swirl each prepared Lady apple in the hot toffee until it is well coated and then set it in a prepared cupcake liner. Sprinkle the toffee coating with additional pink sea salt. Allow the apples to cool to room temperature and the toffee to set firmly before wrapping, about 8 hours or a bit longer if the weather is humid. Store the apples in a wide, deep storage container with a tea towel loosely draped over the top to allow air circulation. Store in a cool, dry place for up to 24 hours, until you are ready to assemble and deliver the gifts.

wrapping it up

Toffee apples wrapped this way will be pristine and perfect when unwrapped. You can add any sort of ribbon and gift tag to the apples. If you would like to use individual apples for place cards or invitations, punch holes in the top and bottom of the cards and slip them over the sticks. The wrapped apples can be set aside in a cool place for 12 to 24 hours before delivering the gifts.

suggested supplies

24 to 26 squares (6 inches each) clear or colored cellophane

24 to 26 wire twist ties

how to wrap a lady apple

Center each apple, still in its cupcake liner, on a square of cellophane.

Carefully gather and twist the cellophane toward the top of the apple stick and then gently push the cellophane down closer to the apple. This allows the cellophane to pouf around the toffee apple without sticking to it. Hold the cellophane in place by wrapping it with a wire twist tie. The "cupcakes" are ready to embellish with ribbon, gift cards, and other elements.

grissini and more *grissini*

Grissini are Italian cracker sticks. This is a labor-intensive project, but it produces a prodigious number of incredibly long, thin grissini for amazing-looking gifts.

8 cups unbleached all-purpose flour

2 to 3 tablespoons fine sea salt

½ cup light olive oil

¼ cup active dry yeast dissolved in ¼ cup lukewarm water

1¾ cups cool water

1 tablespoon extra-virgin olive oil

sea salt flakes (optional)

overall prep time: about 24 hours

active prep time: 2 hours

challenging

inexpensive

uncooked dough freezes well

do not ship

can be doubled

shelf life: 1 week in an airtight container

makes: about 10 to 15 dozen, enough for at least 10 generous gifts

1 Sift the flour with the fine sea salt directly onto a large work surface, forming a wide mound. Place the light olive oil in a small pitcher and drizzle it all over the mound of flour. Use both hands to rub the oil into the flour until the flour is evenly moistened and looks slightly mealy.

2 Gather the flour into a mound again and make a well in the center to hold the yeast mixture. Slowly add the yeast mixture to the center of the well and swirl your fingertips around and around the edge of the well to incorporate the flour into the yeast. Continue to incorporate the yeast mixture, tracing increasingly larger circles from the center outwards with your fingers, until the mixture is thick and pasty. When all of the water has been incorporated, gather up all the bits and knead the dough just until it sticks together. The dough will still be rather rough and lumpy at this stage. Cover the dough with a towel and let it rest for 30 minutes.

3 Knead the dough on a smooth, unfloured work surface for about 10 minutes or until it is elastic and uniform. Form the dough into a ball and rub the extra-virgin olive oil on top. Put the dough ball, oiled side down, in a large, shallow bowl and

recipe continues

smear the bowl with the oil from the dough. Turn the ball right side up in the bowl and cover with plastic wrap. Refrigerate the dough for 18 to 24 hours.

4 Preheat the oven to 400°F and line two 11 × 17-inch sheet pans with parchment paper. Divide the dough ball in half, covering one half with a towel while working with the other. Using a heavy rolling pin and your hands, stretch and roll the first half of the dough to a thickness of ¼ inch. Trim the edges to form a neat 12 × 17-inch rectangle. Using a straightedge and a sharp knife or rotary pastry cutter, cut the dough into strips no wider than ⅓ inch. Carefully place the strips, close but not touching, on the prepared pans. Using a spray bottle, mist the breadsticks with water and, if you like, sprinkle them with the salt flakes.

5 Place the sheet pans on the center two racks of the oven and bake the grissini for 10 minutes. Switch and rotate the pans, spraying with water once again. Bake for another 7 to 8 minutes, until the grissini are a very pale golden brown. Carefully slip the parchment and grissini onto cooling racks and reline the sheet pans with fresh parchment. Repeat the process with the remaining dough. The grissini should be stored in airtight containers until you are ready to assemble and deliver the gifts.

wrapping it up

The long micro-perforated cellophane bags used by supermarket bakeries are the ideal wrap for grissini. If you ask politely, the counterperson will usually give you a few of these bags or at least sell them to you for a nominal price. You could also use long white paper bakery bags or staple together your own bags from clear cellophane.

suggested supplies for each gift

2 strips (3 × 6 inches) card stock, 1 red and 1 green, or ribbons in the same colors and approximate size	1 cellophane bakery bag
	several strands of raffia
1 strip (3 × 8 inches) white card stock	stencils, stamps, markers, or stickers

how to make banner closures for the grissini bags

Fill the cellophane bag with grissini and fold the top tightly over the grissini. Fold the strips of card stock or wide ribbon in half lengthwise. Place the red and green strips over the folded bag top, overlapping them slightly in the middle. Center the longer white strip on top of the red and green strips, so that some of the green card stock is visible on one side and some of the red on the other. Punch five evenly spaced holes across the strips and through the folded bag top, and weave the raffia in and out of the holes, finishing with a bow to the front and center of the white cardstock strip. Use stencils, stamps, markers, or stickers to make a gift greeting on the white center strip of the banner.

cottage-style fresh rhubarb *tea loaves*

These simple, quick loaf cakes are perfect with tea and coffee, iced or hot. The fresh rhubarb adds a tart jam-like flavor and keeps the bread moist for days on end. Even if you think you do not like rhubarb, I think you will enjoy this.

FOR THE LOAVES:

3 cups all-purpose flour

2 cups cake flour

½ cup semolina flour

2½ teaspoons baking powder

½ teaspoon baking soda

1⅛ teaspoon salt

3 cups granulated sugar

1½ cups (3 sticks) butter, melted and cooled to room temperature

5 large eggs, beaten

1 cup buttermilk

1 tablespoon grated orange zest

¼ cup orange juice

4 cups (about 4 stalks) finely diced rhubarb

FOR THE SUGAR CRUMBLE:

1 cup cake flour

¼ cup yellow cornmeal

1 cup light brown sugar

½ teaspoon grated nutmeg

¼ teaspoon ground mace

½ cup (1 stick) unsalted butter, softened

overall prep time: 2 hours

active prep time: 35 minutes

moderately easy

inexpensive

freezes well

ships well

can be doubled

shelf life: 1 week when well wrapped

makes: 10 small loaves

1. Coat ten 3 × 6-inch mini-loaf pans with nonstick cooking spray and place them on two 11 × 17-inch baking sheets. Preheat the oven to 350°F.

2. To make the loaves, in a large bowl combine the three flours, baking powder, baking soda, and salt, and whisk them together. Add all of the remaining loaf ingredients except the rhubarb, and stir the batter until it is evenly blended. Fold the diced rhubarb into the batter with a large spatula. Fill the pans halfway with

recipe continues

batter and arrange them on the baking sheets. Bake the loaf pans on the middle racks of the oven for 20 minutes.

3   To make the sugar crumble: While the loaves bake, combine all of the crumble ingredients in a small bowl and use a fork to press and blend the ingredients into a rough, crumbly mixture. After the loaves have baked for 20 minutes, sprinkle the crumble topping over them, distributing it evenly. Rotate and switch the baking sheets and continue baking the loaves for another 25 minutes.

4   Cool the pans on racks for 20 minutes and then unmold the loaves directly onto the racks. When the loaves are completely cool, wrap them very tightly in plastic wrap. Store the wrapped tea loaves in an airtight container (or freeze them) until you are ready to assemble and deliver the gifts.

wrapping it up

Patterned card stock in a gingham check or other small pattern gives just the right look to these cottage tea loaves.

suggested supplies for each loaf

glassine or wax paper	**cotton twill tape or ribbon**
double-face tape	**1 gift card**
1 rectangle (3 × 12 inches) patterned card stock	

how create a country wrap

Remove the plastic wrap from a loaf and neatly wrap it in glassine or wax paper. Use double-face tape to seal the wrap on the underside of the loaf. Center the rectangle of cardstock on the loaf lengthwise and use the tape to secure the ends of the cardstock to one another and to the glassine paper wrapping. Center a length of twill tape or ribbon over the cardstock band lengthwise and finish with a simple slip knot or bow. Slip the gift card under the tie.

tapenade **for ten**

Although this is a very simple recipe, it includes all the flavorful elements that make tapenade a time-honored staple of Mediterranean kitchens. Jars of tapenade, along with garlic toast or fresh crudités and wooden spreaders packed in small galvanized tin containers, make for an unusual and welcome gift.

overall prep time:
30 minutes

easy

moderately expensive

do not freeze or ship

can be doubled

shelf life: 1 week refrigerated in a tightly sealed jar

makes: ten 8-ounce jars

3 lemons

8 large garlic cloves, peeled

1½ tablespoons minced fresh ginger

2 cups Mediterranean black olives, pitted, rinsed, and patted dry

2 tablespoons green peppercorns (freeze-dried or in brine)

½ cup drained capers

7 anchovy fillets

2 cans (4 ounces each) sardines packed in olive oil

3 vacuum-packed foil packages (7 ounces each) albacore tuna

1 cup tahini paste

2 tablespoons grainy Dijon mustard

¼ cup loosely packed fresh thyme leaves

1 cup loosely packed fresh basil leaves

⅓ cup extra-virgin olive oil

1 Use a swivel-bladed peeler to remove the zest from the lemons. Set the zest aside. Juice the lemons and set the juice aside. Fit a food processor with the steel chopping blade. Turn the processor on, drop the lemon zest, garlic, and ginger through the feed tube, and process until they are finely chopped.

2 Add the olives, peppercorns, and capers, and pulse the machine on and off until the ingredients are very finely chopped but not pureed (about 30 pulses). Empty the olive mixture into a very large bowl.

3 Place all of the remaining ingredients and ⅓ cup of the reserved lemon juice in the processor and pulse the mixture until the ingredients have the consistency of a very rough, thick puree. Add the puree to the olive mixture in the large bowl. Use a wooden spoon to blend the ingredients together.

4 Taste to correct the seasoning, adding salt or additional lemon juice as needed. Pack the tapenade into 8-ounce jars, cover them tightly, and refrigerate the jars for up to 1 week, until you are ready to assemble and deliver the gifts.

wrapping it up

Small galvanized tin pails or tubs abound at craft, garden, and home stores. If you plan to make a lot of tapenade gifts, shop online for very reasonably priced metal pails (see Resources, page 290). For tapenade gifts with crudités, add a small ice pack to the bottoms of the metal containers if you will be making a lot of deliveries.

suggested supplies for each tapenade gift

1 wired manila shipping tag (available at office-supply stores)

1 galvanized tin pail or tub, 5 to 7 inches in diameter

1 small ice pack (if packing crudités)

1 sheet (5 × 8 inches) parchment paper

crackers, Melba toasts, or crudités

1 small wooden knife or spreader

1 square (14 inches) cellophane

raffia or paper ribbon

how to tub a tapenade

Write a gift message on the shipping tag and set it aside. If you are packing crudités with the tapenade, place an ice pack at the bottom of the pail or tub. Line the bottom of the container with the parchment paper. Arrange the crudités in the tub and set the tapenade jar on top. If you are packing toasts or crackers with the tapenade, place the jar of tapenade in the lined tub first and arrange the toast or crackers around it. Insert the knife or spreader, blade first, in the tub. Center the container on the cellophane, then gather the cellophane tightly over the top and twist it very tightly. Secure the twisted cellophane by tightly wrapping the wire end of the shipping tag around it. Wrap a few strands of raffia or ribbon over the wire, tie it in a tight double knot, and trim the ends.

four-plus pounds of *truffles*

Chocolate is temperamental. It can seize, separate, scorch, or turn to sand with little notice or provocation. This recipe, however, is fairly foolproof, all but eliminating any chance of the chocolate turning against you. To ensure success, never let so much as a drop of water come in contact with the chocolate, and use the best-quality chocolate you can find. If you are inexperienced with chocolate, I strongly recommend that you divide the recipe in half and make two batches, because large quantities of chocolate are more challenging to work with.

4 cups heavy cream

⅔ cup golden corn syrup

3 pounds bittersweet chocolate chips

1 cup (2 sticks) unsalted butter, softened

1⅓ cups Dutch-processed cocoa powder

1 cup sanding sugar

overall prep time: about 30 hours

active prep time: 1 to 1½ hours

slightly challenging

expensive

truffles freeze well before coatings are added

do not ship

can be divided but not doubled

shelf life: up to 2 weeks

makes: about 4½ pounds (4 to 5 dozen large, or 8 to 10 dozen small)

1 Combine the cream and corn syrup in a large, heavy saucepan over medium heat, and slowly bring the mixture to a boil.

2 Place the chocolate chips in a large heatproof bowl and pour the boiling cream mixture over the chocolate. Stir the mixture briefly with a clean, dry spoon and set the bowl aside for 3 to 5 minutes. Use the same spoon to stir in the butter, 1 tablespoon at a time. Continue to stir the truffle mixture until it is smooth and glossy. Pour the mixture into four separate bowls and set them aside to cool completely. Tightly cover the bowls with plastic wrap and refrigerate for 4 hours, or until the truffle mixture is very firm.

recipe continues

3 Depending on the size of truffles you want to make, use a small melon baller, a mini cookie scoop, or a tablespoon to scoop portions of the firm truffle mixture onto wax paper–lined trays. Work with one bowl of the truffle mixture at a time, keeping the others in the refrigerator. Put the trays into the freezer for 20 to 30 minutes.

4 Using the palms of your hands, quickly roll the scoops into balls and return them to the lined trays. Refrigerate the truffles for 1 hour (or you can freeze the truffles for up to 3 months at this point).

5 Mix the cocoa and sanding sugar (or other coating variations, below) in a pie pan or a wide, shallow bowl. Roll 5 or 6 chilled truffles in the pan, tilting and shaking the pan (as if you were panning for gold) until the truffles are evenly coated. Return the coated truffles to the lined trays. Loosely cover the trays with plastic wrap and set them aside in a cool place to firm up for at least 24 hours. Store them in the freezer in a large, airtight container in single layers between sheets of parchment until you are ready to assemble the gifts; the truffles should be frozen at least overnight before proceeding and can be stored frozen for up to 3 months, either in the airtight container or wrapped as described below.

COATING VARIATIONS FOR TRUFFLES

Each of these coating variations will cover about 2¼ pounds of truffles, or half the recipe:

- *chai spice truffle coating:* Combine ¼ cup cocoa powder with 1 teaspoon of each of the following ground spices: white pepper, coriander, cloves, cinnamon, allspice, and ginger.

- *espresso truffle coating:* Combine ¼ cup cocoa powder with 3 tablespoons of powdered instant espresso and 2 tablespoons of turbinado sugar.

- *dark and sweet truffle coating:* Combine ¼ cup cocoa powder with 4 tablespoons dark brown sugar and a pinch of sea salt.

wrapping it up

A gift that can be made and wrapped in advance is a definite asset when there are a lot of gifts to make and wrap. These classic chocolate truffles are a perfect example. Not only do the truffles freeze well, so does the gift wrap. You can start making Christmas presents in September or sweet Valentines in November. One more "do-ahead" tip: Make sure to freeze the truffles at least overnight before starting the gift wraps.

Restaurants use white, cylindrical cardboard "hot or cold" containers with matching lids for packing premium ice creams, hot soups, and sauces. They have classic good looks, come in both pint and half-pint sizes, and are very durable. You can find these containers at restaurant-supply stores or online (see Resources, page 290).

suggested supplies for each gift

5-inch squares waxed colored tissue (sometimes called florist tissue or food-service tissue), 1 for each truffle

colored card stock

1 classic white cardboard "hot or cold" container with lid

colored metal brads

1 or 2 paper cupcake liners

1 length (18 to 24 inches) 1-inch-wide (or narrower) wired ribbon

how to make freezable gift containers

Roll each frozen truffle diagonally in a square of waxed tissue and twist the ends in opposite directions, in the manner that salt-water taffy usually is wrapped. Mound the wrapped truffles on a baking sheet and store them in the freezer while you embellish the containers.

Cut the colored card stock into flowers, hearts, gift cards, or any embellishments you fancy. Attach the card stock embellishments to the container and its lid with colored metal brads. To prepare the container for the ribbon, use a craft knife to cut two small parallel slits about ½ inch apart and 1 inch wide at the center of the bottom of the container and two more at the center of the lid.

Line the bottom of the container with a paper cupcake liner; pint-size containers can hold 2 layers of small truffles, with 1 cupcake liner per layer. Fill the cupcake liner or liners with wrapped truffles, and cover the truffles with another square of the waxed tissue. Securely push the container lid in place. Repeat with additional containers and supplies, as desired.

Arrange the containers on baking sheets, allowing plenty of space between containers so the cardstock embellishments are not crushed or wrinkled. Freeze the decorated cartons for up to 3 months.

Add ribbon to the gifts only after you remove them from the freezer. Pass the ribbon through the precut slots on the bottom of the carton. Draw the ends up evenly on either side of the container and pass each end of the ribbon through both of the precut slots in the lid, threading from left to right with the left-hand ribbon and from right to left with the right-hand ribbon. (You might have to compress the ribbons a bit to get them both to fit through the slots.) Tie the ends in a single knot over the center of the lid, between the slots. Finish with a bow.

sticky *butterscotch cakes* in baking baskets

overall prep time: 2 hours

active prep time:
45 minutes

easy

inexpensive

do not freeze

ships well

can be doubled

shelf life: 1 week tightly wrapped

makes: 14 small cakes

Only the cake is sticky; the recipe itself is very smooth going. There are no pans to butter and line (or wash), no icing to whip or spread, and very little gift wrapping to do. These delectable pudding cakes are baked, glazed, and given in very pretty ovenproof Panibois baskets. These wooden baking baskets come with parchment liners, so they do not need to be buttered. They are about 5 × 3½ × 2 inches in size. You can find them at gourmet and craft stores as well as online; see Resources, page 290.

FOR THE CAKES:

3 cups all-purpose flour

3 cups cake flour

1 tablespoon baking powder

1 tablespoon baking soda

1 teaspoon salt

4 large eggs

3 cups light brown sugar

5 tablespoons unsalted butter, melted

3 cups buttermilk

FOR THE GLAZING SAUCE:

1 cup half-and-half or light cream

1 cup dark brown sugar

⅓ cup unsalted butter

1 tablespoon vanilla extract

1 Preheat the oven to 350°F. To make the cakes, in a large bowl combine the flours, baking powder, baking soda, and salt, and use a wire whisk to blend and aerate the dry ingredients. Combine the eggs, brown sugar, melted butter, and buttermilk in a separate bowl and blend them with a wooden spoon.

2 Stir the liquid ingredients into the dry ingredients with the wooden spoon and beat the ingredients very briefly, just until the mixture is evenly moist. Do not overbeat the batter.

3 Arrange 14 Panibois basket molds with their liners on two large sheet pans. Divide the batter among the pans and bake them on the middle racks of the oven for 20 minutes. Switch and rotate the baking sheets and bake the cakes for another 30 minutes, or until they test clean when a wooden skewer is inserted in the centers of the cakes.

4 To make the glazing sauce: While the cakes are baking, combine all of the sauce ingredients in a heavy saucepan and simmer (but do not boil) over low heat, stirring frequently, for 25 to 30 minutes.

5 Pour the hot glazing sauce slowly over the cakes as soon as they come out of the oven. Cool the glazed cakes on the baking sheets and then wrap them tightly in plastic wrap (still in their wooden baking baskets). Store at room temperature; if you are not planning to assemble and deliver the gift within 8 hours, store the cakes in a very large airtight container until you are ready to proceed.

wrapping it up

Accentuate the natural look of the wooden baking baskets and the deep brown of the cakes by choosing "natural" materials like craft paper or unbleached parchment paper, raffia, waxed string, and twine, along with acorns, nuts, or pine cones, for gift wrapping.

suggested supplies

14 rectangles (3¼ × 4¼ inches each) clear cellophane

14 rectangles (4¼ × 11 inches each) parchment or craft paper

invisible tape

large acorns or tiny pine cones

twine, waxed string, or raffia

14 small gift cards

how to put a cake in a sleeve and an acorn on a string

Remove the plastic wrap and cover the top of each cake with a cellophane square. Wrap each cake in a rectangle of paper, joining the edges and taping them on the bottom of each basket.

Use a handheld power craft drill to make small holes in the acorns or pine cones. String up to three of the drilled embellishments onto 4-inch lengths of the twine, string, or raffia and double-knot both ends.

Wind twine, string, or raffia around all 4 sides of each paper-sleeved cake and tie a double knot to the front and center of each cake, keeping the long ends free. Add a few of the "strung" embellishments to the center of the knot and tie a small bow or looped knot over them. Slip a gift card under each bow.

fresh *mint wafers* in julep cups

Fresh mint adds a lovely color and an intriguing flavor to these tiny cookies. The little wafers are almost candy mints, since they are dipped in white chocolate after baking. Pile them high in silvery julep cups to make party favors, place-card holders, or sophisticated Easter gifts. As presented here, the julep cups would work well as favors or place cards for a summer wedding. If inexpensive silver-plated baby cups were substituted for the julep cups, they would be impressive put to the same use at a baby shower.

overall prep time: 3½ to 4 hours

active prep time: 1 hour

easy

inexpensive

uncooked dough can be frozen for a few days

do not ship

can be doubled

shelf life: up to 2 weeks in an airtight container

makes: 9 dozen

1 cup (2 sticks) unsalted butter, softened and cooled

1 cup granulated sugar

2 large egg yolks

3 cups all-purpose flour, plus 2 tablespoons for dusting your hands

2 teaspoons baking powder

⅓ cup light cream

5 teaspoons white crème de menthe

2 cups finely chopped fresh mint leaves

11 ounces white chocolate chips

2 teaspoons vegetable shortening

1 In the bowl of a large mixer, cream the butter and sugar at medium-high speed for 3 minutes. Add the egg yolks one at a time, beating after each addition.

2 Briefly whisk the 3 cups of flour and the baking powder together in a bowl. Combine the light cream and 2 teaspoons of the crème de menthe in a cup. Add half of the flour mixture to the butter mixture, mix briefly, and then add half of

the light-cream mixture to the batter. Mix briefly, then add the remaining flour mixture and light cream mixture to the dough. Mix briefly again.

3 Reduce the mixer speed to low and gradually add the chopped mint. Beat just until the mint is evenly incorporated into the dough. Scrape the dough (it will be very sticky) onto a large sheet of plastic wrap. Seal the wrap tightly around the dough and put it in the freezer for about 1 hour, or until the roll of dough is very firm to the touch.

4 Divide the dough into 4 portions. Lightly dust your hands with the remaining flour and roll each portion into an 8-inch log. Wrap the logs tightly in wax paper, smoothing all the wrinkles out of the paper. Put the logs in the freezer for at least 1 hour (and up to 3 days), until you are ready to slice and bake the wafers.

5 Preheat the oven to 350°F and line several baking sheets with parchment paper. Slice the logs into ¼-inch-thick wafers and place them 1 inch apart on the lined baking sheets. Bake the wafers on the center racks of the oven for 6 minutes. Switch and rotate the pans and continue baking for another 6 minutes. The wafers should be browned around the edges and evenly browned on the bottoms. Cool the baking sheets on racks and store the wafers in airtight containers until you are ready to coat them with white chocolate.

6 Preheat the oven to 200°F. In a heatproof bowl, combine the remaining 3 teaspoons of crème de menthe, the white chocolate chips, and vegetable shortening. Place the bowl in the warm oven to melt the chocolate, stirring the mixture every 6 to 8 minutes until the chocolate is completely melted. Meanwhile, arrange the wafers on baking racks set over baking sheets or parchment paper; the wafers should be close but not touching. Using a small ladle or deep spoon, cover each wafer with the chocolate mixture. Use a pastry scraper to collect the chocolate drippings from under the racks and transfer them back to the bowl of chocolate. When necessary, return the bowl to the warm oven to melt the chocolate again, and continue the process until all the wafers are covered with white chocolate.

7 Set the racks of coated wafers aside in a cool, dry place for 12 to 24 hours. Pack the wafers in single layers between sheets of wax paper in airtight containers until you are ready to assemble and deliver the gifts.

recipe continues

wrapping it up

Julep cups in silver plate or metallic plastic are available at party and craft stores or anyplace else that sells wedding supplies. If you plan to buy at least a dozen julep cups, you can buy silver-plated cups online (see Resources, page 290) for the same price you'd pay for the plastic version at local craft stores.

suggested supplies for each julep cup

1 square (6 inches) parchment paper or pale green vellum

1 small silver-plated or plastic julep cup, no more than 5 inches tall

1 square (9 inches) clear cellophane

1 wire twist tie

1 small 3-leaf cluster or floral pick of wired silky paper leaves (available with florists' materials at craft stores)

pale green silky ribbon

1 small round gift tag

how to fill and wrap a julep cup

Loosely roll the parchment or vellum, set it inside the cup, and let the roll unfurl in the cup. Overfill each cup with mint wafers and gently pinch or fold back the paper collar to reveal the wafers. Center the cup on the cellophane, tightly gather the cellophane over the cup, twist the ends tightly, and secure with the twist tie. Twist one cluster of leaves to the wire twist tie. Wrap and cover the twist tie with the silky ribbon, knotting it tightly, and finish with a loopy little bow and streamers. Punch a hole in the gift tag, string it onto the ribbon streamers, and knot them around the tag to hold the tag in place.

chinese *spiced peanuts* in take-away boxes

Raw peanuts slow roasted in this Far Eastern marinade look like shiny wooden beads. They are spicy, crunchy, and more than slightly addictive.

4 pounds blanched raw peanuts (available at health-food stores and Asian markets as well as online; see Resources, page 290)

4 teaspoons five-spice powder

1 tablespoon kosher salt

1 teaspoon ground coriander

1 tablespoon granulated sugar

½ cup plus 1 tablespoon water

bottled hot sauce to taste

1 Preheat the oven to 350°F. Rinse the peanuts and let them drain in a colander for 10 minutes. Spread them in a single layer over the baking sheets.

2 Whisk all the remaining ingredients together in a 2-cup liquid measure. Add additional water or hot sauce as needed to make a total of ¾ cup marinade. Pour the marinade over the 2 sheets of nuts, and shake the pans to coat the peanuts with the marinade.

3 Bake the nuts on the middle racks of the oven, turning them with a wide spatula every 15 minutes, for 1 hour. Reduce the oven temperature to 325°F and continue to bake the peanuts, turning them with the spatula every 10 minutes, until all the moisture has evaporated and the pans are dry. The peanuts should be shiny and a deep brown color. Put the baking sheets on racks to cool the nuts completely. Store the cooled peanuts in an airtight container until you are ready to assemble and deliver the gifts.

recipe continues

overall prep time: 3 hours

active prep time: 45 minutes

easy

inexpensive

do not freeze

ships well in an airtight container

can be doubled

shelf life: 4 to 6 weeks in an airtight container

makes: 4 pounds

wrapping it up

While you will not have any trouble locating Chinese "take-away" boxes for packaging these spicy nuts, you may have a little trouble deciding which ones to buy. Craft and party-supply stores offer plenty of sizes and colors. Light-colored paper versions enable you to write gift messages directly on the boxes, to simplify the gift-wrapping. Import stores, Asian markets, and specialty paper stores feature renditions of the traditional take-away box in non-traditional materials such as ceramic and clear plastic. If you can lay your hands on a few copies of a Chinese newspaper it will make an excellent liner for your favorite version of the take-away box.

fennel *pickles* with fresh tarragon

Fennel is such an underappreciated vegetable! The crisp texture and the delicate licorice flavor of fresh fennel enable this pickle to stand alone as an hors d'oeuvre. I always keep this on hand; it is easy to make and has so many uses. I add diced fennel pickle to chicken salad, and I heat it gently to use as a garnish for fish or pork dishes. The recipe is designed so that you can make as much or as little as you need. Multiply the ingredients by the number of pints you want to make.

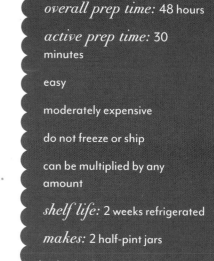

overall prep time: 48 hours

active prep time: 30 minutes

easy

moderately expensive

do not freeze or ship

can be multiplied by any amount

shelf life: 2 weeks refrigerated

makes: 2 half-pint jars

2 large fresh fennel bulbs

4 small lemons

12 sprigs fresh tarragon

coarse sea salt to taste

⅔ cup champagne vinegar

2 tablespoon fennel seeds

2 teaspoons green peppercorns

1 Prepare the fennel bulbs by cutting off the leafy tops and discarding the tough outer stalks (which are often bruised and discolored). Wash and dry the trimmed bulbs. Halve the bulbs lengthwise and trim off the bottoms of each half. Slice the fennel lengthwise in ⅓-inch-thick slices and put the slices in a large colander.

2 Juice 2 of the lemons, reserve the juice, and roughly chop the reamed halves. Add the chopped lemon to the colander along with half of the tarragon, and toss the fennel, lemon pieces, and tarragon with the sea salt. Set the colander aside for 30 minutes.

recipe continues

3 Wash 2 half-pint heat-resistant jars and lids with hot soapy water and place them in a 190°F oven to dry and sterilize.

4 Combine the vinegar and the reserved lemon juice in a small nonreactive saucepan and bring the mixture to a boil. Discard the lemon pieces and the wilted tarragon from the colander. Cut the remaining 2 lemons into ¼-inch slices and pack them with the fennel slices, remaining fresh tarragon sprigs, fennel seeds, and peppercorns in the hot jars. Cover the jars with damp pieces of cheesecloth and pour the hot vinegar mixture into the jars. Use a wooden spoon handle to press any air pockets out of the jars. The jar contents must be totally submerged in the liquid. Cover the jars and store them in a cool, dark place for 48 hours. Refrigerate the pickle until you are ready to assemble and deliver the gifts.

wrapping it up

A translucent vellum label framed in silver surrounding the jar complements the wonderful colors and highlights the beautiful shapes of this pickle. Use an all-surface marker to write out a label on a wide strip of vellum long enough to wrap around the jar.

suggested supplies for each jar

double-face tape

1 vellum label large enough to encircle the jar

thin silver adhesive-backed tape (available at craft stores)

how to make a silver-framed label surround

Apply a strip of double-face tape to the back of the vellum label and press the label into place all around the jar. Remove the protective film from the silver tape and apply it to the top and bottom of the vellum label to frame it. Use a bone folder (or a cuticle stick) to attach the tape firmly to the label and jar.

FENNEL PICKLE

FENNEL PICKLE

...CKLE

cupcakes by the inch, foot, or yard

overall prep time: 1½ hours

active prep time: 45 minutes

easy

inexpensive

freezes well

do not ship

can be doubled or tripled

shelf life: 2 to 3 days in an airtight container

makes: 6 dozen

This cupcake measures up to your fondest childhood memories of parties and after-school treats. It is lighter than air yet moist, with plenty of chocolate punch and an old-fashioned cocoa frosting. As an added bonus when you're cooking in big batches, one very simple batter base makes both the cupcake and the frosting. So, if you like, you can make yards and yards of cupcakes to package by the inch or foot in shipping tubes or in recycled cardboard potato-chip cylinders.

1 package (8 ounces) cream cheese

½ cup (1 stick) unsalted butter, cold

1½ teaspoons vanilla extract

6 cups confectioners' sugar

⅓ cup milk, warmed

⅔ cup cocoa powder

1 teaspoon instant espresso granules

¼ cup unsalted butter, melted

3 eggs, well beaten

¾ cup buttermilk

1¼ cups all-purpose flour

1 cup cake flour

3 teaspoons baking powder

1 teaspoon salt

1 Preheat the oven to 350°F. In the bowl of a stand mixer, combine the cream cheese, cold butter, vanilla, confectioners' sugar, milk, cocoa powder, and espresso granules, and beat on medium speed for 5 minutes. You will have a slightly fluffy batter. Remove approximately one-third of the batter to a small bowl and reserve it for frosting the cupcakes.

2 Continue to beat the remaining batter while you add the melted butter, eggs, and half of the buttermilk.

3 In a small bowl, whisk together the flours, baking powder, and salt. Add half of this mixture to the batter, beating on low speed until the flour mixture is completely incorporated. Continue beating the batter as you add the remaining buttermilk, followed by the remaining flour mixture. At this point, you will have a fairly thick batter.

4 Line muffin pans with paper cupcake liners and fill each one with about 3 tablespoons of batter. Bake the cupcakes for 12 minutes on the two middle racks of the oven. Rotate and switch the pans, and continue baking for another 10 minutes. Remove the cupcakes in their paper liners from the pans and place them on a cooling rack. Repeat with the remaining batter.

5 Once the cupcakes have cooled, top each one with a small amount of the reserved frosting. Use an offset spatula to spread the frosting smooth and flush with the top of the baking cup. Store the frosted cupcakes in an airtight container at room temperature until you are ready to assemble and deliver the gifts.

wrapping it up

Because the cupcakes are so light and are frosted flush with their paper liners they can be stacked between flattened cupcake liners. White or brown cardboard shipping tubes decorated with measuring tape can be adapted to any height of cupcake stack. You can also substitute paper-covered cardboard potato-chip cylinders for the shipping tubes.

suggested supplies

cardboard shipping tubes and extra plastic end pieces (available at office-supply stores)

low-temp hot glue or super-tacky craft glue

paper, plastic, or fabric-ribbon measuring tapes

cupcake liners

double-face tape

how to stack and pack cupcakes by the inch

Shipping tubes are available in several sizes, so it is easy find just the right size for the number (or inches or feet) of cupcakes to be stacked and packed. You can use a craft saw to cut custom lengths from larger tubes, since extra plastic end pieces are available wherever you buy the shipping tubes. Use the glue gun or craft glue to apply measuring tape directly to tubes, or use the tape as a tie for the tubes. Stack the cupcakes between flattened cupcake liners in the tube and seal the tube with the plastic top. Use the double-face tape to attach an inverted cupcake liner to the top and bottom of each tube and tie them in place with a length of measuring tape or other color-coordinated ribbon.

crisp and creamy homemade *candy bars*

These chocolate candy bars have it all—crisp wafers, creamy caramel layers, and rich peanut butter. They are very easy and inexpensive to make, perfect for bake sales, birthday parties, or Halloween treats.

overall prep time: about 6 hours

active prep time: 1 hour

easy

inexpensive

do not freeze

do not ship

can be doubled

shelf life: 1 week in an airtight container stored in a cool place

makes: 32

2½ cups milk chocolate chips

16 ounces buttery rectangular crackers, such as Nabisco Waverly or Keebler Club

2 cups (4 sticks) unsalted butter, cut into thin slices

1 cup whole milk

3⅓ cups fine graham cracker crumbs, from about 30 graham crackers

2 cups firmly packed light brown sugar

⅔ cup granulated sugar

1⅓ cups premium-quality creamy peanut butter

1 Prepare two 9 × 13-inch pans by lightly coating them with cooking spray and lining the bottoms with wax paper. Melt the chocolate in either the microwave or a very low oven. "Paint" the bottom of each prepared pan with a thin layer of melted chocolate, using a pastry brush or icing spatula. Keep the remaining chocolate warm. Cover the melted chocolate with a single layer of crackers and set the pans aside while you make the caramel.

2 Melt the sliced butter in a large saucepan over medium-low heat. Add the milk, graham cracker crumbs, and sugars to the pan. Cook the mixture for 8 to 12 minutes, stirring constantly, until it thickens and turns to caramel. Pour one quarter of the hot caramel mixture over the cracker layer in each pan and use an offset spatula to spread the caramel in a thin layer over the crackers. Cover the

caramel with another layer of crackers. Divide the remaining caramel between the two pans and spread it in a thin layer over the crackers.

3   In the same pan you used for the caramel, gently heat the peanut butter through. Remove the pan from the heat and add about 1 cup of the remaining melted chocolate to the warm peanut butter; stir the mixture until it is smooth. Pour half of this mixture over each pan of candy bars. Spread and smooth this layer with the offset spatula. Refrigerate the pans for 30 to 40 minutes.

4   Gently reheat the remaining chocolate in a microwave oven on Medium, checking it every 30 seconds, until it is melted enough to pour over the chilled pans of candy bars. Working quickly, pour the chocolate evenly over the two pans and spread it with the offset spatula. Cover the pans with plastic wrap, transfer them to the refrigerator, and chill the candy for several hours or overnight, until it is very firm.

5   Unmold the pans onto a cutting board. Peel away the wax paper. Use a long serrated knife to cut each slab in half crosswise and cut each half into bars approximately 1½ × 4½ inches in size. The bars should be individually wrapped in clear cellophane, colored craft foil, or craft or parchment paper immediately. The wrapped bars can be stored in an airtight container in a cool place for up to 2 days until you are ready to assemble and deliver the gifts.

wrapping it up

Sealing the wrapped bars with adhesive labels instead of tape adds a bit of polish to the presentation. If you have the necessary computer skills, you can create custom labels for every conceivable occasion: individual names for party favors, ingredients and a price for bake sales, seasonal images for Halloween or other holidays. Or you can use blank labels and a marker to make handwritten labels.

peel and eat *shortbread* on chocolate cards

overall prep time: 1 hour and 15 minutes

active prep time: 35 minutes

easy

inexpensive

raw dough freezes well; finished shortbread should not be frozen

can be shipped if well cushioned in an airtight container

can be halved (do not double)

shelf life: up to 1 week in an airtight container

makes: about 14 dozen

Classic shortbread dough requires only a few ingredients and very little preparation. Shortbread is incredibly easy to make in very large batches. In this recipe, you use chocolate to "glue" the shortbread squares to simple cards with closing flaps.

2 cups (4 sticks) unsalted butter, chilled and thinly sliced

½ cup light brown sugar

½ cup granulated sugar

5 cups all-purpose flour

¼ cup sanding sugar or granulated sugar

1 Preheat the oven to 325°F. Combine the butter, brown sugar, and the ½ cup of granulated sugar in the bowl of a stand mixer fitted with the wire whip attachment. Cream the mixture for 3 minutes, starting on low speed and gradually increasing the speed. Switch from the wire beater attachment to the paddle attachment and reduce the mixer speed to low. Gradually add all the flour to the creamed butter and sugar, working in ½-cup increments. The mixture will be moist but too crumbly to form a solid mass of dough.

2 Smear a little bit of the dough in the corners and centers of two large (11 × 17-inch) sheet pans, then line the sheet pans with parchment paper. (The dough helps hold the parchment in place as you spread the rest of the dough over it.)

3 Divide the crumbly dough between the two lined sheet pans. Flatten and pat the dough until it covers the entire surface of each pan. A wide, flat dough scraper is a

good tool to use to "squeegee" the dough evenly over the pans. Sprinkle the dough with an even coating of the sanding sugar and gently press the sugar into the dough with the palms of your hands.

4 Use a plastic or metal straightedge to score a grid of 1½-inch squares over the entire surface of the dough (cutting almost but not all the way through). Pierce each outlined square diagonally once with the tines of a fork. Reduce the oven temperature to 300°F and bake the cookies on the middle racks of the oven for 45 minutes. The dough should be a very pale golden beige and firm to the touch. Cool the pans for 5 minutes on racks and then cut through the imprinted grid lines with a sharp knife while the pans are still warm. Let the shortbread cool completely, then separate the squares by hand. Store the shortbread squares in an airtight container until you are ready to assemble and deliver the gifts.

wrapping it up

To make the festive "chocolate cards," you attach a doily or a circle of parchment paper to a piece of cake board or cardboard using chocolate as your glue. Then you coat one side of each shortbread cookie with additional chocolate.

suggested supplies

1 large piece of cake board or cardboard

1 package (12 ounces) bittersweet chocolate chips

paper doilies or parchment-paper circles, 4 to 5 inches in diameter, 1 for each card

6-inch glassine or cellophane bags, 1 for each card

decorative adhesive labels or stickers, 1 for each card

how to wrap a cookie card

Cut the cake board or cardboard into 5-inch squares. Melt the chocolate chips on the stove over very low heat, and allow the chocolate to cool until it is thick but still liquid. Affix a doily or parchment-paper circle to each cardboard square with a dab of the melted chocolate. Use an offset spatula to thinly coat the back of each shortbread square with melted chocolate, and arrange, coated side down, side by side on each prepared cardboard square. Depending on how many gifts you want to make, you can use 6 shortbread squares per card (2 rows of 3), 9 squares per card (3 rows of 3), or any number that works for you. Carefully set the squares aside until the chocolate has cooled completely and the shortbread squares are firmly attached to the cardboard. Once the chocolate has cooled and the shortbread is firmly attached to the doily-lined cardboard, slip each "card" of cookies into a glassine or cellophane gift bag, fold the open ends of the bag together, and seal them with an adhesive label or sticker.

a rich and buttery *yeast dough,* and five *breads* to make with it

I am sure this Swedish recipe for a buttery yeast dough is the Nordic cousin of classic French brioche dough. The recipe is relatively easy, especially when compared to the far more complicated brioche dough. The recipe produces a prodigious quantity of light, rich dough, and there is a seemingly inexhaustible variety of things you can make with it—everything from golden breakfast Danish to chewy and moist cheese-filled breadsticks. I consider this wonderfully versatile dough a godsend to both new and experienced bakers who have a long gift list. The five breads that follow this recipe use this dough and make especially nice gifts.

A word about working with large quantities of rich yeast dough: This recipe yields so many pastries and breads that you may not have enough time, space, or pans to work with more than a portion of the dough at one time. If that is the case, keep the rest of the dough in a flat-bottomed bowl tightly covered with plastic wrap and refrigerate it for up to 24 hours until you, or your kitchen equipment, are available to bake more dough. (Note that because a refrigerated dough is cold, it will take a little longer to undergo its final rising before baking.)

recipe continues

overall prep time: 2 hours

active prep time: 30 to 45 minutes

slightly challenging

moderately expensive

both shaped dough and finished breads freeze well

do not ship

do not double or halve

makes: 1 large batch, enough for any of the 5 recipes that follow

2 packages (2¼ teaspoons each) active dry yeast

1½ cups (3 sticks) unsalted butter, cut in thick slices

2 cups buttermilk

¼ cup granulated sugar

7 cups all-purpose flour

1 Put the yeast in the bowl of a stand mixer. Melt the butter in a small saucepan over low heat, add the buttermilk, and warm the mixture to about 110°F on an instant-read thermometer. Pour the warm buttermilk mixture over the yeast and whisk until the yeast is dissolved.

2 Beat the liquid at low speed using the paddle attachment, while gradually adding the sugar and 3 cups of the flour to the mixer bowl.

3 Increase the mixer speed to medium and gradually beat in the remaining 4 cups of flour. Continue to beat the dough with the paddle attachment until it is satiny smooth and cleanly pulls away from the sides of the bowl. Remove the bowl of dough from the mixer stand, cover it loosely with a tea towel, and set it aside in a warm, draft-free place to rise for 40 minutes, or until it has almost doubled in volume. The dough is now ready to be used in any of the recipes that follow.

sunny orange marmalade danish

Each marmalade Danish looks like a swirling golden sun, making these an appropriate and especially pretty breakfast gift.

Makes 48

1 batch Buttery Yeast Dough, page 113

2 to 3 tablespoons all-purpose flour, for dusting the rolling pin

¼ cup (½ stick) unsalted butter, softened

⅔ cup orange marmalade

1 large egg

½ cup pearl sugar or coarsely crushed sugar cubes

1 Line four cupcake pans (each holding a dozen cupcakes) with paper cupcake liners. Turn the dough out onto a work surface and divide it in half. Lightly flour a heavy rolling pin and roll the first half of the dough into a 12 × 16-inch rectangle. Spread the top of the dough with 2 tablespoons of the butter. Whisk the marmalade to loosen its consistency and spread half of it over the butter.

2 Tightly roll the rectangle from one long side to the other and pinch the dough to seal the roll. Cut the roll into 24 even slices and place each slice in a cupcake liner in the prepared pans. As you fill each pan set it aside to allow the Danish to rise for 30 minutes. Repeat this process with the second half of the dough and the remaining butter and marmalade. While the dough rises, preheat the oven to 425°F.

3 Beat the egg in a small bowl and liberally brush it over each pastry. Sprinkle the pastries with the sugar pearls or crushed sugar cubes. Bake the Danish on the center racks of the oven for 15 minutes. Switch and rotate the pans and continue baking the Danish for another 10 minutes, or until the pastry is golden brown. Cool the pans briefly on racks before transferring the Danish directly to the racks to finish cooling. Store the cooled Danish in an airtight container for up to 24 hours, until you are ready to assemble and deliver the gifts.

greek savory sweet rolls

The combination of onions and raisins may be new to you, but I urge you to try this wonderful roll. It is moist and full of intriguing flavor, making it a wonderful addition to brunches or light lunches.

Makes 48

3 medium-size yellow onions, peeled and sliced as thinly as possible (to make about 1 quart loosely packed sliced onions)

6 tablespoons (¾ stick) unsalted butter

1 tablespoon light brown sugar

⅔ cup golden raisins

2 teaspoons dried thyme leaves

1 batch Buttery Yeast Dough, page 113

2 to 3 tablespoons all-purpose flour

1 Carefully separate the sliced onions into rings. Melt the butter in a large sauté pan over medium-low heat. Add the onions to the pan and cook them slowly, stirring very frequently, until they are reduced to about half their original volume. Add the brown sugar, raisins and thyme to the pan and continue to cook, stirring frequently, until the onions are translucent, golden, and almost a "melted" puree.

2 Remove the pan from the stove and let the onion mixture cool completely. While the mixture cools, line four cupcake pans (each holding a dozen cupcakes) with paper cupcake liners. Turn the dough out onto a work surface and divide it in half. Lightly flour a

heavy rolling pin and roll the first half of the dough into a 12 × 16-inch rectangle.

3 Spread half of the cooled onion mixture over the rolled-out dough. Tightly roll the rectangle from one long side to the other and pinch the dough to seal the roll. Cut the roll into 24 even slices and place each slice in a cupcake liner in the prepared pans. As you fill each pan set it aside to allow the rolls to rise for 30 minutes. Repeat this process with the second half of the dough and the remaining onion mixture. While the dough rises, preheat the oven to 425°F.

4 Bake the rolls on the center racks of the oven for 15 minutes. Switch and rotate the pans and continue baking the rolls for another 10 minutes, or until the pastry is golden brown. Cool the pans briefly on racks before transferring the rolls directly to the racks to finish cooling. Store the rolls in an airtight container for up to 24 hours until you are ready to assemble and deliver the gifts.

black currant buns

Try using parchment "tulip cup" papers instead of the traditional pleated variety for these unusual buns, to make them as impressive in appearance as they are in flavor. Parchment tulip cups are available at most baking-supply stores.

Makes 48

⅔ cup pomace brandy, such as Grappa or Marc

⅔ cup water

1¼ cups dried black currants

1 batch Buttery Yeast Dough, page 113

½ cup turbinado sugar

1 Combine the brandy and water in a 2-quart saucepan with a tight-fitting lid. Cover the pan and bring the liquid to a rolling boil over medium heat. Remove the pan from the heat, add the dried currants to the liquid, cover the pan again, and set it aside to cool completely.

2 Meanwhile, line four cupcake pans (each holding a dozen cupcakes) with paper cupcake liners or parchment tulip cups. When the pan of currants has cooled completely, drain the currants in a colander. Discard the liquid. Spread the drained currants on several paper towels and pat them dry.

3 Roll out the dough into a large rectangle (about 11 by 17 inches) and sprinkle it evenly with the currants. Fold the dough in thirds and knead until the currants are evenly distributed throughout the dough.

4 Preheat the oven to 350°F. Place a portion of dough (approximately ⅓ cup) in each cupcake liner in the prepared pans. Set the filled pans aside to allow the buns to rise for about 45 minutes, or until the dough has risen almost to the top of each paper liner. Use kitchen scissors to cut a deep "X" in the top of each bun and sprinkle the buns liberally with turbinado sugar.

5 Bake the buns on the center racks of the oven for 25 to 30 minutes, or until they are a pale golden brown. Place the pans on racks to cool for 5 minutes, then turn the buns out directly onto the racks to cool completely. Store in an airtight container for up to 24 hours, until you are ready to assemble and deliver the gifts.

wrapping it up:
sunny marmalade danish, greek savory sweet rolls, or black currant buns

These three breads reheat extremely well, so package them in an oven-ready gift wrap with the reheating instructions right on top.

suggested supplies for each gift

1 disposable aluminum foil loaf pan (8 × 4 × 2½ inches)

2 sheets (10 × 14 inches each) parchment paper

12 metal brads

2 rectangles (8 × 18 inches each) clear cellophane

Twine or paper ribbon

1 square (4 inches) card stock

how to make an oven-ready wrap

Center the loaf pan on one sheet of parchment and center the second sheet of parchment over the pan. Use your hands to crease, fold, and press both sheets of parchment to the contours of the pan sandwiched between them; the goal is to camouflage the aluminum foil pan in a crisp, freeform ruffle of parchment. Using a bamboo skewer or similar implement, pierce 12 holes in an evenly spaced pattern around the periphery of the parchment-clad pan, going all the way through the outer parchment, the aluminum foil pan, and the inner parchment. Insert the brads into the holes, opening the wings over the inner lining parchment.

Fill the parchment-lined pan with the Danish, rolls, or buns (it is okay to stack them on top of one another). Wrap the cellophane tightly around the filled pan and wind twine or paper ribbon around the cellophane cover to hold it in place. Write these reheating instructions on the card-stock square: "Preheat the oven to 325°F. Remove the ribbon and cellophane, and reheat the rolls for 15 minutes." Slip the card under the twine or ribbon.

sweet baby brioches

When I found tiny disposable paper brioche molds, available at baking-supply stores and specialty gourmet stores (and online; see Resources, page 290), it inspired this diminutive take on a classic.

Makes 75 to 80

1 batch Buttery Yeast Dough, page 113

75 to 80 miniature paper brioche molds

1 large egg

1 egg yolk

1 tablespoon water

2 tablespoons (¼ stick) unsalted butter, melted and cooled to room temperature

2 to 3 tablespoons sanding or caster sugar

1 Preheat the oven to 375°F.

2 To make each baby brioche, you will need a golf ball–sized portion of dough and a smaller portion about the size of a marble. Roll the larger portion by hand into a round ball and insert your forefinger through the center of the ball, making the ball into the shape of a fat miniature doughnut. Place the shaped dough into a miniature paper brioche mold. Roll the marble-sized piece of dough by hand into a smooth ball and press it deeply and firmly into the hole in the center of the "doughnut." Repeat with remaining dough. All of the mini brioche molds will fit comfortably on two standard baking sheets.

3 Prepare the egg glaze: Whisk the egg and egg yolk with the water until completely blended. Whisk in the melted, cooled butter. Using a small pastry brush, gently and thoroughly glaze each brioche. Reserve the remaining glaze. Set the baking sheets aside for 30 minutes, or until the brioches have risen slightly.

4 Brush the brioches with the remaining glaze and then liberally sprinkle each with the sanding sugar.

5 Place the baking sheets on the center racks of the oven and reduce the temperature to 350°F. Bake the brioches for 10 minutes. Switch and rotate the pans and bake the brioches for another 10 minutes, or until they are a very deep golden brown. Set the pans on racks to cool for 5 minutes, and then set the brioches directly on the racks to cool completely. Gently remove each cooled brioche from its paper pan (which can be discarded). Return the brioches to the racks to cool until you are ready to assemble and deliver the gifts. This gift should be delivered within a few hours of baking.

asiago and pine nut twists

The smooth and complex flavor of Asiago cheese combined with the subtle taste and texture of pine nuts make this one of the best soft bread sticks ever.

Makes 36

1 batch Buttery Yeast Dough, page 113

2 to 3 tablespoons all-purpose flour

3 large eggs

1 cup pine nuts, roughly chopped

2 cups grated Asiago cheese

Coarse sea salt crystals

1 Turn half the dough out onto a work surface. Lightly flour a heavy rolling pin and roll the dough into a 12 × 16-inch rectangle. Using a rotary pastry cutter and a straightedge guide, cut the rectangle into twelve 16-inch-long strips of dough.

2 Beat the eggs in a small bowl to form a smooth glaze. Coat the dough strips with the glaze, reserving any extra glaze. Sprinkle the dough strips with half of the chopped pine nuts and then cover the dough with a little less than half of the grated Asiago. Create pairs of bread sticks by tightly pinching the tops of two adjacent strips together. Very tightly twist the pairs of strips around one another, forming six tight spirals of dough. Cut each spiral into thirds. (You should now have 18 twists each measuring approximately 4 inches in length.) Tightly pinch the ends of each twist so they will not unravel when rising and baking. Arrange the twists about 1 inch apart on parchment-lined baking sheets. As you finish each baking sheet, set it aside to allow the twists to rise for 20 minutes. While the twists rise, preheat the oven to 400°F.

3 Brush the twists with the remaining egg glaze. Sprinkle the glazed bread twists sparingly with some of the remaining grated Asiago cheese and a little coarse sea salt. Place the sheet pans on the center racks of the oven and reduce the oven temperature to 375°F. Bake the twists for 6 minutes. Switch and rotate the pans and continue to bake the twists for another 6 to 8 minutes, until they are golden brown and the cheese is bubbling and brown. Set the pans on cooling racks and do not remove the twists until they are completely cool. Repeat all of the steps with the second half of the dough. The cooled twists can be stored for up to 24 hours in an airtight container until you are ready to assemble and deliver the gifts.

wrapping it up: sweet baby brioches

Sweet Baby Brioches are perfect at room temperature. Neatly aligned in a large white pastry box they make a charming and delicious gift.

suggested supplies for each gift

1 plain full or half sheet-cake box

1 plain full or half sheet-cake board

1 large paper doily to fit the box, or a piece of colored card stock cut to fit the box

bakers' twine or thin ribbon

how to box a big batch of baby brioches

Crease and fold the cake box into shape. Place the cake board in the bottom of the box and cover it with the doily or card stock. Form neat rows of brioches in the box and close it. Tie the twine or ribbon tightly around the box in both directions and finish with a small bow.

wrapping it up: asiago and pine nut twists

The Asiago and Pine Nut Twists are too pretty to cover up. Slender cellophane gift bags are just the thing for showing this gift to its best advantage. A 4 × 6-inch rectangular cellophane gift bag will hold over a dozen bread twists.

suggested supplies

3 or 4 clear cellophane gift bags (4 × 6 inches each), available at party, craft, or paper stores

3 or 4 wire twist ties, 1 for each bag

curling ribbon

3 or 4 large gift tags, 1 for each bag

how to twist and tie pretty bread twists

Fill each cellophane bag with 12 to 16 bread twists and tightly twist the top of the bag closed. Secure each bag top with a wire twist tie. Cover the twist ties with the curly ribbon and tie it in tight double knots. Thread the curly ribbon ends through the holes in the gift tags and tie another knot to secure the tags to the gifts.

vanilla *sugar tubes*

This is one of the simplest big-batch gifts you could ever hope to find. It is perfect for members of a cookie exchange club or for any group of friends that enjoys cooking. I give these as favors to my cooking students. Vanilla beans are sold in supermarkets, but they can be expensive there. You can buy them more economically in bulk online (see Resources, page 290). The 12-inch plastic tubes are about 1 inch in diameter; they are available at some craft stores and are easy to find online (see Resources, page 290). The recipe can be easily increased; simply multiply the ingredients by the number of tubes you want to fill.

overall prep time: 2 weeks

active prep time: less than 3 minutes per tube

easy

inexpensive

do not freeze

ships well when tubes are sufficiently protected

can be multiplied to create any quantity of gifts

shelf life: 1 year

makes: one 12-inch tube

2 whole vanilla beans	1 plastic tube, 12 inches long and about 1 inch in diameter, sealed at one end and with a cap for the other	about ⅔ cup granulated sugar

1 Put 2 vanilla beans in the plastic tube, and fill the tube with sugar. Seal the tube with its cap.

2 Set the tube in a cool, dry place for 2 weeks, shaking it occasionally so the vanilla flavor and aroma permeate the sugar. Store in a cool, dry place until you are ready to assemble and deliver the gift.

wrapping it up

This is one of those all-in-one wraps that are so handy when you have a lot of gifts to make. A sheet of colored 8½ × 11-inch paper or card stock will wrap the sugar tube and also serve as a gift card. On the reverse side you can list some of the uses for vanilla sugar; use either your word-processing design skills or your calligraphy skills to write the list.

suggested supplies for each vanilla sugar tube

1 sheet (8½ × 11 inches) colored paper or card stock

1 elasticized gift cord

1 miniature cookie cutter (optional)

how to make a three-in-one wrap

On one side of the paper or card stock create a gift message and any desired other embellishments across the upper third of the short side of the sheet. Turn the sheet over and write or type a list of uses for the sugar; these uses might include sweetening espresso or hot chocolate, garnishing cookies before baking, sprinkling on top of hot oatmeal, or tossing over chilled berries or stone fruit.

Roll the vanilla sugar tube tightly in the paper or card stock (make sure the list side is facing in). Wind a length of elasticized gift cord tightly around the paper a couple of times and secure it with a double knot. You can finish with a simple bow, or, if you like, you can thread a miniature cookie cutter onto the free ends of the cord and finish with a slipknot.

We all know it is the thought that counts. It takes a little extra thought, creativity, and ingenuity to make a modestly priced present into something really special. You can make and wrap each gift in this chapter for less than $15.

These recipes will help you stretch your budget by utilizing larger amounts of affordable staples like flour and eggs, making original and creative use of "everyday" produce including carrots, eggplant, apples, and oranges, and focusing on seasonal price reductions.

Great-looking gift wraps can be as costly as gifts, but the presentations in this chapter stay "outside of the box" by using commonly available materials in uncommon ways. Some of the suggested containers and gift wraps in this chapter feature materials that are repurposed or recycled, making your gifts both earth- and budget-friendly.

The price of a gift has absolutely nothing to do with its value. Nothing is more valuable than the care and time you invest in making these terrific presents.

things to keep in mind

Keep it simple. Simple materials, ingredients, and packages always look more expensive than overly fussy ones.

If you are trying to save money, avoid gourmet markets and craft stores because they are the most expensive places to shop. Instead, learn to see the potential and perfection in everyday ingredients available at the supermarket and at discount stores. Shop for unusual packaging materials and containers at the hardware store, resale shops, and tag sales. Check online for real bargains if you need craft supplies and harder-to-find ingredients.

Selectively repurpose and creatively recycle items like jars, gift boxes, ribbons, and tote bags. Use only those items that show no wear and that need just a simple touch of your own to make them fresh and stylish.

amaretti cookie clone

Amaretti, those little Italian cookies in the beautiful orange tin, are very expensive. The high price must be due to import taxes or the colorful tin, because the ingredients are few and not very costly. This recipe is for the exact same cookie: dark nut brown with a crackling bite that melts into a distinctive sugary almond flavor. I have successfully cloned the cookie at a fraction of the original's price, but a wise woman knows her limits, and I will never be a tinsmith or a lithographer. So these amaretti are packaged in an "industrial chic" style—otherwise known as a repurposed paint can.

Piping the cookies with a pastry bag and garnishing them with pearl sugar are the key steps in making an exact clone of amaretti. You can, however, drop the batter from a spoon and substitute crushed sugar cubes for a good imitation.

7 ounces almond paste

1 cup granulated sugar

2 large egg whites

3 tablespoons pearl sugar (see Resources, page 290), or substitute crushed sugar cubes

1 Preheat the oven to 325°F and line two baking sheets with parchment paper.

2 Finely dice the almond paste and combine it with the granulated sugar in a large bowl. Beat this mixture with a handheld mixer at medium speed until it resembles wet sand. Add the egg whites, increase the mixer speed to medium-high, and continue to beat the batter until it is perfectly smooth and very thick.

recipe continues

Handy opener

3 Scoop the amaretti batter into a large pastry bag fitted with a 3/16-inch plain tip and pipe quarter-sized mounds of batter 2/3 inch apart on the lined baking sheets, or drop scant teaspoonfuls of the batter onto the lined baking sheets. Sprinkle the cookies with the pearl sugar or crushed sugar cubes.

4 Bake the amaretti on the middle racks of the oven for 10 minutes. Rotate and switch the pans and continue baking for another 7 minutes. Reduce the temperature to 200°F, prop the oven door slightly ajar with a wooden spoon, and bake the amaretti for another 20 minutes. Turn off the oven and leave the amaretti undisturbed until they have cooled completely. Store the cooled amaretti in airtight containers until you are ready to assemble and deliver the gift.

wrapping it up

To wrap the amaretti, you could repurpose a cake or cookie tin with a newly painted or papered exterior, but the tin may just look like a poor imitation of the original Italian box. The simple wrap below goes in an entirely different direction—that Italian lithographed tin may be a stunner, but it doesn't have a handle!—with a shiny metal washer "reinforcement ring" on the gift card that is handy for opening the paint can.

suggested supplies

tissue paper

1 paint can, 1 gallon size (available at hardware, home improvement, and craft stores; see Resources, page 290)

card stock

1 large metal washer

thin cord

how to make a gift card with a "reinforcement ring"

Cut the tissue paper in 6-inch squares. Put two cookies together, bottom to bottom, place them on a tissue square, and wrap them tightly by twisting the ends in opposite directions (like a candy wrapper). Wrap all of the amaretti in this way and place them in the can; cover the can tightly with its lid. Cut a large gift tag from the card stock and punch a hole in one end. Center the metal washer over the punch hole and glue it in place. (I often write "Handy Opener" on the card, with an arrow pointing to the washer.) Thread the cord through the washer hole and tie it to the paint can handle.

nectarine *crostata* in a tissue ruffle

Crostata is a rustic, free-form version of an open fruit tart, requiring no tart pan. The wide golden crust surrounding the juicy nectarine filling, set in clouds of ruffled tissue, is prettier than any traditional pie could ever be—and a lot easier to make. This foolproof pastry recipe, a favorite of mine, is substantial enough for a free-form tart like a crostata but still tender and flaky.

FOR THE FLAKY AND FOOLPROOF PASTRY DOUGH:

¾ cup cake flour

1½ cups unbleached all-purpose flour

¼ teaspoon salt

¼ teaspoon baking powder

¾ cup (1½ sticks) unsalted butter, cut in very small pieces and frozen

8½ tablespoons cream cheese

3 tablespoons heavy cream

1 tablespoon lemon juice

FOR THE CROSTATA:

1 tablespoon semolina flour

⅓ cup cake, bread, or cookie crumbs

1 tablespoon unsalted butter, softened

½ teaspoon ground mace

4 tablespoons turbinado sugar

4 small ripe nectarines, halved, pitted, and cut into wedges

1 egg yolk beaten with 1 tablespoon water

1 tablespoon unsalted butter, chilled and thinly sliced

recipe continues

overall prep time: slightly over 3 hours

active prep time: 35 to 40 minutes

moderately easy

inexpensive

do not freeze or ship

can be doubled or tripled

shelf life: 3 days refrigerated for pastry dough; 24 hours for completed crostata

makes: one 9-inch crostata

1 To make the pastry dough, combine and sift the cake flour and all-purpose flour into the bowl of a stand mixer. Remove and reserve ¼ cup of the mixed flour. Add the salt and baking powder to the bowl. Use the paddle attachment to stir the dry ingredients on the lowest speed while adding a few bits of frozen butter at a time. Continue to beat the mixture until the largest bits of butter are reduced to the size of dried lentils. Add the cream cheese to the mixer bowl, one tablespoon at a time, and continue beating at low speed until the mixture resembles cornflakes.

2 Whisk the cream, lemon juice, and ¼ cup reserved flour together in a small bowl until the mixture forms a smooth paste. Add the paste to the mixer bowl and continue to beat the dough at the lowest speed until it balls up around the beater.

3 Lightly mist a work surface with water and lay a 10-inch square of plastic wrap on the damp surface (the water helps hold it in place). Turn the dough out onto the plastic wrap. Use your fingertips and the heels of your hands to form the dough into a rough disc 6 to 8 inches in diameter and 2 inches thick. Wrap the dough tightly in the plastic wrap and refrigerate it for at least 2 hours and up to 3 days before using it.

4 To make the crostata, preheat the oven to 375°F. Sprinkle a 13 × 17-inch sheet of parchment paper with the semolina. Put the chilled dough on the parchment and roll the dough into a circle 11 inches in diameter. Slide the dough and parchment onto a baking sheet.

5 Using your fingertips or a pastry blender, combine the crumbs, soft butter, mace, and 3 tablespoons of the turbinado sugar in a small bowl. Cover all but the outermost edge of the dough circle with the crumbs.

6 Arrange the nectarine wedges in a tightly spiraled pinwheel pattern over the crumbs, stopping 3 or 4 inches from the edge. Gather the pastry edges up and over the nectarines and gently press the dough around the fruit, leaving an opening in the center about 5 inches in diameter. Brush the entire surface with the egg yolk wash, sprinkle the crostata with the remaining tablespoon of turbinado sugar, and distribute the cold butter slices evenly over the fruit.

7 Bake the crostata on the middle rack of the oven for 20 minutes. Rotate the pan and continue baking for another 20 to 25 minutes, or until the fruit is bubbling and the crust is a deep golden brown. Cool the crostata on a rack until you are ready to assemble and deliver the gift.

wrapping it up

A colorful ruffle of tissue surrounds the tart; a smear of melted chocolate holds the tart in place; and an overwrap of cellophane protects it.

suggested supplies

double-face tape

1 cake board, 10 inches in diameter

4 rectangles (4 × 18 inches each) tissue paper

1 square (20 to 24 inches) cellophane

melted white or dark chocolate

1 wire twist tie

ribbon

1 gift card

how to make a tissue ruffle tart surround

Turn the cake board upside down. Make a large "X" of double-face tape on the center of the inverted cake board and apply two lines of double-face tape to the outer edges of the same side. Press the tissue sheets onto the taped "X." Pinch and fold rectangles of tissue paper onto the tape around the edge so they form a ruffle around the edge of the cake board, and press the tissue paper into place. Turn the ruffled cake board over and center it on a large sheet of cellophane; the edges of the ruffled tissue should curl around the edges of the inverted board. Apply double-face tape about 1 inch from the edge around the upper surface of the cake board. Press and fold the tissue to this tape, forming a ruffle. Dab the middle of the cake board with melted chocolate and center the crostata on the chocolate. Enclose the ruffled crostata in the cellophane by twisting the cellophane over the top of the crostata. Secure the twisted cellophane with a wire twist tie and cover the twist tie with a ribbon, finishing in a bow and attaching a gift card.

gingerbread turned on its head

overall prep time: 1 hour and 20 minutes

active prep time: 20 to 30 minutes

easy

inexpensive

freezes well

do not ship

can be doubled or tripled

shelf life: 2 days in an airtight container

makes: 10

If you turn tradition on its head, you can gain a whole new perspective, or, as in this case, taste and presentation. Unlike traditional dark and dense gingerbread, this white gingerbread is ethereally light in color, flavor, and texture. The cupcakes stand on their heads, which are wreathed in crystallized ginger.

¾ cup (1½ sticks) unsalted butter, melted, for preparing the cupcake liners and for the sugar coating

1 large egg, well beaten

½ cup whole milk

½ cup unbleached all-purpose flour

1 cup cake flour

1½ teaspoons baking powder

½ teaspoon sea salt

½ teaspoon ground ginger

⅓ cup unsalted butter, cool (not cold)

½ cup granulated sugar

½ cup sanding sugar or additional granulated sugar

4 or 5 pieces crystallized ginger

1. Preheat the oven to 350°F. Prepare 10 small (⅔-cup capacity) paper cupcake liners by brushing them lightly with ¼ cup of the melted butter. Place the buttered liners in a muffin tin.

2. Combine the egg and milk in a 1-cup liquid measure or a small pitcher and thoroughly whisk them together. Combine the all-purpose flour, cake flour, baking powder, salt, and ground ginger in a bowl and "sift" them by stirring with a wire whisk. Put the ⅓ cup cool butter and the ½ cup granulated sugar in the work bowl of a food processor and process for 1 minute. With the processor still running, add half the flour mixture through the feed tube and slowly pour in all of the milk and

egg mixture. Add the remaining flour and continue to process the batter for 30 to 40 seconds.

3 Fill each cupcake liner halfway (about ⅓ cup of batter). Bake the cupcakes on the middle rack of the oven for 10 minutes. Rotate the pan and bake for another 10 to 15 minutes, until the cupcakes are a very pale golden yellow and yield slightly to pressure. Cool the cupcakes on a baking rack for 5 minutes.

4 Meanwhile, combine the sanding sugar and crystallized ginger on a small cutting board and chop the ginger very finely. Place the mixture in small shallow bowl.

5 As soon as the cupcakes are cool enough to handle, peel off the cupcake liners. Use a dry pastry brush to remove loose crumbs from the inverted cakes. Dip the flat bottom (which now is the top) of each cupcake in the remaining ½ cup melted butter, then gently press it into the saucer of sugar and ginger until it has a generous coating of the mixture. Place the inverted cakes on a baking rack to cool completely. Store them in a single layer in an airtight container until you are ready to assemble and deliver the gift.

wrapping it up

These upside-down cupcakes glow in ruffled nests of inside-out paper cupcake liners.

suggested supplies

20 paper cupcake liners

2 tablespoons marmalade, such as ginger, lemon, or orange

double-face tape

1 round corrugated cake board (12 to 14 inches)

pale yellow or clear cellophane

1 wire twist tie

wired ribbon

how to make a cupcake nest

Stack 2 cupcake liners together and turn them inside out. Spread a little marmalade in the center and place an upside-down cupcake in the marmalade. Repeat with the remaining 9 cakes and set them aside.

Cover the cake board tightly with cellophane and secure the cellophane on the bottom of the board with the double-face tape. Cut a sheet of clear or colored cellophane 15 inches taller and wider than the cake board and lay it out flat. Add 2 or 3 strips of double-face tape to the center of the cellophane square and press the cake board in place. Use additional double-face tape to attach the bottoms of the lined cupcakes to the board. Gather the cellophane up around the board and secure with a wire twist tie. Cover the wire with ribbon and a bow.

strawberry shortcake *trifle*

Strawberry shortcake is the all-American summer dessert. Adapting it to a trifle presentation makes it both portable and very pretty. You can give someone a whole lot of summer for very little money. This trifle combines three recipes, which are wonderful basics you can add to your personal repertoire of "always dependable" recipes.

overall prep time: 2 hours

active prep time:
45 minutes

easy

inexpensive

do not freeze or ship

can be doubled or tripled

shelf life: 48 hours refrigerated in a tightly sealed jar

makes: one 1-quart trifle

1 recipe My One and Only Biscuits (page 135)

1 recipe Almost Everlasting Whipped Cream (page 137)

1 recipe Macerated Strawberries (page 136)

½ cup strawberry jam

1 jar (4- to 6-cup capacity), with a wide mouth and a tight-fitting lid

ground cinnamon

1 Drain the strawberries in a colander, reserving the juices for another purpose (such as pouring over ice cream or pound cake), and set them aside.

2 Generously spread the jam on the split biscuit halves and gently press the halves back together. Put any remaining jam in the bottom of the jar. Put a biscuit in the jar, top side down and flat side up. Cut another biscuit into pieces that will fit around the whole biscuit to make a complete layer that covers the bottom of the jar. Spoon some berries over the biscuit layer, followed by a large dollop of whipped cream. Neatly spread the whipped cream with a long-handled spatula to cover the berries. Sprinkle a little cinnamon over the whipped cream.

my one and only biscuits

These are the only biscuits I have ever made; I dare not change it because the recipe has been so completely foolproof over the years. The dough is extremely versatile – good for shortcakes, cobblers, and potpies. Of course, I use it for biscuits, too, plain or embellished with grated cheese, fresh herbs, spices, or flavored sugars.

1 cup sifted all-purpose flour

1 teaspoon baking powder

½ teaspoon baking soda

½ teaspoon sea salt

2½ tablespoons shortening, chilled

½ cup plus 2 tablespoons buttermilk

2 tablespoons granulated sugar

1　Sift the flour, baking powder, baking soda, and salt onto a clean work surface and scoop them into a mound. Use your fingertips to rub the shortening into the mounded flour, continuing until the mixture looks like moist, gravelly sand. Make a well in the center of the flour mixture and add ¼ cup of the buttermilk. Work the drier edges of the well into the wet center and continue mixing with your fingers. When the ¼ cup of buttermilk is completely absorbed into the flour, gradually add more until ½ cup of buttermilk has been added. Knead the dough just enough to make it form a cohesive mass that can be formed into a thick round disc. Tightly seal the dough in plastic wrap and refrigerate it for 35 to 40 minutes.

recipe continues

3　Add another layer of upside-down biscuit and biscuit pieces in the same way and gently press the biscuits into the whipped cream beneath. Continue to fill the jar with the layers, gently compressing the biscuits as you go. The final layer should be whipped cream. Cover the jar tightly and wipe it down with a damp cloth before assembling and delivering the gift.

2 Preheat the oven to 400°F. Roll the dough out on a floured work surface to a ⅓-inch thickness. Cut the dough into rounds just a bit smaller than the mouth of the jar you have chosen for your trifle. Place the biscuits on an ungreased heavy-duty baking sheet. Brush the biscuit tops with the remaining 2 tablespoons of buttermilk and sprinkle with sugar. Bake the biscuits on the middle rack of the oven for 6 minutes, and rotate the pan. The total baking time depends on the size of the biscuits: Standard 2½- to 3-inch round biscuits take another 6 minutes and larger ones up to another 9 minutes, so adjust your baking time accordingly. It is easy to judge when the biscuits are done by their color, which should be a brilliant golden brown.

3 Cool the pan on a baking rack for 10 minutes, and then transfer the biscuits directly to the rack. When the biscuits are completely cooled, split them with a fork and set them aside on the rack. While the biscuits are baking and cooling, you can prepare the strawberries.

macerated strawberries

These luscious berries can also be used as a sauce for plain cake or vanilla ice cream.

2 pints firm, evenly sized ripe strawberries

juice and finely grated zest of 1 small orange

½ to ⅔ cup granulated sugar, depending on the sweetness of the berries

2 tablespoons Triple Sec or other orange liqueur

1 Wash the berries and pat them dry. Stem the berries and cut them in halves or quarters, depending on their size. In a large bowl, combine the berries with the orange zest and juice, ½ cup of sugar, and the liqueur. Stir the berries and set them aside for 10 minutes.

2 Taste the berries for sweetness and add more sugar if needed, keeping in mind that the whipped cream in the trifle is very sweet. Cover the bowl and refrigerate the berries for up to 24 hours. You can make the whipped cream up to 24 hours ahead of time as well, if you use the following recipe.

almost everlasting whipped cream

If you follow these directions to the letter, it is almost impossible to overwhip the cream, and it will not separate. The whipped cream holds its shape and stays very firm for 2 days.

1 pint ultra-pasteurized heavy whipping cream

⅔ cup granulated sugar

2 teaspoons vanilla extract

1 Combine the cream and the sugar in a bowl and stir until most of the sugar has dissolved. Set the cream and sugar aside to rest for 5 minutes.

2 Put the cream mixture in the work bowl of a food processor. Add the vanilla extract. Process the cream mixture until it is stiff enough to stand away from the processor blade. Refrigerate the whipped cream until you are ready to assemble and deliver the trifle.

wrapping it up

If the trifle is assembled in a good-looking jar with a clamp lid, your gift needs little more than a card. You can camouflage a metal jar lid with a circle of checkered tissue held in place with waxed string.

suggested supplies

1 circle (6 to 7 inches in diameter) solid red or gingham-checked tissue paper

red waxed string or thin twill tape

how to dress up a trifle

Center the tissue circle over the lid of the trifle jar and press it evenly down and around the lid. Wind the string or twill tape tightly under the lid rim to hold the tissue in place. Finish with a double knot and simple loop or bow.

green tea *cookies* in a paper lantern

The green tea makes these buttery and tender seeded cookies pleasingly different to eat. The paper lantern cookie "jar" makes them special gifts.

overall prep time: 3½ hours

active prep time: 30 minutes

moderately easy

inexpensive

raw dough and finished cookies freeze well

ships well in an airtight container

can be doubled or tripled

shelf life: 1 week in an airtight container

makes: about 30

¾ cup (1½ sticks) unsalted butter

1¼ cups packed light brown sugar

3 tablespoons finely crumbled green tea leaves

¼ cup boiling water

1 large egg

3 cups sifted all-purpose flour

2¼ teaspoons baking powder

pinch of sea salt

½ cup sesame seeds

½ cup sanding sugar or raw sugar

1. Preheat the oven to 400°F. In a large bowl, using a handheld mixer set on medium-high speed, cream the butter and brown sugar for 3 minutes.

2. Steep the crumbled tea leaves in the boiling water in a medium bowl. When the bowl is cool enough to touch, add the egg and beat well. Add this mixture to the butter mixture.

3. Sift the flour, baking powder, and salt together into a bowl and add this to the butter mixture in three increments, beating well after each addition. Cover the bowl with plastic wrap and chill it for at least 2 hours and up to 48 hours.

4 Form the dough into 1-inch balls. Place the sanding sugar in a pie pan or other shallow dish and the sesame seeds in a saucer. Roll 4 or 5 of the dough balls at a time in the sugar until they are well coated. Press the top of each sugared dough ball into the sesame seeds. Space the dough balls, sesame side up, 1 inch apart on parchment-lined cookie sheets. Press a chopstick or wooden skewer across each cookie several times to make a pattern of lines and to flatten the top slightly.

5 Bake the cookies for 6 minutes on the middle racks of the oven, then switch and rotate the pans. Continue baking the cookies for another 5 to 7 minutes, or until the edges are pale gold. Place the cookie sheets on racks and let the cookies cool completely. Gently remove the cooled cookies from the parchment. Store the cooled cookies in an airtight container until you are ready to assemble and deliver the gift.

wrapping it up

A paper lantern is an inexpensive container with a lot of creative potential. You can keep it sleek and simple or go all out with embellishments. It is important that you select a paper lantern that comes with an interior wire brace to keep the lantern fully expanded. Eight-inch round paper lanterns, plain or fancy, are easy to find at party-supply and import stores, and they're usually quite inexpensive.

suggested supplies

1 round paper lantern (8 inches)

colored poster board

low-temp glue gun

tissue paper or cellophane

how to make a lantern into a cookie jar

Expand and brace the lantern, then trace the bottom of the lantern onto the poster board. Cut out the traced shape. Use the glue gun to attach the poster board cut-out to the bottom of the paper lantern. Line the lantern with tissue paper or cellophane, then add the cookies. Crumple one or two additional sheets of tissue paper or cellophane to cover the cookies and fill in the top of the lantern.

a lavish *lavash*

Incredibly large sheets of lighter-than-air crackers primly wrapped in craft paper make a very grand hostess gift for very little money. You will love working with this dough, but, since there is a lot of dough to work with, use a stand mixer if you have one.

overall prep time:
just under 3 hours

active prep time:
45 minutes to 1 hour

slightly challenging

inexpensive

do not freeze or ship

can be doubled or tripled

shelf life: 2 to 3 days in an airtight container

makes: 2 large sheets

1¾ cups unbleached all-purpose flour, plus ⅓ cup for dusting the work surface and rolling the dough

1 tablespoon whole wheat flour

⅓ cup vegetable shortening

1 teaspoon kosher salt

¼ teaspoon granulated sugar

⅔ cup lukewarm water

½ tablespoon beaten egg, from less than 1 whole egg

¼ cup (½ stick) unsalted butter, melted

1 teaspoon finely minced garlic

2 teaspoons any combination of the following: white sesame seeds, black sesame seeds, slightly crushed cumin seeds, flax seeds, roughly chopped sunflower seeds

¼ cup finely grated Asiago cheese

1 Combine the unbleached and whole-wheat flours with the shortening, salt, and sugar in the bowl of a stand mixer fitted with the dough hook attachment. Mix the ingredients at medium speed until the mixture resembles cornmeal.

2 Add the water and egg to the bowl and mix for 5 minutes at medium speed. The dough will be very sticky at this point. Scrape down the sides of the mixer bowl and cover the bowl with plastic wrap. Allow the dough to rest at room temperature for 2 hours.

3 Position the oven racks in the upper and lower thirds of the oven and preheat the oven to 350°F.

4 Combine 2 tablespoons of the melted butter with the garlic in a small bowl and set aside. Using a pastry brush, coat two 11 × 17-inch baking sheets with the remaining 2 tablespoons of melted butter.

5 Turn the dough out onto a well-floured work surface. Divide the dough in half and use a heavily floured rolling pin to roll each half into a 10 × 7-inch rectangle. Dust your hands with flour, work your hands under one dough rectangle, and lift it over a buttered baking sheet. Gently lay the dough in the pan and stretch the dough to fit the pan, making as even a layer as possible. Work the dough gently and press it into the sides and corners of the pan. Repair any holes in the dough by pinching and pressing the edges of the holes together. Repeat this process with the second half of the dough and the second baking sheet.

6 Brush the top of the dough with the melted butter and garlic. Sprinkle the seeds over the two sheets of dough and gently press them into the surface. Sprinkle the cheese evenly over the dough.

7 Bake the lavash on the upper and lower racks of the oven for 12 minutes. Switch and rotate the pans and continue baking the lavash for another 12 minutes. Cool the pans completely on racks; the lavash will crisp as it cools.

8 Break each sheet of cooled cracker bread into three or four pieces. Store the lavash in an airtight container until you are ready to assemble and deliver the gift.

recipe continues

wrapping it up

This is a chic, simple, and practical wrap that makes serving the large sheets of lavash a breeze: Unwind the string closure, unfold the flaps, and serve. This wrap keeps the lavash pieces from being broken into smaller pieces, and it collects all the crumbs as well.

suggested supplies

1 square (30 inches) brown or white craft paper

1 rectangle (10 × 16 inches) cardboard (sheet-cake cardboard, available at craft and cake-decorating stores, is ideal)

2 sheets waxed tissue paper

2 circles (2 inches each) heavy card stock

2 plain or decorative metal brads

1 length (16 inches) string, thin ribbon, or cord

how to lavishly wrap lavash

Place the craft-paper square diagonally in front of you on a work surface, so you have a corner at the top, bottom, left, and right. Center the rectangle of cardboard on the craft paper with the long sides on the left and right. Gently wrap the lavash in the tissue paper and place it on the cardboard rectangle.

Form four overlapping flaps to cover the lavash by folding the left and right corner points of the craft paper over the lavash, then folding the bottom and top corner points over the crackers. Use your fingertips to gently press the folded outer edges of the craft paper to maintain and sharpen the shape.

Use a craft awl or a sharp skewer to pierce a small hole centered on the left-right axis and 3 inches above the corner point of the top flap. Make another hole in the bottom flap centered on the left-right axis and 6 inches below the corner point.

Use a marking pen to write a gift message around one or both of the card-stock circles and then punch a metal brad through the center of each circle. Insert the sharp end of one of the brads into the hole you made on the top flap, then open the brad prongs on the underside of the top flap to secure the circle to the top of the flap. Repeat with the remaining brad and card-stock circle in the hole on the bottom flap of the package.

Fold the string in half to find the center. Slip the string at this center point around the brad (and under the card-stock circle) that is on the bottom flap of the packet and wind the string in opposite directions around the brad twice. Wind the ends in opposite directions around the brad on the top flap of the packet in exactly the same way. Join the two free ends of the string with a simple slipknot.

faux escargot *pastry swirls* in a garden trowel

These flaky pastry "garden snails" taste like classic escargot. But no real snails are involved in the making of this hors d'oeuvre, just lots and lots of garlic, butter, and parsley—which is what most people like about escargot anyway. Don't omit the anchovies unless you absolutely hate them.

¼ cup (½ stick) unsalted butter

9 garlic cloves, finely minced (you can use more or less, according to taste)

1 large shallot, finely minced

leaves from 3 or 4 sprigs thyme

2 anchovy fillets

1 cup finely chopped fresh flat-leaf parsley

1 recipe Flaky and Foolproof Pastry Dough (page 129), well chilled

1 large egg beaten with 1 tablespoon water

sea salt flakes, such as Maldon

overall prep time: 4 hours

active prep time: 45 minutes

easy

inexpensive

uncooked rolls, ready to slice and bake, freeze well

ships well

can be doubled

shelf life: 3 or 4 days in an airtight container

makes: 2½ to 3 dozen

1 Melt the butter in a medium sauté pan over medium heat. Add the garlic and shallot to the butter and gently sauté them until they are translucent and soft, 3 to 4 minutes. Add the thyme, anchovies, and parsley and continue sautéing the mixture, stirring constantly, for another 2 minutes. Remove from the heat and set aside to cool while you roll out the pastry.

2 Roll the pastry into a 9 × 13-inch rectangle. Brush egg wash over the entire surface of the pastry. Spread the cooled parsley mixture over the egg wash all the way to the edges of the pastry. Reserve the remaining egg wash in the refrigerator.

3 Tightly roll the pastry from one short end of the rectangle, stopping 2 inches from the opposite short end. Fold the edge opposite the roll in half over the filling and

recipe continues

toward the roll and then press the roll into the folded edge to seal it, so that you have a tight roll with about ¼ inch of folded pastry along the edge of the tightly rolled pastry (this will be the "snail's head"). Transfer the roll to a tray lined with parchment paper and place it in the freezer for 30 to 45 minutes. Meanwhile, preheat the oven to 350°F.

4 Use a serrated knife to slice the frozen pastry roll into ¼-inch-wide swirls. Place the swirls on a parchment-lined baking sheet. Use your fingers to press and shape the "head" of each "snail" swirl and flatten each swirl with the heel of your hand. Brush the pastry swirls with the reserved egg wash and sprinkle them with sea salt flakes.

5 Put the baking sheet on the middle rack of the oven and bake for 12 minutes. Rotate the pan and continue baking for another 15 to 20 minutes, or until the swirls are a very deep golden brown. Cool the baking sheet on a rack for 5 minutes before transferring the pastries directly to the rack to finish cooling. The cooled pastries should be stored in an airtight container until you are ready to assemble and deliver the gift.

wrapping it up

A shiny new garden trowel lined with tissue paper and filled with the "snails" makes an adorable gift, especially for a gardener.

suggested supplies

1 rectangle (8 × 10 inches) tissue paper

1 new large garden trowel

1 square (18 inches) clear cellophane

1 wire twist tie

ribbon

1 gift card

how to make a garden trowel gift package

Put the sheet of tissue paper diagonally over the top of the trowel and place the trowel on a large square of cellophane. Fill the tissue-lined trowel to overflowing with the pastry swirls, gather the cellophane tightly around the handle of the trowel, and secure the cellophane with the wire twist tie. Cut away all the excess cellophane as close to the twist tie as possible. Tie a ribbon around the twist tie and finish with a bow and gift card.

buckwheat and black currant *cookie roll*

overall prep time: 3 hours

active prep time:
45 minutes

slightly challenging

inexpensive

unbaked rolls of cookie dough
can be frozen for months

do not ship

can be doubled or tripled

shelf life: 3 to 4 days well
wrapped

makes: two 6-inch cookie
rolls, to yield a total of 20 to 24
cookies

Instead of a slice-and-bake roll of cookie dough, this is a bake-and-slice roll—you bake the roll of dough and the gift recipient slices off individual cookies. Buckwheat flour and black currant jam make this a far-from-ordinary sweet. A simple gift presentation that includes a serrated knife means the slicing and sampling can start without delay.

¾ cup (1½ sticks) unsalted butter or salted margarine

2 tablespoons light brown sugar

1 large egg

1½ cups sifted cake flour

½ cup buckwheat flour

¼ teaspoon salt

1 teaspoon baking powder

¼ cup ice water

12 ounces black currant jam, whisked until smooth

2 egg whites beaten with 1 tablespoon water

½ cup granulated or turbinado sugar

1 In a large bowl, using an electric mixer on medium-high speed, cream the butter and brown sugar for 3 minutes. Add the egg, and beat the mixture for 1 minute more.

2 Combine the flours, salt, and baking powder in a small bowl and whisk them together. Add the dry ingredients to the butter mixture and beat on low speed for about 1 minute.

3 Add the ice water to the cookie dough and continue to beat on low speed until the dough starts to mass itself around the beaters. Knead the dough very briefly on a lightly floured work surface and form it into a 4 × 5-inch rectangle. Sandwich the

dough between 12-inch squares of parchment paper and refrigerate it for at least 30 minutes and up to 24 hours.

4 Preheat the oven to 325°F. Roll out the dough between the sheets of parchment paper to an 8 × 12-inch rectangle. If the dough becomes sticky, refrigerate it for a half an hour to firm it up a bit.

5 Peel the top sheet of parchment from the rectangle of dough and spread the jam over the dough, all the way to the edges. Roll the jam-covered dough tightly from one long side to the other, forming a tight roll. Cut the roll in half and place the halves side by side about 2 inches apart on one of the sheets of parchment. Slide the parchment onto a baking sheet. Brush the logs with the egg white mixture and sprinkle heavily with granulated sugar.

6 Bake the rolls on the middle rack of the oven for 1 hour. They should be firm to the touch and pale nut-brown in color. Place the baking sheet on a cooling rack for 2 to 3 hours, then remove the cookie rolls and store them in an airtight container until you are ready to assemble and deliver the gift.

wrapping it up

Wrap the cookie rolls on a rickrack-trimmed "cutting board" with an inexpensive serrated knife.

suggested supplies

foam-core board

super-tacky craft or fabric glue

1 length (about 2 yards) wide rickrack, available at fabric and craft stores

1 serrated knife (4 to 6 inches long)

cellophane

1 wire twist tie

how to make a cookie roll cutting board

Use a straight edge and a craft knife to cut a rectangle from the foam-core board large enough—about 8 × 10 inches—to accommodate the cookie rolls and a knife. Attach the rickrack to the cut edges of the rectangle with the craft glue. Center the trimmed foam core on a rectangle of cellophane twice as large as the foam core. Place the cookie rolls and knife on the trimmed foam core and gather the cellophane tightly over the cookie rolls and knife. Twist the cellophane tightly before securing it with a twist tie. Cover the twist tie with a length of rickrack, which can then be knotted or tied in a simple bow.

cardamom coffee can *cake*

overall prep time: almost 3 hours

active prep time: 30 minutes

easy

inexpensive

baked coffee cakes can be frozen, if removed from cans

can be shipped overnight

do not double

shelf life: 2 days

makes: 2 coffee cakes

If you own a food processor but not a single bread pan, you are probably a good cook who lacks baking confidence! Working with yeast dough can be rewarding, and it need not be intimidating. Cardamom Coffee Can Cake is a great place to start building your skills with yeast dough. This recipe involves no guesswork, no kneading—and no bread pans. You will need the food processor and three hours of time, start to finish. You can make the starched burlap bows for the cans while the bread is rising and baking.

FOR THE CANS:

2 coffee cans (1 pound size)

3 tablespoons soft unsalted butter

FOR THE DOUGH:

½ cup buttermilk

½ cup (1 stick) unsalted butter, cool but not chilled, cut into 1-inch slices

⅔ cup warm water (like a baby's bathwater)

1 teaspoon granulated sugar

1 package (2¼ teaspoons) active dry yeast

3 cups all-purpose flour

¼ teaspoon ground cardamom

¼ cup light brown sugar

½ teaspoon sea salt

2 large eggs

½ cup golden raisins

FOR THE TOPPING:

⅓ cup unsalted butter

5 tablespoons granulated sugar

1 teaspoon ground cardamom

½ teaspoon ground cinnamon

1 Soak the coffee cans in hot soapy water to clean them and remove the labels and glue. Dry the cans thoroughly in a warm oven. Heavily coat the interior of the cans with the soft butter once they have cooled.

recipe continues

2 To make the dough, combine the buttermilk and butter slices in a small saucepan over medium heat and warm the mixture until the butter slices start to melt. Set the pan aside. Combine the warm water, granulated sugar, and yeast in a 4-cup liquid measure and stir until the sugar is dissolved. Set the mixture aside.

3 Put the flour and the cardamom in the work bowl of a food processor fitted with the dough blade or the steel chopping blade. Pulse the machine on and off three times. Add the brown sugar, salt, eggs, and yeast mixture to the flour mixture and process for 1 full minute. With the machine still running, slowly pour the buttermilk mixture through the feed tube, then immediately turn off the processor. Scrape down the sides of the work bowl and add the raisins. Pulse the processor on and off several times or until the raisins are distributed throughout the dough. Divide the batter between the two prepared coffee cans.

4 Cover the cans with a tea towel and set them in a warm, draft-free place to rise for 45 minutes, or until the dough has risen to within 1 inch of the can tops. When the dough has finished rising, remove all but the lowest rack from the oven and preheat the oven to 350°F.

5 To make the topping, melt the ⅓ cup butter and brush it over the top of each coffee cake. Combine the sugar and spices and liberally sprinkle each cake with half of the mixture.

6 Bake the cakes in their cans for 35 minutes, or until the tops are a dark golden brown. Thump the tops as you would a melon and listen for a hollow sound, like a ripe melon. If you do not hear a hollow sound, bake the cakes for another 8 minutes and test again. Cool the cans for 1 hour on a rack, then unmold them.

7 Wash and dry the interiors of the cans. Roll each cooled coffee cake in a strip of parchment paper and put the cakes back in the cans once the cans are dry. The finished cakes should be tightly wrapped in plastic wrap until you are ready to assemble and deliver the gift.

wrapping it up

Cover the cake tops with 9- or 10-inch squares of parchment paper. Attach the four corners of the paper to the sides of the can with a small strip of double-face tape, pressing the corners firmly to the can. Once the cake tops are securely covered with parchment paper, the cans can be simply or elaborately embellished. If you are pressed for time, just wind colored twine around the parchment and slip a gift card between the twine and the parchment. But in the time it takes the coffee cakes to rise and bake, you can make these big stiff burlap bows for the cans.

suggested supplies

4 strips (about 18 × 2 inches each) burlap or other loosely woven cotton or linen fabric thin-gauge craft or floral wire

spray fabric stiffener (available at craft stores)

double face tape

glue gun

how to make starched burlap bows

Use a pin or sharp skewer to unravel three or four rows of thread from each edge of each burlap or other fabric strip. Use 2 of the strips to make 2 bows; pinch the fabric strip tightly at the center with one hand, forming the bow loops with the other hand and adding them to the pinched center. Wrap wire around the pinched center of the bow and twist it tightly to accentuate and secure the bow's shape. Apply the fabric stiffener according to the manufacturer's directions, and put the bows in a well-ventilated place to dry.

Apply a 9-inch strip of double-face tape along the middle of the remaining strips of burlap, leaving about 4 inches of untaped burlap on either end of the strip. Wrap a taped burlap strip around each can, just covering the tips of the parchment paper. Press the taped burlap firmly onto the cans so it is secure, and tightly knot the free ends of the strip.

When the bows are dry, press them in place over the knotted center of the burlap can surrounds and use the free ends of the knotted surrounds to tie the bow in place. If the bows are too wobbly, give them additional stability with strategically placed dabs of hot glue.

got muesli?
cherry almond *muesli* in a milk bottle

overall prep time:
45 minutes

active prep time: 15 minutes

easy

inexpensive

freezes well

ships well in an airtight container

can be doubled or tripled

shelf life: up to 2 months in an airtight container

makes: 1 quart

I'm not a big believer in "health food"; I think all food is healthy, if consumed in reasonable quantities. But this Cherry Almond Muesli really is good for you, and tasty, too. In the witty milk-bottle presentation I suggest here, this cereal is a great gift for just about anyone who eats breakfast or likes yogurt, whether they swear by "health food" or not.

. . . .

3 cups rolled oats

½ cup wheat germ

3 tablespoons sesame seeds

⅔ cup sunflower seeds

⅔ cup sliced almonds

⅓ cup flax seeds

2 tablespoons safflower oil

3 tablespoons honey, preferably organic

1 cup dried cherries, roughly chopped

. . . .

1 Preheat the oven to 325°F. Combine all of the ingredients in a large bowl and toss them together until the oil and honey are evenly distributed through the dry ingredients.

2 Line a baking sheet with heavy-duty foil and spread the muesli evenly over the foil. Bake the muesli on the middle rack of the oven for 35 minutes, stirring it every 10 minutes so it browns evenly. (Europeans tend to like muesli barely golden. This

recipe makes a muesli that is toasted to a deep golden brown, closer to a granola. For a more European-style muesli, reduce the time in the oven to 20 to 25 minutes.)

3 Remove the muesli from the oven and let it cool it on the baking sheet for 1 hour. Store it in an airtight container until you are ready to assemble and deliver the gift.

wrapping it up

An old-fashioned milk bottle full of cereal may be a tongue-in-cheek presentation, but it keeps the muesli very fresh and makes it easy to pour. You can substitute any glass jar for the milk bottle, if you prefer, and decorate it a little differently.

suggested supplies

1 glass milk bottle (at least 1 quart)

adhesive letters

1 foil cupcake liner

double-face tape

silver elastic gift cord

1 gift tag

how to bottle muesli

Label the bottle with the adhesive letters. Use a wide-mouth funnel to fill the bottle with the cooled muesli, and seal the bottle with its lid. To make a covering for the bottle lid that looks like one of those old-fashioned foil milk-bottle caps, place double-face tape in the inside of the foil cupcake liner, invert it over the lid, and press it in place. Tie a thin piece of silver elastic gift cord around the edge of the foil lid to hold it in place, and knot the cord tightly. Attach the gift tag to the end of the gift cord.

two sisters, side by side: cumin *tortilla chips* and black bean—fresh corn *salsa*

overall prep time: 35 to 40 minutes

active prep time: 30 minutes

easy

inexpensive

do not freeze or ship

can be doubled or tripled

shelf life: 1 week refrigerated for salsa; 1 week in an airtight container for chips

makes: 4 dozen tortilla chips and 1 quart salsa

Early Native American cultures called corn, beans, and squash the "three sisters." Two of the sisters are teamed up here in crisp cumin-dusted corn tortilla chips and a chunky salsa of beans and fresh corn. The cornhusk-covered can and matching jar dress these two sisters up to perfection.

FOR THE SALSA:

3 cups freshly cooked or canned black beans

4 tablespoons olive oil

1½ cups fresh corn kernels (frozen kernels can be substituted in a pinch)

4 garlic cloves, minced

¾ cup finely chopped yellow onion

1 large green jalapeño pepper, seeded and minced

1 heaping tablespoon minced fresh oregano leaves

1 tablespoon chili powder

juice and finely grated zest of 1 small lime

FOR THE TORTILLA CHIPS:

6 tablespoons unsalted butter, melted

¼ teaspoon ground turmeric

¼ teaspoon sweet paprika

½ teaspoon ground cumin

½ teaspoon garlic salt

12 corn tortillas (6 inches each)

recipe continues

1 To make the salsa, put the beans in a colander, thoroughly rinse them under cold running water, and set the colander aside to drain.

2 Heat 2 tablespoons of the olive oil in a large heavy sauté pan over medium-high heat. Add the corn kernels and cook them, stirring constantly, for 2 minutes. Add the garlic, onion, jalapeño, oregano, and chili powder to the corn and continue to cook, stirring frequently, until the corn is evenly browned, about 8 to 12 minutes. (Fresh corn varies in sugar content; corn with a higher sugar content will brown faster.)

3 Pour the contents of the pan into a large bowl. Mix in the beans, the remaining olive oil, and the lime juice and zest. Pack the salsa tightly in a wide-mouth quart jar and cover it tightly. Refrigerate the salsa while you make the tortilla chips and until you are ready to assemble and deliver the gift.

4 To make the tortilla chips: Preheat the oven to 375°F. Line two heavy baking sheets with parchment paper. In a small bowl, combine the melted butter with all the seasonings. Use a small pastry brush to coat one side of each tortilla with the butter mixture.

5 Cut each tortilla into 4 wedges and place them on the lined baking sheets. Bake the tortilla wedges on the middle racks of the oven for 5 minutes, then rotate the sheets and continue baking for another 6 minutes, or until the tortilla wedges are evenly browned and crisp.

6 Cool the baking sheets on racks, and store the cooled chips in an airtight container until you are ready to assemble and deliver the gift.

wrapping it up

A large tin can with a tight-fitting plastic lid (a coffee can for example) will keep the tortilla chips crisp. Covering the can in cornhusks is inexpensive but it looks like a million.

suggested supplies

1 large tin can with a tight-fitting plastic lid, such as a coffee can

1 package cornhusks (found in the ethnic food section of large supermarkets)

spray bottle of water

low-temp glue gun and glue sticks

raffia or brown-paper curling ribbon

1 card-stock square or round gift tag

1 sheet tissue paper, for lining the can

heavy duty red-line double-face tape

how to cover a can with cornhusks

Arrange the cornhusks in a single layer on a tray or baking sheet. Using a spray bottle filled with water, moisten the cornhusks thoroughly. Set them aside for about 20 minutes, or until they are almost dry to the touch. Blot the cornhusks of excess moisture and glue a flat layer of husks to the can in a slightly overlapping pattern.

Once the can is covered in a flat layer of cornhusks, start adding dimension to the design with layers of overlapping cornhusks, starting at the top of the can. (But reserve several cornhusks for embellishing the salsa jar; see below.) You can mist the husks with additional sprays of water to make them more malleable as you work, so they can be twisted and curved inward over the can opening and folded back like husks on ripening corn. Set the can aside to dry completely.

Cut several strands of raffia or ribbon long enough to encircle the can with 6 to 8 inches to spare. Twist or plait the strands together and knot them around the middle of the husk-covered can. Slip a card-stock gift tag behind the knotted raffia.

Line the inside of the can with tissue and fill it with the chips. Seal the can with the plastic lid, concealing the lid with the uppermost cornhusks on the can.

Attach several cornhusks to the salsa jar lid with red-line tape in a spokelike pattern, with the tips of the husks trailing downward over the jar. Wind several strands of raffia or ribbon tightly under the lip of the lid to pull the husks down over the jar and hold them in place. Knot the raffia or ribbon tightly and form a single loop slipknot, then cut away any excess raffia.

oven-roasted *ratatouille*

overall prep time: 2½ hours

active prep time: 1 hour

easy

inexpensive

do not freeze or ship

do not double

shelf life: 2 weeks refrigerated in tightly covered jars

makes: about 7 cups

At the height of summer, sweet red peppers, plum tomatoes, eggplant, and all the other ingredients needed for ratatouille are inexpensive and available in abundance. Couple that affordability with this simplified oven-roasted version of this Mediterranean classic, and you have a wonderful and versatile gift. Ratatouille is good with so many things—as a side dish for everything from roast chicken to grilled fish, as a garnish for pasta or pizza, or served alongside a sliced baguette and an apéritif wine.

4 small firm eggplants

1½ tablespoons coarse sea salt

4 pounds sweet red bell peppers

1⅔ cups extra-virgin olive oil

4 to 5 pounds Roma tomatoes, stemmed and quartered

10 garlic cloves, peeled and smashed

2 teaspoons fine sea salt

3 large sprigs fresh thyme

3 large sprigs fresh marjoram

⅔ teaspoon dried red pepper flakes

1 Stem the eggplants and cut them into 1½-inch cubes. Toss the cubes with the coarse sea salt and set them aside in a colander to drain.

2 Cut the peppers in half and remove the stems, the pithy white interiors, and all of the seeds.

3 Place an oven rack 4 to 6 inches from the broiler and preheat the broiler. Prepare a large roasting pan by lining it with an extra-large sheet of heavy-duty foil, folding the excess over the sides of the pan. Coat the bottom of the lined roaster with 1 teaspoon of the olive oil. Arrange the peppers, cut side down, in a single layer in the

roaster. Broil the peppers about 10 minutes, watching them very carefully. The skins should be charred and blistered and the peppers should be slightly shriveled. Remove the roasting pan from the oven and set it aside; turn off the broiler. Using oven mitts, fold the excess foil tightly around the peppers, and allow them to steam for 20 minutes. Move the oven rack to the center position and preheat the oven to 400°F.

4 Remove the foil-wrapped peppers from the pan and set aside. Remove the seeds from the quartered tomatoes and put the tomatoes in the roasting pan. Rinse the eggplant, pat it dry with paper towels, and spread the eggplant pieces in the roasting pan.

5 Unwrap the peppers and peel away the charred skin. Discard any accumulated juices, cut the peppers into 2-inch-long pieces, and add them to the roasting pan.

6 Add the garlic, the remaining olive oil, fine sea salt, fresh herbs, and red pepper flakes to the roaster and mix the vegetables well, coating them with the oil and seasonings.

7 Roast the vegetables on the center rack of the oven for 20 minutes, stir, and cook for another 20 minutes. Stir the vegetables again and cook for another 20 minutes, or until the vegetables are meltingly tender. Let cool and discard the sprigs of herbs before putting the ratatouille in clean jars or crocks. Cover the containers tightly and refrigerate them until you are ready to assemble and deliver the gift.

wrapping it up

Wide-mouthed crocks can be repurposed for the ratatouille and are often found at tag sales and consignment shops. Any glass jar with a wide mouth and tight-fitting lid can be used as well; whatever suits your budget will work. If you use crocks, they only need a simple shipping tag on colored twine tied around them. The jars also would look good in tissue-paper pouches (see wrapping instructions for Blond Biscotti on page 270).

black and white *olives*

overall prep time: 25 to 36 hours

active prep time: 30 minutes

easy

inexpensive

do not freeze or ship

can be doubled or tripled

shelf life: 10 days refrigerated in a tightly sealed jar

makes: about 14 ounces (enough to fill a 1½- to 2-cup jar)

What is black, white, and delicious all over? These olives answer the question in spades. Not only are they delicious, they're simple and economical, and everyone loves them. The shopping list is short and simple, and the prep time is under an hour, yet the outcome is surprisingly upscale. Bring the olives to room temperature before giving or serving them.

12 ounces extra-large pitted black California olives

4 ounces feta cheese

1 teaspoon dried oregano

4 garlic cloves

6 fresh or dried bay leaves

½ to ⅔ cup olive oil

1   Drain the olives and rinse them under cold water. Lay the olives out on a tray lined with paper towels and set them aside.

2   Drain the feta in a strainer or colander. Using a large fork, mash it with the dried oregano until it forms a smooth paste. Using your hands, stuff the pitted olives with the feta mixture. Alternatively, you can put a "dab" of cheese mixture on the fat end of a chopstick and use that to stuff the olives. Wipe any excess cheese from the olives with a damp paper towel. Set the stuffed olives on the paper towel–lined tray and cover them loosely. Put the olives in a cool, dry place to cure for 24 hours.

3   Sterilize a wide-mouthed glass jar and lid (1½- to 2-cup capacity) by washing it in hot, soapy water and drying it in a 190°F oven.

4   Peel the garlic cloves and split them in half. Layer the olives, garlic, and bay leaves in the warm jar and fill the jar with the olive oil. Cover the jar tightly and store the olives in a dark, cool place for 24 hours. Refrigerate the jar until you are ready to assemble and deliver the gift. The olives should be stored in the refrigerator but served at room temperature.

wrapping it up

A simple coil of craft wire embellishes the gift jar and provides a fun, practical way to hold cocktail picks in place.

suggested supplies

1 length (about 30 inches) 22- to 26-gauge craft wire (available at craft and art supply stores)

12 to 16 small wooden cocktail picks or flat toothpicks

clear cellophane

1 wire twist tie

black and white ribbon

how to make a coiled wire pick holder

Use flat needle-nose craft pliers to tightly wind about ⅓ of the craft wire into a flat spiral.

Put your index finger in the center of the spiral and push slightly outward, until there is enough space between each pair of concentric circles to tightly hold a cocktail pick. Wrap the uncoiled portion of the wire around the neck of the jar and twist the remaining wire to secure the coil to the jar.

Lace the cocktail picks through the wire coil, like rays emanating from an iconic mid-century modern sunburst. Center the jar on a sheet of cellophane large enough to wrap the jar. Gather the cellophane loosely up over the jar lid and gently twist the ends of the cellophane tightly enough to be secured with the wire twist tie. Cover the twist tie with the ribbon, knot it, and finish with a simple bow.

january first black-eyed-pea *relish*

overall prep time: 3 hours

active prep time: 1¼ hours

moderately easy

inexpensive

do not freeze or ship

can be doubled

shelf life: 5 to 7 days
refrigerated

makes: a generous 2 quarts

Give someone luck and prosperity for the coming year and a jar of good relish to boot. You can even wrap it in a calendar page to remind them of the day it must be eaten for the magic to work. You can bring two people phenomenal luck, giving each a whole quart of relish, or four people very good luck, with a pint for each of them. You could also serve the relish as part of a New Year's Eve midnight supper or a New Year's Day brunch, and then give everyone a little jar to take home.

½ cup olive oil

4 medium red bell peppers, seeded and finely diced

4 celery stalks with tops, finely diced

2 sweet yellow onions, such as Vidalia, finely diced

½ pound ham (about 2 thick slices), diced

2 bags (10 ounces each) frozen black-eyed peas

¼ teaspoon red pepper flakes, or more to taste

1 bay leaf

1 quart low-sodium organic vegetable stock

⅔ cup cider vinegar

6 tablespoons finely chopped fresh flat-leaf parsley

2 tablespoons fresh thyme leaves, roughly chopped

1 teaspoon Tabasco or other hot sauce, or to taste

salt and freshly ground black pepper to taste

/ Heat the olive oil in a large saucepan or Dutch oven over medium heat for 3 to 4 minutes. Add the bell peppers, celery, and onions and cook, stirring frequently, for 6 to 7 minutes, until the vegetables begin to soften.

2 Add the ham, black-eyed peas, red pepper flakes, and bay leaf and continue cooking, stirring frequently, for another 5 minutes. Increase the heat to high, add the vegetable stock, and bring the mixture to a boil, stirring occasionally. Reduce the heat and allow the mixture to simmer for 30 minutes, or until the peas are tender.

3 Strain the relish in a mesh strainer, reserving the liquid. Set the relish aside and return the liquid to the cooking pot. Boil the liquid over moderately high heat until it has reduced by three-quarters, to about ⅔ cup. Add the vinegar, parsley, thyme, and strained relish. Stir the mixture gently with a large wooden spoon, taste, and add Tabasco, salt, and pepper as desired.

4 Pack the relish in jars with tight-fitting lids. Let it cool, uncovered, to room temperature, then cover the jars and refrigerate until you are ready to assemble and deliver the gift. The relish should be stored in the refrigerator but served at room temperature.

wrapping it up

Download, scan, copy, or create a January calendar page and use it to wrap the jar up to the neck. Tie a ribbon around the jar neck to hold the calendar page in place.

sugar pumpkin *chutney* in a paper pumpkin cage

overall prep time: 1½ hours

active prep time:
35 minutes

easy

inexpensive

do not freeze

ships well

can be doubled or tripled

shelf life: 2 to 3 weeks
refrigerated

makes: about 3 cups

Sugar pumpkin chutney is wonderful to serve alongside a holiday turkey or ham, and even better with sandwiches the next day. I like to serve this with a wedge of aged cheddar and toasted bread rounds with fall cocktails. The gift-wrapped jar is disguised as a fat little pumpkin.

1 pound peeled and seeded sugar pumpkin, cut into 1-inch cubes

1 cup granulated sugar

⅔ cup light brown sugar

1 cup freshly squeezed lemon juice

1 small yellow onion, thinly sliced

⅓ cup golden raisins

3 tablespoons grated lemon zest

1 tablespoon grated orange zest

1 piece (½ inch) peeled fresh ginger, cut into fine slivers

1 Combine all of the ingredients in a large Dutch oven or a small stockpot and allow them to macerate for 30 minutes. Place over medium heat and bring to a simmer, stirring frequently to prevent scorching, cover, reduce the heat to low, and simmer the chutney for 10 minutes.

2 Remove the cover and continue to cook the chutney for another 15 to 20 minutes, stirring frequently, until the pumpkin flesh is very soft and easily pierced with a fork and most of the liquid has cooked away. Allow the mixture to cool slightly. Meanwhile, wash a glass jar or jars (this recipe makes enough to fill three 8-ounce jars) in hot soapy water and dry in a 190°F oven.

3 Spoon the warm chutney into the hot jar, let cool, and cover tightly. Store in the refrigerator until you are ready to assemble and deliver the gift.

wrapping it up

A pumpkin costume makes the chutney an entirely charming gift for any fall occasion. The supply list and directions that follow apply to an 8-ounce jar approximately 4 inches high and 3 inches wide. You can adjust the supplies and directions to accommodate just about any jar; simply make sure that the diameter of the orange paper circle is four times the height of the jar. For example, a jar that is 4 inches in height requires a circle of orange paper that is 16 inches in diameter.

suggested supplies for each 4-inch jar

1 circle (16 inches) orange construction paper or lightweight poster paper

2 sheets dark-orange tissue paper

double-face tape

2 circles (3 inches each) brown construction paper

3 paper or fabric autumn leaves

1 length (10 to 12 inches) curly paper or paper raffia ribbon in green or brown

how to turn a jar into a pumpkin

If you can envision folding circles of paper to make snowflakes, the construction of this pumpkin cage will be easy. Fold the orange paper circle in half, then in half again. Unfold the circle and smooth it out on a work surface. Using the two intersecting crease lines as your guide, center the chutney jar on the paper circle and trace

recipe continues

around the bottom of the jar. Remove the jar and refold the circle into quarters. Fold the quarter circle in half, and then in half again, so that you have folded the circle into 16 parts. (Remember, this is just like folding a paper snowflake.) Use small pointed craft scissors to round off the sharp corners of the folded circle's outer edge. Unfold the paper circle and smooth it out once again on the work surface, revealing a large circular shape with 16 scallops around the circumference. Starting at the outside of the circle, use the pointed craft scissors to cut along each of the 16 creased lines all the way to the outside of the traced center circle. The big orange circle should now resemble a floppy daisy with 16 petals.

Center the chutney jar on 2 sheets of slightly crumpled tissue paper and gather the tissue loosely over the jar, not only to cover the jar but to give it a rounder shape. Apply a large "X" of double-face tape to the jar lid and press the tissue into the tape to keep it place over the jar. Apply another large "X" of double-face tape to one of the brown paper circles and center it, tape side down, over the top of the jar to neatly cover the orange tissue on the jar lid. Now apply double-face tape all around the perimeter of this brown paper circle. Center the tissue-wrapped, brown-circle-topped jar of chutney on the orange "daisy." Bring each "petal," one after the other, just over the rim of the jar lid and press it into the double-face–tape perimeter of the brown circle. Each consecutive petal should overlap about one-third of the previous petal. Proceed all the way around the jar in this fashion. When you are finished, you will have a jar of chutney surrounded by a paper pumpkin "cage."

Apply a couple of large "X"s of double-face tape to the remaining circle of brown construction paper, and apply this circle, tape side down, to the top of the pumpkin cage to further secure the pumpkin "petals" and cover the construction of your wrap. Use double-face tape or super-tacky craft glue to apply the autumn leaves and some curly-paper or raffia "vine" to the pumpkin for a finishing touch.

indescribable *eggplant* in won ton origami cups

Asian recipes that pique my interest often end up a little less Asian by the time I'm finished with them. An example is this eggplant spread. The starting point was Barbara Tropp's recipe from her book *China Moon* (Workman, 1992), which has evolved into a kind of fusion baba ghanoush. In the process it has become, hands down, my favorite eggplant recipe. Present it in a bamboo steamer; a two-tiered steamer stacks the eggplant spread and won ton cups into one very nice gift and provides a stylish way to serve them. The sauté phase of this recipe goes very quickly, so it is important to assemble the seasoning and sauce elements in small bowls before you begin that step. The little "cups" of crisp won ton wrapper resemble origami and make the perfect receptacle for the eggplant spread. They are also incredibly easy to prepare if you have a silicone mini-cupcake pan. If you don't have a silicone pan, you can use a metal one; spray it generously with nonstick cooking spray.

overall prep time: about 24 hours

active prep time: 1¼ hours

slightly challenging

inexpensive

do not freeze or ship

can be doubled or tripled

shelf life: 2 weeks refrigerated for eggplant spread; 24 hours in an airtight container for won ton cups

makes: a generous 2 cups of eggplant spread and 36 won ton cups

FOR THE EGGPLANT SPREAD:

2 medium eggplants (1¼ pounds total weight)

4 tablespoons extra-virgin olive oil

6 garlic cloves, minced

2 tablespoons grated fresh ginger

1 cup thinly sliced scallions (white and green parts)

1 dried red chile pepper, cut in small pieces

½ cup roughly chopped fresh basil leaves

3 tablespoons soy sauce

3 tablespoons dark brown sugar

2 tablespoons white balsamic vinegar

2 teaspoons boiling water

FOR THE WON TON ORIGAMI CUPS:

36 won ton wrappers

recipe continues

2 Combine the olive oil, garlic, ginger, scallions, chile pepper, and basil in a bowl. Combine the soy sauce, brown sugar, vinegar, and boiling water in a second bowl. Place a deep sauté pan over medium-high heat, and, when the pan is hot, add the seasoned olive oil mixture. Stir the seasonings constantly with a wooden spoon so they do not burn. As soon as the scallions start to soften, reduce the heat and add the eggplant to the pan. Continue to cook the mixture, stirring constantly, for 3 to 4 minutes, until the eggplant is warmed through. Add the soy sauce mixture to the eggplant and continue to cook, stirring constantly, until all the liquid has been absorbed and the eggplant is a deep mahogany brown, about 3 to 4 minutes more.

3 Puree the hot eggplant mixture in a food processor. Allow it to cool completely before refrigerating it in an airtight container overnight. Keep the spread refrigerated until you are ready to assemble and deliver the gift.

4 While the eggplant spread chills, make the won ton cups: Preheat the oven to 350°F. Line each compartment of a silicone mini-cupcake pan with a square won ton wrapper; depending on the configuration of your pans, you will need anywhere from two to six mini-cupcake pans. Use your fingertips to press the wrapper into the mini-cupcake form. Bake the wrappers for 10 minutes, or until the edges of each wrapper are a dark golden brown and the cups are crisp. Place the mini-cupcake pans on a rack to cool completely before removing the won ton cups.

1 Preheat the oven to 425°F. Use a meat fork to pierce the eggplants in several places. Remove the stems and leaves, and place the eggplants on a parchment-lined baking sheet. Bake the eggplants on the middle rack of the oven for 1½ hours, or until they are very soft. When the eggplants are cool enough to handle, halve them and scoop the flesh into a bowl. Coarsely chop any large pieces of eggplant.

wrapping it up

An 8- to 10-inch bamboo stacked steamer basket is so well suited to this gift there is little to do but shop for the right steamer at the right price. These can usually be found at Asian food markets and import stores. They are cheaper still online; see Resources (page 290).

see Resources (page 290)

suggested supplies

1 two-tier bamboo steamer basket (8 to 10 inches)

parchment paper

savoy cabbage leaves, for lining one tier of the steamer

¼ cup fresh cilantro or flat-leaf parsley

4 lengths (36 inches each) raffia, plus several additional 12-inch lengths

1 or 2 disposable bamboo spoons (available in upscale supermarkets and import stores, and online; see Resources, page 290)

1 square (about 30 inches) cellophane

1 wire twist tie

1 square (5 inches) origami paper or other decorative paper

how to make a steamer into a server

Trace around the bottom of each steamer-basket tier onto two sheets of parchment paper and cut out the two circles of parchment. Line the bottom of each tier with a parchment paper circle.

Cover the parchment in the bottom tier with overlapping leaves from the cabbage, and arrange smaller cupped leaves around the edges of the tier. Spoon the eggplant spread into this leaf-lined tier. Pile the won ton cups high in the second parchment-lined tier. Sprinkle the eggplant spread with cilantro or parsley leaves. Stack the won ton tier over the eggplant tier and loosely cover with the bamboo lid.

Divide the 36-inch raffia lengths into two pairs. Knot the ends of each pair together. Form an "X" with knotted pairs of raffia and center the stacked tiers on the raffia "X." Bring the opposite ends of each raffia length up the sides of the steamer, passing the ends through the looped handle on the steamer lid. Tie the ends in a slipknot, being careful not to tie them so tightly as to crush the won ton cups. Slip the spoons through the looped lid handle or tie them to the basket handle.

Center the assembled steamer on the cellophane square and gently gather the cellophane up and over the steamer, lid, and spoons. Carefully twist the cellophane to tighten it around the gift, and secure the twisted cellophane with the wire twist tie. Gather the 12-inch strands of raffia and wrap them around the twist tie to cover it, finishing with a tight double knot.

Write serving instructions on the decorative-paper square: "Use the bamboo spoons to fill the won ton origami cups with eggplant spread." Add any gift message you would like. Roll the decorative paper into a tiny scroll. Knot the scroll in the ends of the raffia to secure it to the gift.

vidalia *confit*

These caramelized sweet Vidalia onions add a rich taste and color to everything they grace. The ultra-chic corrugated surround with onion beads on tasseled raffia only *looks* expensive.

overall prep time:
45 minutes

active prep time:
10 minutes

moderately easy

inexpensive

do not freeze

can be shipped

can be doubled

shelf life: 4 to 6 weeks
refrigerated

makes: about 3 cups

6 medium Vidalia onions (or other sweet onions, such as Texas 1015 or Maui)

¼ cup unsalted butter

1 tablespoon extra-virgin olive oil

2 large sprigs fresh thyme and 4 fresh bay leaves, wrapped tightly in cheesecloth

2 teaspoons light brown sugar

1 Peel the onions and cut them into uniform slices ¼ inch thick. In a deep sauté pan set over medium-high heat, melt the butter with the olive oil. Add the sliced onions to the pan, toss them gently in the butter and oil until they are thoroughly coated, and cook them for 5 minutes, stirring frequently, until they are slightly translucent. Reduce the heat to medium and add the bundled herbs to the pan. Cook the onions, stirring very frequently, for 15 minutes.

2 Reduce the heat to low, sprinkle the onions with the brown sugar, and continue to cook them another 20 to 25 minutes, stirring very frequently, until the onions are very soft and a deep caramel brown. Set the pan aside to cool completely, then remove and discard the bundled herbs.

3 Pack the cooled confit into a glass jar with at least a 3-cup capacity and cover tightly. Refrigerate the confit until you are ready to assemble and deliver the gift. The Vidalia confit should be stored in the refrigerator but served at room temperature.

wrapping it up

A corrugated-paper surround gives the confit a crisp, tailored look. The onion tassels are a subtle hint about what the jar inside contains.

suggested supplies

1 sheet corrugated paper (available at craft and paper stores)

double-face tape

1 length (2 yards) raffia

2 large unpainted wooden beads

1 gift card

how to put onions on a string

Measure the jar of confit and cut a rectangle of corrugated paper 1 inch taller than the jar and 3 inches longer than the jar diameter. Line the corrugated paper with three horizontal strips of double-face tape. Tightly roll the jar in the paper, overlapping the end. Tie a knot at the center of the raffia, then knot the raffia strands together at several irregular intervals on either side of the center knot. String a wooden bead on each end of the knotted raffia and form double knots on either side of the beads to hold them in place. Closely trim the raffia ends so they resemble onion roots or tassels. Wrap the beaded raffia around the jar several times and finish with a slipknot at the point where the corrugated surround overlaps. Tuck a gift card between the raffia and the corrugated paper.

hot and sour
carrot-coin *pickles*

Carrots never had it so good! This bright-orange pickle is extra crunchy, with gingery heat and a pleasant pucker. The pickles will nicely fill the empty space next to a sandwich, and they add interest to almost any salad. The carrot coins also make a colorful garnish for poached fish or grilled chicken. I add them to stews, pot roasts, and meatloaf mixtures instead of raw carrots.

overall prep time: 4 days

active prep time: 30 to 40 minutes

easy

inexpensive

do not freeze or ship

can be doubled or tripled

shelf life: 6 weeks refrigerated

makes: 1 quart

2 fresh green jalapeño peppers

1 fresh red jalapeño pepper

1¾ cups water

2 teaspoons sea salt

4 large carrots, peeled and cut into ⅓-inch-thick rounds

1 large sweet yellow onion, such as Vidalia, peeled and cut into ¼-inch-thick slices

¼ cup cider vinegar

6 whole black peppercorns

1 piece (3 inches) fresh ginger, peeled and cut into matchstick julienne

1 Cut the jalapeños into quarters lengthwise and remove the seeds and white pith. Put the water and salt in a medium nonreactive stockpot over high heat and bring it to a rapid boil. Add the carrots, onion, and jalapeños. Reduce the heat and simmer the mixture for 4 to 5 minutes. The carrots will be noticeably brighter in color and the onion rings almost translucent.

2 Remove the pan from the heat and add the vinegar, peppercorns, and ginger. Cover the pan with a tea towel and let it stand at room temperature overnight.

3 Sterilize a quart jar by washing it in hot soapy water and drying it in a 190°F oven. Pour the vegetables and their brine into a colander set over a large bowl. Set the

vegetables in the colander aside and pour the brine through a fine-mesh strainer back into the cooking pot. Bring the brine to a simmer over medium heat, while you pack the vegetables into the warm quart jar. Pour the simmering brine over the vegetables, filling the jar to within ½ inch of the rim. Set the jar aside to

cool completely, then cover the jar tightly and wipe it with a damp cloth. Refrigerate the pickled carrots for at least 3 days, to allow the flavors to develop. Keep the jar in the refrigerator until you are ready to assemble and deliver the gift.

wrapping it up

A scrap of fabric and some cotton embroidery floss are the only things you need to make this cottage-style cap cover. If needlecrafts are your forte, you will think of many different ways to make these little caps even cuter.

suggested supplies

1 fabric scrap (at least 8 to 10 inches square)   **four-ply embroidery floss**

how to make a fabric cap cover

Assuming that your jar lid measures a little less than 4 inches in diameter (most of them do), trace an 8-inch-diameter circle onto the back of the fabric. Trace a 5½-inch circle in the center of the 8-inch circle. Use pinking shears to cut around the 8-inch circle. Starting the needle on the right side of the fabric and following the traced inner circle, sew large running stitches ½ inch long and ½ inch apart all the way around the inner circle, finishing with the needle about ½ inch from where you started. Leave at least 6 inches of floss on either end. Center the cover over the jar's lid, fabric right side up. Pull both ends of the floss to gather the cloth tightly around the jar lid, and tie it tightly with a simple bow.

herb-stuffed *eggs* in a wheat grass nest

overall prep time: 2 to 3 hours

active prep time: 45 minutes

easy

inexpensive

do not freeze or ship

can be doubled or tripled

shelf life: 24 hours refrigerated

makes: 2 dozen

Using butter in place of mayonnaise produces a prettier stuffed egg that has a creamier texture and stays fresh longer. Fresh wheat grass adds a lot of organic texture and bright color to the gift for very little money.

....

12 extra-large eggs

5 tablespoons unsalted butter, softened

4 tablespoons finely minced fresh flat-leaf parsley

3 tablespoons finely minced fresh chives or tarragon

½ teaspoon sea salt

pinch of ground white pepper

....

1 Place the eggs in a deep saucepan and cover them with cold water. Bring the water to a boil over medium heat. As soon as the water comes to a boil, remove the pan from the heat and cover it. Set the pan aside until the water is tepid to the touch.

2 Drain the eggs and gently crack the shells in several places. Put the cracked eggs in a bowl of ice water for 10 minutes, and then carefully peel them. Cut the eggs in half lengthwise, remove the yolks to a small bowl, and add the butter, herbs, salt, and pepper to the bowl. Set the egg-white halves aside.

3 Using a fork, mash the yolks with the butter and seasonings, and then whisk them until the mixture is smooth. Spoon the yolk mixture into the egg-white halves and level the yolk filling with the edge of the white, using a small metal spatula. Wipe the eggs with a damp paper towel to remove any yolk smears. Cover the eggs loosely with plastic wrap and refrigerate them until you are ready to assemble and deliver the gift.

wrapping it up

Use an empty egg carton, with nests of wheat grass in the cavities, for the stuffed eggs. Clear plastic cartons are especially nice for this presentation, but any egg carton will do.

suggested supplies

1 bunch of fresh wheat grass (available wherever organic produce is sold)

1 egg carton

parchment paper or waxed tissue paper

raffia or waxed string

how to build nests in an egg carton

Fill each carton cavity with a small bunch of wheat grass. Gently press the soft grass so it conforms to the egg-shaped cavity. Nestle two stuffed egg halves, with their yolks facing the front of the carton, in each nest. Close the carton, wrap it with parchment paper or waxed tissue, and tie the wrapped carton closed with a simple bow of raffia or string.

ten-minute chocolate *mousse*

overall prep time: 4 hours

active prep time:
10 minutes

easy

inexpensive

freezes well

do not ship

do not double

shelf life: 1 week refrigerated in a tightly covered container

makes: 8 servings

An ideal gift for any practicing chocoholic, this unbelievably easy dessert is everything a perfect chocolate mousse should be: dense and rich with a superbly silken texture. All that perfection takes only 10 minutes, and the finished product freezes beautifully. If frozen solid, the mousse will survive the perils of delivery unscathed.

This recipe will make two gifts, each serving four if your recipient is inclined to share it (by no means a sure thing). You will need to decide on containers before you begin, and you have several options to consider. Simple white ramekins can be purchased inexpensively in several sizes from major discount stores; while these are the most suitable, they may push the budget a bit. Glass or plastic jars will also work and should cost less. Simple white-paper ice cream cartons are the least expensive option and one of the most attractive, but they can be difficult to find. I have located a good source online, and the standard delivery parcels usually go out the day they are ordered (see Resources, page 290).

1 cup granulated sugar

1 cup water

1 package (12 ounces) dark chocolate chips

4 large eggs

⅓ cup brandy, rum, or Triple Sec

¼ cup very strong brewed coffee

1 tablespoon vanilla extract

2 cups whipping cream or heavy cream

1 Combine the sugar and water in a heavy saucepan and stir until the sugar is dissolved. Bring the mixture to a boil over medium heat, without stirring. Once the mixture begins to boil, cover the pan and very slightly lower the heat. Continue to boil for 6 minutes, or until the bubbles are thick and slow and the consistency is slightly syrupy.

2 Meanwhile, place the chocolate chips and the eggs in the bowl of a food processor and process them for 25 seconds. Add the brandy, coffee, and vanilla to the bowl of the food processor. Process the mixture, then continue to run the machine while you carefully pour the boiling sugar syrup through the feed tube in a slow, steady stream. Continue to process the mousse base until it is very smooth and shiny.

3 Pour the mousse base into a large mixing bowl. Return the work bowl to the processor base, pour in the cream, and process until the cream is thick but not stiff. It should have the same consistency as the chocolate mixture. Pour the whipped cream on top of the chocolate mixture and use a rubber spatula to fold the cream gently into the chocolate until there are no streaks of white. Pour the mousse into two or more containers and place them in the freezer for at least 4 hours. Once the mousse has set, tightly cover the containers and return them to the freezer until you are ready to assemble and deliver the gift. Allow the frozen mousse to thaw for 1 hour in the refrigerator before serving.

wrapping it up

Your decoration will depend on the container you have chosen. Ramekins can be covered with large circles of white parchment paper, which can be held in place with silver or white elastic gift cord. Jars can be covered with a wide band of glassine paper, while the white lidded cartons can be wound with paper ribbon knotted tightly over the center of the lid and finished with either a flouncy or simple bow.

chic french *milk jam*

overall prep time: 3 to 4 hours

active prep time: 30 minutes

easy

inexpensive

do not freeze or ship

can be doubled

shelf life: 2 weeks refrigerated in a tightly covered jar

makes: 3 cups

This jam, which the French call *confiture de lait*, is like a Spanish *dulce de leche* but slightly less sweet and with less of a deeply caramel flavor. The French version is richer, too, and has a smoother texture. Milk jam can be used as a dessert sauce for cake, ice cream, or fresh or poached fruit. It is fabulous on a toasted brioche or as a filling for éclairs. A tall glass of iced coffee sweetened with milk jam, accompanied by assorted cookies, makes a fine summer dessert. A little milk jam goes a long way, so you could easily divide this into two smaller gifts.

| 2 quarts whole milk | 2 cups granulated sugar | 2 vanilla beans |

1 Combine the milk and sugar in a heavy saucepan. Stir the milk until the sugar is dissolved. Cut the vanilla beans in half lengthwise and add them to the saucepan. Bring this mixture to a full boil over medium heat, stirring frequently. Reduce the heat to low and allow the mixture to simmer very gently, uncovered, for 3 to 4 hours. Stir the mixture frequently and adjust the heat as needed to maintain a gentle simmer and prevent the bottom from scorching. The milk jam has finished cooking when it reaches the consistency of a thick yogurt. Sometimes the mixture separates during cooking, but this will be resolved when you puree the mixture in the next step.

2 Remove the saucepan from the stove and set aside to allow the contents to cool slightly. When the vanilla beans are cool enough to handle, remove them and squeeze the pods over the saucepan so that all of the black seeds fall into the milk

jam. Puree the warm mixture in a food processor or blender for 2 minutes. The mixture should be silky smooth; if it is not, let it cool for another 5 to 10 minutes and then process it until smooth.

3 Pour the milk jam into a heat-resistant glass jar and set aside to cool completely before covering and refrigerating the jar. Store the milk jam in the refrigerator until you are ready to assemble and deliver the gift.

wrapping it up

A jar of milk jam, while delicious to eat, is not very exciting to look at. It's just beige. For some reason, anything French and beige reminds me of Chanel, so I cover the lid with a black pouf of tissue held in place with silky tasseled ribbon. I add a classic black-and-white label (à la Chanel No. 5). Pearls would be a bit much.

suggested supplies

1 large sheet black tissue paper

1 elastic band

black and white thin silky ribbons

1 black bead with a large hole

1 plain white adhesive label

how to make a Chanel-style jar

Measure the circumference of the jar lid. Cut the tissue paper into a 5- or 6-inch-wide strip 1 or 2 inches longer than that measurement and fold it in half lengthwise. Crumple the leftover tissue scrap into a ball and set it aside. Wrap the tissue-paper strip around the jar with the top of the strip approximately flush with the top of the jar and slip the elastic band over the jar into the channel between the jar and lid. Set the crumpled ball of tissue on top of the jar and pull the lower part of the wide strip up over the lid and elastic, twisting it closed gently into a fat little pouf over the lid. Wrap several strands of the black and white ribbons tightly around the twisted tissue top, and then tie them together tightly with a double knot. Make a tassel by sliding the ribbon ends through the black bead and knotting the ribbon ends again to hold the bead in place. Trim the ribbon ends evenly. Use a straightedge and a black marker to create a border on your adhesive label. Write the label with the black marker and carefully attach it to the jar.

another dozen *eggs* (for dessert this time)

Imagine cracking an egg and peeling off the shell to find a perfect bite-sized genoise cake inside. This old French *truc*, or trick, delights everyone who encounters it. This is a very inexpensive gift, and cakes in eggs are surprisingly easy to make; they're only time-consuming until you get the hang of it. I have made 6 dozen at a time for party favors, box lunches, picnics, tailgates, and Easter baskets. If you write names on the egg shells, they make very special place cards when set on little mounds of moss or inside miniature bird's nests (found at craft stores). Just think how much money an industrious bride could save on her wedding cake with this idea!

12 large eggs

1 cup coarse salt

3 tablespoons corn oil or safflower oil

½ cup (1 stick) unsalted butter, cool but not chilled

½ cup granulated sugar

2 teaspoons vanilla extract

¾ cup all-purpose flour

1 teaspoon baking powder

2 tablespoons heavy cream

overall prep time: 3 hours

active prep time: 1 hour

slightly challenging

inexpensive

do not freeze or ship

can be doubled or tripled

shelf life: 3 days individually wrapped in plastic wrap at room temperature

makes: 12 small egg-shaped cakes

Use a push pin to pierce the wider bottom end of each egg. Carefully enlarge the holes with a pair of small sharp-pointed scissors until they are a little more than ¼ inch in diameter. Use a wooden skewer to stir and break up the yolks inside the shells. Place a coarse-mesh strainer over a small bowl and shake the eggs out well over the strainer. Set the strainer and bowl aside while you prepare the shells.

recipe continues

2 Rinse the eggs out with warm water and place them gently in a large flat-bottomed bowl with the salt. Add enough water to cover the eggs, filling each egg with salt water so that it stays submerged. Set the bowl aside for 1 hour.

3 Rinse the eggs out very thoroughly again with warm water and invert them onto a paper towel–lined tray to drain and dry. Pour a little oil into each dry eggshell and roll the shells with your hands until the interiors of the shells are completely coated with oil. Invert each shell as you finish it on the paper towel–lined tray to drain any excess oil. Crumple 2 or 3 foil cupcake liners around the narrow end of each eggshell and set the shells, hole side up, in the cups of a cupcake pan. Adjust the shells and foil so the shells stand upright and level.

4 Preheat the oven to 350°F. Using an electric mixer, in a large bowl cream the butter and sugar for 3 minutes. Force the reserved eggs through the strainer with the back of a wooden spoon. Measure out 1 cup of the strained eggs, saving the rest for another purpose, and add them to the creamed butter and sugar along with the vanilla; beat for 1 minute. Slowly beat the flour and baking powder into the batter at low speed until completely blended. Add the cream to the batter and continue beating at low speed for 1 minute.

5 Use a pastry bag fitted with a 3/16-inch plain tip to fill each egg with about 3 tablespoons of the batter. Each egg should be three-fourths full of batter.

6 Bake the eggs for 25 to 30 minutes, or until a wooden skewer inserted into the center of the eggs comes out clean. Place the cupcake pan on a baking rack until the eggs are completely cool. Use a damp paper towel to wipe any splatters off each egg and remove batter that may have overflowed. Store the eggs in an airtight container until you are ready to assemble and deliver the gift.

wrapping it up

Although you can always buy miniature nests at craft stores, it is easier and less expensive to make your own, using raffia.

suggested supplies

white paper cupcake liners in various sizes

thin natural raffia

cellophane

how to make nests for little cakes

Each "nest" can hold 1 to 4 cake eggs, depending on the size of cupcake liner you use. Wind a small bunch of raffia around your fingertips and arrange it in a paper cupcake liner. Add the cake egg or eggs, filling in any gaps with more raffia. Individual eggs in a nest can be wrapped tightly with cellophane; twist the cellophane tightly into a nub on the underside of the nest and tie it tightly with a few strands of raffia. Larger nests with 3 or more eggs need to be overwrapped with cellophane twisted over the top of the nest and finished with wire twist ties and raffia or ribbon.

pound foolish

You can wrack your brain and ruin your financial peace of mind trying to come up with a gift for someone who has everything, knowing that no matter what you buy, if the recipient really wanted it he or she would already own it. For that person, an indulgent gift of food is the perfect solution.

The gifts in this chapter are all expensive, some far more than others. They use "exclusive" ingredients to create gourmet gifts in equally superb presentations. Almost all of these gifts require a larger investment of your time, as well as money. But the fun of cooking and creating when price is no object is your reward. Each of the recipes in this chapter will produce a truly special offering guaranteed to delight even the most jaded palate or jaundiced eye.

things to keep in mind

Be prepared to spend some time finding the perfect container or packaging for your gift. It must not only be fittingly luxurious but perfectly suited to the gift you are preparing. The ideal presentation should echo the quality of the contents.

Think through the gift and its presentation completely. Include all the little things that will facilitate the enjoyment of the items you have prepared. These thoughtful touches add another layer of luxury to your gift.

You might consider giving the recipient a little advance warning if you are preparing a gift on a really grand scale or of a more perishable nature. In other words, to take two examples from this chapter, it is probably not a good idea to show up unannounced on someone's doorstep with a complete Greens Goddess, page 201, or Caviar Sampler, page 205. After all, it would be a shame for your effort and expense to go to waste, and you want your gift to bring the maximum enjoyment to the recipient.

gravlax and *limpa* in a fisherman's creel

overall prep time: 48 to 72 hours

active prep time: 2 hours

moderately easy

expensive

do not freeze or ship

can be doubled or tripled

shelf life: 2 weeks refrigerated and tightly wrapped for gravlax; 4 days for bread (but it's best within 48 hours)

makes: about 5 pounds gravlax and 2 generous loaves limpa bread

For centuries the Swedish have preserved salmon using large quantities of fresh dill and heavy pine planks to compress the fish while it is curing. The result is called gravlax. A really good gravlax is similar to smoked salmon in texture and color, but the taste is much fresher and the texture is firmer. It is virtually impossible to buy top-quality gravlax in the U.S. Wild salmon is very expensive, but it has the firm, dense consistency essential to success with this recipe. You will also need a lot of fresh dill; long-branched bunches are usually available at upscale gourmet supermarkets. This recipe makes two large fillets, enough to justify keeping one for yourself, if you like; the gift, when packaged as described below, includes one fillet.

Swedish limpa is a fine-textured light rye bread that is traditionally flavored with orange zest. But I think lemon makes the limpa pair better with the gravlax.

FOR THE GRAVLAX:

30 full branches (8 to 10 inches long) fresh dill, about 1 large bunch

2 center-cut skin-on wild salmon fillets, about 2½ pounds each

¾ cup granulated sugar

5 tablespoons turbinado sugar

1 cup coarse sea salt

3 tablespoons dried dill leaves

FOR THE LIMPA BREAD:

½ cup buttermilk

⅓ cup water

1 package active dry yeast

⅓ cup dark brown sugar

finely grated zest and juice of 1 medium lemon

1 teaspoon sea salt

¼ cup (½ stick) unsalted butter, melted

2 cups rye flour, plus 2 tablespoons for the baking sheet

2 cups unbleached all-purpose flour, plus up to ¼ cup for kneading the dough

2 tablespoons unsalted butter, softened

1 egg white beaten with 1 tablespoon water

¼ cup fennel, rye, or anise seeds

1. To make the gravlax, wash the dill branches and tie them in two or three bundles by the woody stems. Hang the bundles upside down to dry outside or over a sink.

2. Lay the salmon fillets, skin side down, on a large sheet of wax paper. Slowly run your index finger against the grain of each fillet, checking for any small bones, which, if found, should be removed with a small pair of kitchen pliers.

3. Stir together the granulated and turbinado sugars, the salt, and the dried dill in a mixing bowl. Sprinkle a handful of this mixture evenly over the skinless side of each fillet. Vigorously rub the seasonings into the salmon. Keep adding the seasoning mixture a handful at a time and rubbing it into the fillets until they are thickly coated with seasonings. Depending on the size and texture of your salmon fillets, you may not require

recipe continues

all the seasoning salt; any leftover seasonings can be rubbed into the skin of each fillet. Loosely cover the fillets and set them aside while preparing the fresh dill.

4 Untie the bundles of fresh dill, and cut off and discard the woody stems at the base of each stalk; keep only the tender green stalks full of leaves. Line the bottom of a 9 × 12-inch glass or ceramic casserole dish with half of these leafy stalks. Lay one fillet, skin side down, on the dill. Cover the fillet with a thick, even layer of dill, using almost all of the remaining stalks; reserve 2 or 3 small sprigs for garnish. Lay the second fillet, skin side up, over the dill, with the thickest portion of the second fillet on top of the thinnest part of the first fillet, so that the two fillets contour to one another and form a more level layer to hold the weights. Place a similar-sized dish on top of the two salmon fillets and fill it with heavy cans or other heavy items to weight the salmon and press it into the dill. Cover the entire assemblage of pans, salmon, and weights in plastic wrap and refrigerate it for 24 to 36 hours.

5 Unwrap the dishes and remove the weighted dish. Turn the fillets over in the dill-lined dish and replace the weights. Rewrap and refrigerate the gravlax and weights for an additional 24 to 36 hours.

6 Remove the salmon fillets from the baking dish and discard all the dill. Scrape off and discard the seasoning mixture from the fillets and wipe them clean with damp paper towels. Lay the reserved fresh sprigs of dill and thin slices of lemon at the center of each fillet and wrap the fillets very tightly in plastic wrap. Refrigerate the wrapped fillets until you are ready to assemble and deliver the gift.

7 To make the limpa bread, combine the buttermilk and water in a small saucepan and gently warm the mixture over low heat until it registers 100° to 105°F on an instant-read thermometer. Pour the warm liquid into a large mixing bowl or the bowl of a stand mixer. Sprinkle the yeast over the liquid and whisk until the yeast is dissolved. Add the brown sugar, lemon zest and juice, salt, and melted butter to the yeast mixture and continue to whisk until the sugar is dissolved.

8 Add the 2 cups of rye flour to the yeast mixture and beat by hand with a wooden spoon or with the paddle attachment of the stand mixer at medium speed until you have a smooth, sticky batter. Reduce the mixer speed to low, and add the 2 cups of all-purpose flour, 1 cup at a time, beating well after each addition. Stop beating the dough once it is dry enough to pull away cleanly from the sides of the bowl.

9 Lightly flour a work surface using a small amount of the additional flour. Turn the dough out onto the floured work surface and knead it for about 8 minutes, using more of the additional flour as needed (up to ¼ cup) for your hands and the work surface if they become sticky. Continue to knead the dough until it is smooth and resilient, springing back to the touch. Heavily coat a large bowl with the softened butter, place the dough in the bowl, and swirl the dough several times so the entire surface of the dough is coated with butter. Cover the bowl with a tea towel

and set it aside in a warm, draft-free area to rise for 2 hours, or until the dough has doubled in volume.

10 Turn the dough onto a lightly floured work surface and divide it in half. Use a heavy rolling pin to flatten each dough portion into a thick oval and cover the ovals with a tea towel to rest for 15 minutes. Meanwhile, line a baking sheet with parchment paper and sprinkle it with the remaining 2 tablespoons rye flour.

11 Roll each dough oval out until it is about 1 inch thick. Fold the long sides to the center of the oval and then join the folded edges by pinching them together, forming slender baguette-shaped loaves. Transfer the loaves to the prepared pan, cover them with a tea towel, and set the pan aside in a warm, draft-free area for 45 minutes.

12 Preheat the oven to 350°F. Make several diagonal slashes across each loaf with a very sharp paring knife. Brush the loaves with the egg white mixture and sprinkle the loaves with the seeds. Bake the breads on the center rack of the oven for 50 minutes, or until they are a deep brown and echo like ripe melons when thumped with your fingers. Cool the breads on a rack and then loosely wrap them until you are ready to assemble the gift.

recipe continues

wrapping it up

A fishing creel filled with gravlax and limpa is a beautiful gift. Traditional creels, woven like baskets, are available at sporting-goods stores and outdoor-sports outfitters; less expensive decorative versions (available at home-goods and craft stores) are fairly easy to find. It is important to incorporate an ice pack in the wrap because the gravlax must be kept very cold at all times. Depending on how much you want to spend, consider adding a smoked-salmon knife to the gift. These knives are designed to make slicing cured and smoked salmon properly a lot easier.

suggested supplies

1 fishing creel

1 ice pack

cotton fish net (available at craft and fabric stores)

kitchen twine

parchment paper or craft paper

1 plain shipping tag with string

how to ice and wrap the gravlax

Spread out a rectangle of fish net smoothly on the work surface. Center one plastic-wrapped gravlax on the fish net, skin side up, and place the ice pack on top. Tightly wrap the gravlax and ice pack in the fish net. The gravlax will hide the ice pack when it's placed skin side down in the creel. Knot the ends of the fish net tightly around the fish and ice pack, or twist the net tightly and secure it with the kitchen twine. Set aside. Roll the limpa loaves diagonally in the parchment or craft paper and arrange the breads and the wrapped gravlax in the creel. Use the shipping tag as a gift card and tie it to the creel handle. On the shipping tag write:

SERVING INSTRUCTIONS

Gravlax should be sliced very thin. Use a long serrated knife with a flexible blade. Lay the center of the blade almost flat and parallel to the center of the gravlax fillet. Use a gentle, back and forth sawing motion, keeping the blade almost flat and parallel to the fillet, to slice the gravlax. The long, thin slices should be spiraled onto thin slices of the limpa bread. Sour cream or lemon wedges can be used to garnish the open-faced sandwiches.

baby artichokes
braised in olive oil

Here's a big gift that is nothing short of flat-out gorgeous: a huge glass jar filled with tiny artichokes, swimming in deep-green olive oil, surrounded by herbs and lemon slices. It makes a perfect edible centerpiece for casual dinner parties or impromptu cocktail gatherings. Baby artichokes are usually available during two brief seasons, in late spring and early fall. These tiny artichokes have no fibrous choke, and the young stem and all but the very outermost leaves are tender enough to eat. Artichokes this small and tender are considered a delicacy, which is usually reflected in their price.

overall prep time: 2 hours

active prep time: 1½ hours

easy

expensive

do not freeze or ship

can be divided

shelf life: 6 weeks refrigerated in a tightly sealed jar

makes: 1 gallon

7 lemons

2 quarts cold water

1 tablespoon coarse sea salt

24 baby artichokes

6 to 7 cups extra-virgin olive oil

1 French-style canning jar (about 1 gallon capacity) with glass lid and wire bale

10 to 12 large sprigs fresh thyme, washed and patted dry

1 Juice 2 of the lemons and use a swivel-bladed peeler to remove the yellow outer rind from the juiced lemons, leaving the bitter white pith behind.

recipe continues

2 Prepare an acidulated water bath for the artichokes by combining the cold water, salt, and the lemon juice and rinds. Rinse the artichokes well under running water. Peel and discard any discolored or bruised portions from the stem of each artichoke with the peeler. Starting at the base of each artichoke, break off the dark green outer leaves until you reach the tender edible leaves, which are almost yellow in color. Using a pair of kitchen scissors, cut a small V-shaped notch in the top of the remaining leaves, to remove the tiny barbs from their tips. As each artichoke is prepared, add it to the water bath.

3 Heat 2 cups of the olive oil in a large Dutch oven or a wide, short stockpot over medium heat. Juice 3 more of the lemons and coarsely chop the reamed halves. Add the lemon juice and chopped rinds to the olive oil.

4 Unless you have a very wide Dutch oven or stockpot and an equally large burner, the artichokes must be braised in batches. Transfer the prepared artichokes to the Dutch oven and arrange them in a single layer over the bottom of the pan. Braise the artichokes in the olive oil, turning them frequently in the simmering oil, for 30 to 40 minutes, or until the center of each artichoke can be easily pierced with a sharp knife.

5 When all the artichokes have been braised, discard the braising oil along with the chopped lemon pieces. Wash the canning jar in hot soapy water, rinse it, and dry the jar in a 190°F oven. Wash the rubber jar gasket in hot soapy water, rinse it, dry it with paper towels, and set it aside.

6 Thickly slice the remaining 2 lemons and place 4 or 5 slices in the hot jar. Pack the jar with the prepared artichokes, the remaining lemon slices, and the sprigs of thyme to within an inch of the jar top. (Depending on the size of the baby artichokes, you may not be able to fit all 24 in the jar.) Pour the remaining 4 to 5 cups of olive oil over the packed artichokes. Use the handle of a wooden spoon to remove any air pockets from the jar, and add more olive oil as needed to fill to 1 inch from the top. The artichokes, lemon slices, and thyme should be submerged in the oil. Attach the rubber gasket to the jar lid and clamp the jar closed. Set the jar aside to cool completely, then store it in the refrigerator until you are ready to assemble and deliver the gift. (The oil congeals and clouds when refrigerated, so the artichoke jar needs to be brought to room temperature before being given or served.)

wrapping it up

The artichokes in the glass jar are so stunning, they do not need decoration. But your recipient might need some information on how to serve and store them, as well as a long pair of tongs for removing them from their jar.

suggested supplies

printer-weight card stock

pale-green paper ribbon or thick twine

1 pair long wooden tongs

1 large decorative brad

how to make "informative" tongs

Make an information sheet with storage and serving suggestions on the card stock. The suggestions might read: "As long as the artichokes are submerged in the olive oil they will keep for 6 weeks refrigerated. The jar should rest at room temperature before the artichokes are served. Serve them with fresh lemon slices, coarse sea salt, and freshly ground black pepper." Tightly roll the instruction sheet into a thin scroll and tie it up with paper ribbon or twine. Using a craft drill, make a small hole near the joint of the tongs. Squeeze the tongs together, slip the scroll over them, and release the tongs, allowing the resulting tension to hold the scroll in place. Using the hole that you drilled, string the tongs onto another length of ribbon or twine long enough to encircle the jar neck. Run the ribbon or twine around the jar neck and tie a simple bow.

filled mocha *macarons* on a french pastry stand

There is only one place on earth with a macaron this big, this beautiful, and this good. It happens to be in Paris, at a tearoom called Ladurée. This is my own recipe for macarons inspired by the style of Ladurée. Show off these pretty filled macarons on a tiered pastry stand.

overall prep time: 2 hours

active prep time: 45 minutes

challenging

expensive

do not freeze or ship

do not double

shelf life: 1 day in an airtight container

makes: 18

FOR THE COOKIES:

8 ounces shelled hazelnuts

4 cups confectioners' sugar

⅓ cup Dutch-processed cocoa powder

2 teaspoons instant espresso powder

6 large egg whites, at room temperature

pinch of fine sea salt

FOR THE GANACHE FILLING:

8 ounces bittersweet chocolate, finely chopped, or 8 ounces bittersweet chocolate chips

1 cup crème fraîche (page 46, or use store-bought)

1½ teaspoons vanilla extract

1½ tablespoons instant espresso powder

1. To make the cookies, toast the hazelnuts in a heavy sauté pan over medium-high heat, stirring and turning them constantly, for 5 to 6 minutes, until they are golden and aromatic. Transfer the hazelnuts to a shallow dish and set them aside to cool completely. Meanwhile, line two heavy-duty baking sheets with parchment paper.

2. Place the nuts and 2 cups of the confectioners' sugar in the bowl of a food processor. Pulse the machine repeatedly to grind the nuts to a coarse powder. Sift the hazelnut powder through a coarse-mesh strainer onto an 11 × 17-inch sheet of parchment paper. Add the cocoa and espresso powder, and stir briefly to combine.

Resift the hazelnut powder through the same coarse-mesh strainer into a bowl and set it aside.

3 Sift the remaining 2 cups of confectioners' sugar into a bowl; set aside. With an electric mixer, beat the egg whites at low speed until they are foamy. Add the pinch of salt. Increase the mixer speed to medium-high and beat the egg whites for 2 to 3 minutes, until they form soft peaks.

4 Increase the mixer speed to high and gradually add the sifted confectioners' sugar to the egg whites until they form stiff, shiny peaks, about 5 to 6 minutes. Scrape down the sides of the bowl and beat the egg whites for another 30 to 45 seconds.

5 Preheat the oven to 325°F. Add the hazelnut powder to the egg whites and gently fold the powder through the egg whites with a large spatula. Do not overfold the batter. Put half of the macaron batter into a large pastry bag fitted with a ½-inch plain pastry tip. Pipe 18 evenly spaced rounds, about 1½ inches in diameter and ¼ inch high, onto one of the parchment-lined baking sheets. Refill the pastry bag and repeat with the remaining batter and the second baking sheet. Wash and dry the pastry bag and tip so they are ready to use for the ganache filling.

6 Place the baking sheets on the middle racks of the oven and bake the macarons for 10 minutes. Rotate and switch the baking sheets and bake for another 8 minutes. Turn off the oven, prop the oven door slightly ajar with a wooden spoon, and leave the macarons in the oven for another 10 minutes. Cool the baking sheets on racks for 10 minutes. Using a large offset spatula, carefully peel the macarons off the parchment and transfer them directly to racks to cool completely. Store the cooled macarons in an airtight container. Filled macarons will have a shelf life of about 24 hours, so do not prepare the ganache or fill the macarons until you are ready to assemble and deliver the gift.

7 To make the ganache filling, put the chocolate in a heatproof bowl and set it in a warm (200° to 250°F) oven to soften while you prepare the remaining ganache ingredients.

8 Combine the crème fraîche, vanilla, and espresso powder in a small saucepan. Bring the mixture slowly to a boil, stirring frequently. Pour the boiling mixture over the softened chocolate. Stir until the chocolate has melted and the mixture is a smooth, glossy brown.

9 Refrigerate the ganache until it has thickened and holds its shape, 45 minutes to 1 hour. The consistency should be similar to that of chocolate mousse. Using the large pastry bag and ½-inch plain pastry tip, pipe a generous dollop of ganache onto the flat bottoms of one half of the cooled macarons. Place the flat bottom of a second macaron on top of the ganache and press the two halves together until the ganache filling reaches the edges of the macarons. Arrange the filled macarons in single layers in airtight containers and set them in a cool, dry place until you are ready to assemble and deliver the gift.

recipe continues

wrapping it up

Small two-tiered pastry display stands made of ceramic, Lucite, woven wire, polished nickel, or silver plate can be found at gourmet and home-accessory stores as well as online (see Resources, page 290). Expect to pay between $30 and $75 for a very nice stand. Stands such as these prove indispensable for people with too many things; they can help organize small miscellaneous items such as corks, toothpicks, piping tips, and what have you when the macarons are only a memory.

suggested supplies

18 large white paper cupcake liners, stacked in pairs of two

18 squares (8 inches each) glassine, tissue paper, or cellophane

18 wire twist ties

18 lengths (8 to 9 inches each) thin silk ribbon or twill tape

double-face tape

1 two-tiered pastry display stand

how to make a pastry stand full of macarons

Stand two filled macarons on edge side by side in each double cupcake liner. Center each lined pair of macarons on a square of glassine and tightly twist the square over the macarons, securing the twisted paper with a wire twist tie. Cover the twist tie with ribbon or twill tape, knot it tightly, and finish with a tiny bow. Apply a small piece of double-face tape to the bottom of each wrapped macaron package. Arrange the macarons on the tiered stand, making sure the tape is holding each macaron package in place. You can overwrap the pastry stand in clear or colored cellophane, too, if you like.

the star attraction: *sugar cookies* in a champagne bucket

There is a charming but completely apocryphal story that attributes the invention of Champagne to a blind Benedictine cellar master, Dom Pérignon. "Come quickly! I am drinking stars!" the monk supposedly exclaimed upon tasting the world's first glass of bubbly. Although the oft-told story has been discredited, the bottles that bear Dom Pérignon's name today contain a truly creditable version of the fabled drink. A bottle of Dom Pérignon (or any other premium brand of Champagne) surrounded by a galaxy of gleaming sugar-cookie stars, all presented in a star-studded Champagne bucket, makes for a charming adjunct to a charming story.

The dough for these sugar cookies is superb for rolled and cut cookies; the finished cookies retain all the definition and detail of the cookie cutters. To make the cookies especially suited for pairing with Champagne, I use less sugar than one normally would, and I add an extra measure of orange zest. To make the star shapes, you will need 3 sizes of star-shaped cookie cutters.

overall prep time: 1½ hours

active prep time: 50 minutes

slightly challenging

moderately expensive

raw dough and baked cookies freeze well

cookies ship well when packed in an airtight tin with layers of tissue paper

can be doubled

shelf life: 1 week in an airtight container

makes: 3 to 4 dozen

2 cups all-purpose flour

1 cup cake flour

1½ teaspoons baking powder

½ teaspoon salt

1 cup (2 sticks) unsalted butter, softened but cool

1 cup granulated sugar

Finely grated zest of 1 orange

1 large egg

1 egg white beaten with 2 teaspoons water

⅓ cup sanding sugar or sparkling crystal sugar

recipe continues

1 Whisk together the flours, baking powder, and salt in a bowl and set aside. Using a stand mixer with the whisk attachment, cream the butter, granulated sugar, and orange zest at medium-high speed for 3 minutes. Add the egg and continue to beat for 1 minute more.

2 Add the dry ingredients to the mixer bowl. Using the paddle attachment, beat the cookie dough at medium speed for 1 minute, scrape down the sides of the bowl, and beat the dough for another minute.

3 Divide the dough in thirds and sandwich each portion between two 11 × 17-inch sheets of parchment paper. Use a rolling pin to roll the dough out to the edges of the parchment paper, stack the portions of dough on a tray or baking sheet, and refrigerate for 30 minutes. Meanwhile, preheat the oven to 350°F.

4 Put one portion of the chilled dough in its parchment sheets on a large baking sheet. Peel away the top sheet of parchment and use the largest star to cut out cookies about ½ inch apart. Peel away the scraps and refrigerate them. Using a pastry brush, coat the cookies with the egg white wash and sprinkle them with about one-third of the sanding sugar.

5 Bake the cookies on the center rack of the oven for 5 minutes. Rotate the pan and bake the cookies for another 3 to 5 minutes, until the edges are golden. Cool the pan on a rack for 5 minutes and then transfer the cookies directly to the rack to cool completely before storing them in an airtight container.

6 Repeat the process with the remaining two sheets of rolled dough, using a successively smaller cutter on each sheet. Smaller stars will take a little less time to bake. Combine all the refrigerated scraps, sandwich them between two sheets of parchment, and roll, cut, and bake them in the same way, using whichever size cutter you like.

wrapping it up

It is surprisingly simple to craft this elegant etched-glass Champagne bucket as a container for the star cookies and the bottle of bubbly. Small gold and silver star stickers are available at office-supply stores that sell teachers' materials and school supplies. Note that while every etching cream I have found is food safe, you should read the package carefully before buying and using the cream.

suggested supplies

1 clear glass champagne bucket or wine cooler

star stickers in one or several sizes

1 bottle (2 ounces) etching cream, available at craft stores

clear cellophane

1 bottle Dom Pérignon or other premium Champagne

1 wire twist tie

1 star cut from a 4-inch square of card stock

several varying lengths (6 to 10 inches) curling ribbon

how to make an etched champagne bucket with a shooting-star topper

Starting at the bottom, apply the star stickers to the inside of the bucket in a random pattern. Space the stickers closely at the bottom, then gradually increase the space between the stickers as you ascend to the top of the bucket. (If you use several sizes of star stickers, start with the largest at the base of the bucket.) Follow the manufacturer's directions for applying, rinsing, and drying the etching cream and removing the stickers.

Cushion the bottom of the bucket with a couple of tightly crumpled sheets of cellophane. Add the bottle of Champagne to the bucket and surround the bottle with the star cookies. The cookies should almost overflow the top of the bucket. Center the filled bucket on a large sheet of cellophane and gather the cellophane tightly to the top of the bucket. Tightly twist the cellophane and secure it with a wire twist tie.

Punch a small hole in the center of the card stock star, and write a gift message on the star. Stack the ribbons together at their midpoints and fold the stack in half. Push the fold through the center hole in the star. Pull the folded ribbon through the other side of the star until you have a loop large enough to fit over the twist tie closure on the cellophane. Place the loop over the closure and tighten the loop by pulling the ribbon ends from the opposite side of the star. Curl the ribbon ends with a scissors blade or a metal straightedge.

greens goddess

A garden trug or a wire basket holding a still-life arrangement of fresh vegetables, fruit, herbs, and edible flowers in every shade of green might look almost too beautiful to eat. But looks can be deceiving: Each item in this still life has been prepared in advance for the salad bowl, and a bottle of classic green goddess dressing helps to tempt all those great greens out of the trug and onto the table.

Wooden garden trugs are expensive because they are handmade. They are very useful as well as lovely to look at. Trugs range in size from approximately 14 × 7 × 9 inches to 20 × 12 × 10 inches, and the prices reflect the materials used as well as the size. You can find trugs in upscale florist shops or home stores as well as in luxury gardening catalogs and online (see Resources, page 290). Alternatively, a wire basket makes an equally attractive and much less expensive container for this gift.

overall prep time:
60 minutes

easy

moderately expensive

do not freeze or ship

can be doubled or tripled

shelf life: 3 days refrigerated in a tightly sealed bottle for dressing; 2 hours with ice packs for greens

makes: slightly more than 3 cups of dressing and as many greens as you choose to include

FOR THE GREEN GODDESS DRESSING:

½ ripe avocado, peeled and seeded

3 tablespoons fresh lemon juice

2 scallions, green and white parts, thinly sliced

3 tablespoons fresh tarragon leaves

¼ cup tightly packed fresh parsley leaves

½ cup tightly packed fresh watercress leaves

2 anchovy fillets

¼ teaspoon coarse sea salt, or more to taste

1 cup mayonnaise

½ cup sour cream

⅓ cup whole buttermilk

½ teaspoon ground white pepper, or more to taste

recipe continues

a selection of salad greens, such as a full head of curly endive, Belgian endive leaves, a full head of Boston or butter lettuce, and hearts of romaine or baby romaine leaves

whole small English or Syrian cucumbers

haricots verts or tender baby green beans

pencil-thin asparagus, trimmed

sprigs of fresh herbs, such as Italian flat-leaf parsley, basil (preferably young and with small leaves), tarragon, marjoram, or chervil

1 large bunch long chives

edible flowers, such as nasturtiums, pansies, marigolds, or borage

clusters of green seedless grapes

. . . .

1 To make the green goddess dressing, chop the avocado coarsely and combine it with the lemon juice in a large bowl with a flat bottom. Use a fork to mash the avocado pulp with the lemon juice into a rough puree and set it aside.

2 Place the scallions, tarragon, parsley, watercress, and anchovy fillets on a cutting board and sprinkle them with the ¼ teaspoon of sea salt. Chop the herbs and anchovies very finely with a wide-bladed chef's knife until the mixture is almost a paste.

3 Add the herb mixture to the avocado puree along with the mayonnaise, sour cream, buttermilk, and white pepper. Whisk the ingredients together until they are well blended into a thick and chunky dressing. Taste for salt and pepper, and adjust the seasonings if you like. Transfer the dressing into an attractive bottle with a tight-fitting lid or stopper, and refrigerate until you are ready to assemble and deliver the gift.

4 Prepare the trug or basket of produce: The goal is to create a breathtaking arrangement, all green, all edible, and all fully "prepped."

- The curly endive and Boston or butter lettuce can be washed and dried while keeping the heads intact. Plunge them headfirst into a sink full of tepid water and allow them to soak for 1 hour. Drain the lettuce heads in a colander and spray them with tepid water to remove any soil clinging to the bases of the leaves. Wrap the heads individually in thin cotton towels and tightly knot the towels over the core of each lettuce head. Hang the bundled lettuces upside down outdoors or over a sink for a couple of hours to drain and dry completely. Belgian endive and romaine leaves must be washed and dried individually. Arrange the leaves on a double layer of paper towels and gently roll them up in the paper towels. Put the rolls in a plastic storage bags and refrigerate until you are ready to assemble the gift.

- The cucumbers should be thinly sliced almost all the way through, so they appear to be whole but can easily be pulled apart when the salad is served. Gently roll each sliced cucumber in a double layer of paper towels. Put each one in a plastic storage bag and refrigerate them until you are ready to assemble the gift.

- The haricots verts (or other green beans) and asparagus should be blanched in a large pot of boiling water for a very brief time. The blanching time depends on the size and age of the beans or asparagus. To make them tender enough to eat yet crisp enough to hold their shape, 2 to 3 minutes in boiling water is usually sufficient. Blanch only a few vegetables at time and immediately plunge them into a large basin of ice and water. When the vegetables are cooled, drain them in a single layer on trays lined with several sheets of paper towels. Gently blot the vegetables dry, cover the trays with more paper towels and with plastic wrap, and refrigerate the vegetables for at least 2 hours and as many as 6 hours, to make sure they are thoroughly chilled and dry before assembling the gift.

- The herb sprigs, chives, and edible flowers should be very gently washed and patted dry. You can put the stems in glasses of water and set them aside at room temperature until you are ready to assemble the gift.

- Wash the grape clusters and set them aside to dry in a colander or on paper towels. Refrigerate until you are ready to assemble the gift.

recipe continues

wrapping it up

Nature has done most of the work; all you have to do is artfully fill the trug or basket with the beautiful items you have so carefully prepared. The arrangement should be done at the very last minute possible, so that it will be at its freshest when you give it as a gift.

suggested supplies

1 piece (approximately 1½ square yards) mosquito netting or fine tulle

1 wooden garden trug or wire basket

ice packs (optional)

1 green cloth napkin or tea towel

craft wire or 1 large covered elastic band

green raffia or curly paper ribbon

how to compose a greens goddess

Spread out the mosquito netting or tulle carefully on a work surface and center the trug or basket on it. Organize all the vegetables on your work space. Tie the asparagus or beans in small bundles with the long chives. (If you have no long chives, use some of the green raffia or curly paper ribbon, or simple cotton cooking twine.)

If your gift will not be refrigerated for several hours, place the ice packs in the trug. Line the trug with the napkin or tea towel (covering the ice packs, if using). Form the base of your arrangement with the heads of lettuce and lettuce leaves. The bottle of dressing should go in next, resting against the salad greens for support. Use larger items next, like the cucumbers and grape clusters, and then the bundled items like beans and asparagus. Finish the arrangement with the most delicate items, such as herbs and flowers.

Gather the netting or tulle over the trug handle or the top of the wire basket and twist the netting until it is tightly stretched over the top, becoming almost transparent in the process. Secure the twisted netting or tulle with craft wire or an elastic band and cut off all but 2 or 3 inches of the excess netting.

Cover the wire or elastic with the green raffia or ribbon and finish with a simple looped knot.

caviar sampler with *crème fraîche* crumpets

It may seem a little odd that a gift this luxurious starts with a mundane muffin tin, but the muffin tin is the keystone of the presentation. Some of the individual muffin compartments hold tiny bottles of vodka in frozen suspension and make perfect iced beds for the jars of caviar. The remaining compartments are filled with crème fraîche crumpets. These crumpets travel better than toast points or blini—the usual caviar platforms—and their lightness and tenderness partner perfectly with the caviar. Altogether, it makes for a self-contained caviar bar for two.

You will need to clear a wide, flat space in your freezer before beginning this project. For the caviar sampler palette, you will need a metal baking pan designed to bake 6 extra-large muffins. This type of pan is widely available and should measure approximately 8 × 12 inches; the muffin compartments should be at least 3 inches in diameter and 2 inches deep.

overall prep time: 24 hours

active prep time: 30 minutes

easy

expensive

baked crumpets can be frozen; refresh thawed crumpets in a 325°f oven for 5 minutes

do not ship

can be doubled or tripled

shelf life: 12 hours

makes: 2 dozen crumpets

FOR THE CAVIAR SAMPLER PALETTE:

1 metal muffin pan (6 muffin capacity), for extra-large muffins

2 lengths (16 to 20 inches each) silver or black craft wire

2 small caviar spoons (spoons made of horn, bone, mother of pearl, or stainless steel are all suitable for caviar; do not use silver or silver plate, brass, copper, or bronze spoons)

6 miniature (50 ml each) bottles imported vodka, 1 to 1⅛ inches in diameter each

nonstick cooking spray

2 small jars premium imported or domestic caviar (50-gram jars usually measure less than 3 inches in diameter)

recipe continues

FOR THE CRÈME FRAÎCHE CRUMPETS:

2 cups self-rising flour

1 cup (2 sticks) unsalted butter, melted

1 cup crème fraîche (page 46, or use store-bought)

¼ teaspoon salt

1 Prepare the caviar sampler palette. First, make spoon "handles" for the muffin pan. Use a craft awl or metal punch to make a small hole in the center of both short sides of the muffin pan. Using needle-nose pliers, tightly coil about 2 inches of each strand of wire into a nub larger than the pierced hole. Insert the straight end of one wire through one of the punched holes from the underside of the pan; repeat on the other side of the pan with the other wire. Pull the strands through the holes until the coiled nub is flush with the bottom of the pan and stops the wire. Wrap one wire around each caviar spoon and roll the spoons in the wires until they are flush against the pan, forming handles for each side of the muffin pan. The wire should not be wound so tight that it is difficult for the gift recipient to remove and replace the spoons as needed.

2 Next, make ice "beds" for the caviar and the vodka. Lightly coat the lower half of the miniature vodka bottles with cooking spray. Put the muffin pan on a baking sheet and cluster 3 bottles of the vodka in each of the 2 center compartments in the muffin pan. Slowly add water around the vodka bottles until the compartments are full. Fill 2 more of the muffin compartments with 4 tablespoons of water each (for icing the caviar). Freeze the muffin pan and vodkas for 24 hours.

3 Meanwhile, prepare the crumpets. Preheat the oven to 350°F. Combine the flour, butter, crème fraîche, and salt in a large bowl and beat with a wooden spoon until the ingredients form a smooth batter.

4 Spoon the batter into 24 ungreased 3-inch tart pans arranged on a baking sheet, or pour the batter into a mini tartlet pan with 24 forms. Bake the crumpets in the center of the oven for 25 minutes. Cool the pan or pans for 5 to 10 minutes on a rack before unmolding the crumpets directly onto the rack to finish cooling.

wrapping it up

The bulk of the presentation work is behind you once you have prepared the muffin pan and frozen its contents. You only need to fill the pan compartments with caviar and crumpets, protect the gift with a cellophane gift bag, and swiftly deliver the sampler.

suggested supplies

2 extra-large paper cupcake liners

1 glassine bag or small covered tin for any extra crème fraîche crumpets

1 extra-large cellophane gift bag (available at craft stores)

1 wire twist tie

1 length (½ to ⅔ yard) thin ribbon or raffia

how to fill and wrap a caviar sampler palette

To assemble the sampler, put 1 jar of caviar in each of the 2 ice compartments of the sampler palette. Fill the remaining 2 muffin cups with the paper liners and as many of the crème fraîche crumpets as will fit comfortably. Put any extra crumpets in the glassine bag or small tin and set them on top of the filled muffin tin.

Place an extra-large cellophane gift bag on a work surface and slide the filled muffin tin inside the bag, keeping it flat and level. Tightly twist the opening of the bag until the bag is stretched tightly over the muffin tin. Secure the twisted opening with the wire twist tie, cover the wire by wrapping it with the ribbon or raffia, and tie the ribbon or raffia with a simple bow. Your gift is ready to deliver, but remember that the ice in the muffin compartments will stay solid for only about 30 to 45 minutes, depending on the ambient temperature, so don't assemble this gift until the very last minute. If you have a large ice chest, I recommend putting the assembled tray on ice for delivery.

fa-la-la-fabulous: *kumquat pomanders* in christmas cognac punch

overall prep time: 6 to 8 weeks

active prep time: 1 hour

easy

expensive

do not freeze or ship

can be multiplied

shelf life: 6 weeks in a beverage dispenser protected from strong sunlight

makes: 1½ quarts

Clove-studded kumquats are often found on the Christmas tree—but seldom in the Christmas punch. In this punch, the tiny pomanders infuse the cognac with sweet citrus and mellow spice. The cognac punch is wonderful with sparkling water on the rocks or mixed with hot water and honey in a mug. A word of friendly advice: This was originally my father's recipe, and he called it "Knock Out Punch." I have made it much prettier but no less potent. The recipe can be multiplied easily to fit whatever kind of container you want to use for the gift. You can give the punch in a simple French canning jar or a larger and more ornate apothecary jar with a fitted lid. Or you can opt for the ultimate container: a large glass beverage dispenser with a stainless steel spigot. Whichever container you choose, this is a very pretty holiday gift. Start this project well in advance because it takes several weeks for the cognac to absorb the citrus and spice flavors. My dad always started his Christmas Day punch on Halloween.

1 cup whole cloves

3 cinnamon sticks

1 whole nutmeg, broken or crushed into several pieces

1 pint Grand Marnier or other orange liqueur

12 to 14 fresh kumquats

1 fifth cognac

1 Put the cloves in a strainer and rinse them under cold water for several minutes to remove any dust or small broken pieces. Spread the cloves on a tray lined with paper towels and set aside. Rinse the cinnamon sticks under running water and tightly bundle and tie them in cheesecloth along with the crushed nutmeg.

2 In a small saucepan, heat the Grand Marnier and the cinnamon bundle over low heat. When the Grand Marnier begins to simmer, cover the pan, remove it from the heat, and set it aside to cool.

3 Starting at the stem end of each kumquat, make a clove-studded spiral around each fruit all the way to its blossom end. Combine the studded pomanders with the cognac in a tall, wide-mouthed glass or ceramic container. Add the Grand Marnier and the cinnamon bundle to the mixture. Put a small saucer inside the container to keep the kumquats submerged in the cognac. Tightly cover the container with plastic wrap and a lid or plate, and store in a dark, cool cellar or closet for 6 to 8 weeks. Do not stir or otherwise agitate the mixture during that time.

4 When you are ready to fill your gift container, remove the pomanders and rinse them under cold running water. Place them in the clean, dry glass gift container. Discard the cinnamon bundle and ladle the cognac punch through a fine-mesh strainer lined with several layers of cheesecloth into a pitcher. Rinse the cheesecloth and reline the strainer with it. Slowly pour the pitcher of punch through the lined strainer into the gift container. Store at cool room temperature out of direct sunlight until you are ready to assemble and deliver the gift.

wrapping it up

The embellishments depend on the container you choose, of course, but very little is needed to dress up such a pretty holiday gift. If the lid of your jar doesn't fit tightly, it should be secured with tape, and the tape should be hidden with ribbon. A garland of kumquats, bay leaves, and cranberries looped around the container is a colorful surround for the punch.

suggested supplies

1 length (at least 1½ yards) transparent monofilament	12 small kumquats
large tapestry needle	24 fresh bay leaves
	36 firm fresh cranberries

how to string kumquats

Knot one end of the monofilament onto the tapestry needle, then string a sequence of kumquats, bay leaves, and cranberries in a pattern that is pleasing to you. Knot the other end of the monofilament and loop it around the cognac container. Tie the ends of the monofilament together. Use more monofilament, if necessary, to secure the strand of kumquats to the jar or container.

al fresco *feast* in a wine-crate hamper

overall prep time: 5 hours

active prep time: 2 hours

moderately challenging

expensive

do not freeze or ship

can be doubled

shelf life: 24 hours

makes: 1

A 10-inch wreath of crusty bread, laden with dried figs and peppery prosciutto and surrounding a ramekin of extra virgin olive (for dipping), is an impressive main-course centerpiece for an afternoon or evening meal *al fresco*. The wine-crate hamper is large enough to hold cheese, olives, pears, and wine as well as the pull-apart loaf. No utensils needed!

The batch of dough for the bread in this recipe is very large and stiff, and is easiest to prepare if you use a heavy-duty stand mixer with a paddle attachment.

1 package active dry yeast

1 cup warm water (100 to 110°F)

2 tablespoons light brown sugar

3 tablespoons extra-virgin olive oil

⅔ cup diced dried figs

⅔ cup diced prosciutto

1 tablespoon cracked white peppercorns

1 tablespoon minced fresh rosemary or 2 teaspoons crumbled dry rosemary

3½ cups unbleached all-purpose flour

1 cup semolina flour

1 teaspoon salt

1 ovenproof ramekin, 3 to 4 inches in diameter

1 Combine the yeast, warm water, and brown sugar in the bowl of a stand mixer and whisk them together. Once the yeast has dissolved, add 2 tablespoons of the olive oil to the mixture and whisk the mixture briefly. Cover the bowl with a tea towel and let it rest for 10 minutes.

recipe continues

2 Toss the figs and prosciutto with the cracked pepper and rosemary in a small bowl and set aside. Combine the flour, semolina, and salt in a bowl and whisk them together. Using the paddle attachment, with the mixer set on low speed gradually add the flour mixture to the yeast mixture. Once all the flour has been added, increase the mixer speed to medium and beat for 2 or 3 minutes, or until the mixture forms a rough dough. Add the fig mixture to the dough and continue to beat at medium speed until it is smooth and pulls away cleanly from the sides of the mixing bowl.

3 Turn the dough out onto a lightly floured work surface and knead it for 5 minutes, or until it becomes smooth and resilient. If the dough is sticky, add a little flour to your hands and continue to knead for several more minutes.

4 Pour the remaining 1 tablespoon of olive oil into a large bowl, place the ball of dough in the bowl, and swirl the dough until it is coated with the oil. Cover the bowl loosely with a tea towel and set it aside to rise in a warm, draft-free area for 30 to 45 minutes, or until it has doubled in volume.

5 Turn the dough out again onto a lightly floured work surface and, using your hands, roll the dough back and forth until it forms a fat log 15 to 16 inches long. Cover the roll of dough loosely a tea towel and allow it to rest for 10 minutes.

6 Line a large, heavy baking sheet with parchment paper. Coat the outer sides of the ramekin with olive oil and put it in the center of the baking sheet.

7 Slice the log of dough into 14 equal portions and stand the slices on end all around the oiled ramekin. Make sure that the inner edge of each slice is resting up against the ramekin. Compress the wreath of dough slices around the ramekin so that they are evenly shaped and fit snugly together. Cover the baking sheet with a tea towel and let the bread rise for 30 minutes. Meanwhile, preheat the oven to 450°F.

8 Fill the ramekin with hot water and place the baking sheet on the center rack of the oven. Reduce the oven temperature to 375°F and bake the bread for 20 minutes. Rotate the pan and bake the bread for another 30 to 40 minutes, or until it is a deep golden brown. (Thump the bread wreath with your fingers, and if the sound is hollow like a ripe melon, the bread is ready.) Place the baking sheet on a rack and allow the bread to cool completely, at least a couple of hours.

9 Gently twist and loosen the ramekin from the wreath's center and remove it. Wash and dry the ramekin and set it aside to include in the wine crate when the gift is assembled. Transfer the bread wreath directly to the baking rack until you are ready to assemble and deliver the gift.

wrapping it up

If you are on good terms with your local wine merchant, it will be easy for you acquire a wooden wine crate. If not, craft stores and online packaging stores carry several styles of wooden crates and bins of a similar size (see Resources, page 290).

suggested supplies

1 wooden wine crate, or other wooden crate of similar size

2 lengths (about 10 inches each) thin hemp rope

1 large rectangle (about 20 × 24 inches) fabric, or a beach or yoga mat, for lining the hamper

1 bottle extra-virgin olive oil

thick slices Asiago or Parmigiano-Reggiano cheese wrapped in cheesecloth

dry-cured cracked green olives in a jar

ripe pears

1 bottle robust red wine and some wine glasses

1 ovenproof ramekin (the one used for baking the bread)

how to transform a crate into a hamper

Begin by making rope handles for the crate: Mark and drill 2 small holes about 3 inches apart on either side of the center of both short ends of the crate. Double-knot the end of one length of rope, and, starting from the inside of the crate, thread it through the first hole and pull the rope tightly toward the outside of the crate. Thread the rope back through the second hole from the outside of the crate to the inside, then tie another double knot. Cut off any excess rope. Make an identical handle for the opposite side of the crate.

Next, create a hamper-like effect by lining the crate with fabric. You can hem four sides of a rectangular length of cloth, or you can buy a beach or yoga mat and cut it to size, or even use a table runner. Center the liner over the hamper and then press it flat against the bottom and sides. Fill the hamper with the bread wreath, olive oil, cheese, olives, pears, wine, wine glasses, and ramekin. Fold the ends of the liner over the food and wine. To serve the bread, put the ramekin in the center of the wreath and pour some of the olive oil into the ramekin. The bread sections easily pull apart for dipping in the olive oil.

seckel *pears* in beaujolais nouveau

overall prep time: 2 hours

active prep time: 1 hour

slightly challenging

expensive

do not freeze or ship

can be doubled or tripled

shelf life: 1 month unopened in refrigerator; 10 days to 2 weeks in refrigerator after opening

makes: 1½ to 2 quarts poached pears

In late autumn, a good deal of fanfare heralds the first shipment of Beaujolais Nouveau wine to American merchants. Seckel pears ship to our supermarkets around the same time, but with considerably less hoopla. These two are made for one another. Fruity and unpretentious, Beaujolais is an ideal wine for poaching pears. Tiny and firm, Seckels are the perfect size and texture for poaching. So there you have it: a match made in autumn that can be enjoyed long after November.

1 bottle Beaujolais Nouveau wine

1½ cups superfine sugar

1 orange, preferably Valencia

2 cinnamon sticks

6 whole cloves

10 whole allspice berries

3 green cardamom pods

2 quarts cold water

juice of 1 lemon

12 to 14 Seckel pears

½ cup triple sec or Grand Marnier

⅓ cup red currant jelly

1 Combine the wine and sugar in a large nonreactive saucepan and stir until the sugar has dissolved. Cover the pan and bring the wine to a boil over medium heat.

2 Use a swivel-bladed peeler to carefully remove the orange peel (take care to avoid the bitter, white pith), making one long, spiraling piece if possible. Juice the orange and add the juice, along with the spiral of peel, to the wine once it has begun to boil. Leave the pan uncovered and reduce the heat to medium-low. Add the cinnamon, cloves, allspice, and cardamom to the wine. Keep the wine at a very gentle simmer while you prepare the pears.

3 Combine the water and lemon juice in a large bowl. Using a tiny melon baller or cherry pitter, carefully remove the pear cores from the bottom of the fruit to a depth of about 1 inch; it is important to keep the pears and their stems intact for the most attractive presentation. Peel the pears with a sharp swivel-bladed peeler and put them in the water bath to keep them from discoloring. When all the pears have been cored and peeled, transfer them from the water bath to the simmering wine.

4 Cover the pan and simmer the pears for 10 to 15 minutes, gently shaking the pan frequently to make sure the pears cook and color evenly in the syrup; the pears are done when they can be pierced with the tip of a dinner knife. Remove the pears from the wine with a slotted spoon to a covered dish and set them aside.

5 Add the triple sec to the wine. Reduce the heat to low and barely simmer the wine mixture, uncovered, for 25 to 30 minutes, or until the volume has been reduced to 1¾ cups of liquid. Stir the red currant jelly into the wine and set the mixture aside.

6 Meanwhile, wash a 2- to 3-quart wide-mouthed jar in hot soapy water and dry the jar and lid in a 190°F oven. Line a fine-mesh strainer with a double thickness of damp cheesecloth and strain the hot wine syrup into a heat-resistant pitcher or spouted bowl. Rinse the spices and orange peel in the strainer under running water for 4 or 5 minutes.

7 Pack the hot jar with the pears and the rinsed spices and orange peel. Slowly fill the jar with the strained syrup to 1 inch from the top. Using a chopstick or the handle of a thin wooden spoon, dislodge any air bubbles. Add more syrup if needed to cover the pears completely and close the jar tightly. Set the jar aside to cool completely. Refrigerate the jar until you are ready to assemble and deliver the gift.

wrapping it up

A small, pink, pear-shaped gift label impaled on a vintage pickle fork adds just the right touch of whimsy and charm to the jar of Seckel pears.

suggested supplies

pale-rose or deep-coral silk cord or twill tape

1 long-handled pickle fork

1 square (about 3 inches) pink card stock

how to pierce a pear with a pickle fork

Knot the silk cord around the handle of the pickle fork just under the tines and tie it to the neck of the jar, tightly knotting the ends to hold the fork in place. Finish with a simple bow.

Draw or trace a pear-shaped outline about 2 inches tall onto the pink card stock and cut it out. Write out either a label or a gift message on the pear-shaped cutout. Gently push the card onto the tines of the pickle fork far enough to hold it securely in place.

portable *bellini* bar

The Bellini, a combination of white-peach puree and the Italian white sparkling wine Prosecco, is deservedly one of the world's most famous cocktails. The legendary Harry's Bar in Venice is justly famous for its Bellinis, but Venice is a long way to go—and Harry's doesn't have the recipe for the toasted rosemary almonds that are part of this gift package.

overall prep time: 3½ hours

active prep time: 1 hour

easy

expensive

do not freeze or ship

can be doubled or tripled

shelf life: 4 days refrigerated for peach puree; 1 week in an airtight container stored in a cool place for almonds

makes: about 3 cups peach puree and 2 cups rosemary almonds

FOR THE ROSEMARY ALMONDS:

2 cups blanched almonds

3 tablespoons unsalted butter, melted

2 tablespoons crushed dried rosemary

2 teaspoons salt

2½ teaspoons granulated sugar

¼ teaspoon finely ground white pepper

FOR THE WHITE-PEACH PUREE:

1 cup granulated sugar

1 cup water

6 or 7 cherries, slightly crushed

4 white peaches

1 Preheat the oven to its lowest setting. To make the rosemary almonds, combine all of the almond ingredients in a large bowl and stir them gently with a wooden spoon until the nuts are well coated. Line an 11 × 17-inch baking sheet with parchment paper and spread the almonds on it in a single layer. Put the baking sheet on the center rack of the oven, prop the door of the oven slightly ajar with a wooden spoon, and let the almonds dry for 2 hours.

2 To make the white-peach puree, combine the sugar and water in a saucepan and stir until the sugar is dissolved. Cover the pan and bring the mixture to a boil over medium heat. Bundle the cherries tightly in knotted cheesecloth and add them to the boiling syrup. Continue boiling the syrup, uncovered, for 7 minutes without

stirring, then set the saucepan aside to cool. Remove and discard the cherry bundle once the syrup has cooled.

3 Peel, pit, and roughly chop the peaches. Puree them in a blender or food processor while pouring the cooled syrup through the opening on the top of the blender or the feed tube for the food processor. Funnel the puree into a bottle, seal it, and refrigerate until you are ready to assemble the gift.

4 After the almonds have dried for 2 hours, remove the baking sheet from the oven and increase the oven temperature to 350°F. Return the baking sheet to the oven and bake the almonds for 8 minutes. Stir the almonds, rotate the pan, and bake for another 6 minutes. Cool the pan on a rack for at least 1 hour, until the almonds are completely cooled. Store the almonds in an airtight container until you are ready to assemble and deliver the gift.

wrapping it up

A chilled bottle of Prosecco, a chilled bottle of white-peach puree, two stemmed cocktail flutes, and bags of rosemary almonds will fit perfectly in a wire bottle caddy with six compartments. Several versions of bottle caddies are available online (see Resources, page 290), and they can also be found in antique stores and gourmet kitchen stores from time to time.

suggested supplies

2 or 3 small glassine or cellophane bags

2 or 3 wire twist ties (1 for each bag)

ribbon

1 wire bottle caddy with 6 compartments

2 Champagne flutes

1 bottle Prosecco sparkling wine

1 pocket guidebook to Venice, available at bookstores (optional)

1 square (4 inches) card stock

how to make a portable bellini bar

Fill the glassine or cellophane bags with just enough almonds to allow each bag to fit into one compartment of the caddie. Tightly twist the bags closed, securing them with wire twist ties; cover the twist ties with the ribbon and tie it in small bows. Fill the compartments of the caddy with the bagged almonds, the Champagne flutes, the Prosecco, and the peach puree. For an extra touch, if you like, add a pocket guidebook to Venice.

Be sure to write this recipe for Bellini cocktails on the card stock and include it with the gift.

RECIPE FOR BELLINI COCKTAIL:
Shake the white-peach puree well, add 1 to 2 tablespoons to each cocktail flute, and top off the glasses with chilled Prosecco.

mumbai *mixed nuts* in a tiffin box

overall prep time: about 10 hours

active prep time: 45 minutes

moderately easy

expensive

do not freeze

ships well in an airtight container with adequate cushioning

can be doubled

shelf life: 1 month in an airtight container

makes: a generous 6 cups

Tiffin boxes are metal, multi-tiered containers used to transport hot meals in India. Here in the States, I find they make very useful and decorative accessories. I use many styles and sizes of tiffin boxes throughout my home for storing such various and sundry items as remote controls, sewing notions, and, in the kitchen and pantry, spices and nuts. The nuts in this recipe are both slow-roasted and dried, giving them an incomparable crackly crisp coating of exotic spices that range from mellow heat to slightly sweet. These mixed nuts are irresistible, I think, especially in such a stylish container.

scant ⅔ cup turbinado sugar or raw sugar

1 tablespoon finely ground sea salt

2 teaspoons onion powder

2 teaspoons garlic powder

2 tablespoons ground cumin

2 teaspoons ground cayenne pepper

2 teaspoons ground cinnamon

2 teaspoons ground white pepper

2 cups whole roasted unsalted almonds

1 cup walnut halves

2 cups whole roasted unsalted cashews

1 cup shelled unsalted pistachio nuts

2 large egg whites

1 Preheat the oven to 250°F. Combine the sugar, salt, onion and garlic powders, cumin, cayenne, cinnamon, and white pepper in a small bowl. Combine all the nuts in a large shallow casserole. Beat the egg whites until they are frothy and pour

recipe continues

them over the nuts. Toss the nuts in the egg whites until they are well coated and no egg white remains at the bottom of the casserole. Add the sugar-spice mixture and continue to toss and mix the nuts until they are thickly coated with spices.

2 Line a large (11 × 17-inch) baking sheet with parchment paper. Transfer the nuts to the baking sheet and gently flatten them into a compact solid layer that covers the entire surface of the pan.

3 Roast the nuts on the middle rack of the oven for 20 minutes. Rotate the pan and roast the nuts for another 25 minutes. Remove the nuts from the oven, reduce the oven temperature to 140°F, and prop the oven door slightly ajar with a wooden spoon. Use a large metal spatula to turn the large clumps of nuts over in the pan. Return the nuts to the oven and allow them to dry for 5 hours.

4 Cool the pan on a rack for at least 3 hours, until completely cool. Break the nuts by hand into bite-sized clusters and place them in an airtight container. Keep the container in a cool, dry area until you are ready to assemble and deliver the gift.

wrapping it up

Tiffin boxes can be found at South Asian ethnic markets and at import and home-accessory stores. The Internet offers a mind-boggling array of tiffin boxes, too, if you can't locate one in your area (see Resources, page 290). Tiffin boxes range in price from $5 to $50, depending on the material and finish. A two-tiered tiffin box with a diameter of about 8 inches and lined with parchment paper will hold all the nuts and keep them very fresh.

gouda *palmiers* in a coaster-covered tin

Hiding this handsome tin until 5:00 p.m. is the only way to guarantee that cheese wafers this good will be around for cocktails. The recipe calls for a high-quality aged Gouda, which bears no resemblance to those red-wax–covered pincushions of processed Gouda. The aged version is drier, with an almost crumbly texture, and the taste is more mellow and complex.

Note that the "roll, fold, turn" technique used for the puff-pastry dough in this recipe makes it more challenging to prepare than regular pastry dough. Your efforts will be rewarded with exceptionally tender and flaky wafers that resemble golden palm fronds. If you enjoy baking but have never tried your hand at classic puff pastry, you can start to familiarize yourself with the technique with this recipe. Just take your time, and stop and refrigerate the dough for 20 or 30 minutes whenever you or the dough need to rest.

overall prep time: about 12 hours

active prep time: 45 minutes

challenging

moderately expensive

dough can be frozen at any stage of its preparation

ships well, with care

do not double

shelf life: 2 weeks in an airtight tin

makes: 2½ dozen

4 ounces aged Gouda cheese

4 ounces Neufchâtel cheese or cream cheese, cold

¼ cup (½ stick) unsalted butter, cold

¼ cup (½ stick) margarine, cold

1 teaspoon ground mustard

¼ teaspoon salt

½ cup cake flour

1⅓ cups all-purpose flour

1 cup finely grated good Parmesan cheese, such as Parmigiano-Reggiano

1 large egg

1 tablespoon buttermilk

recipe continues

1 Coarsely grate the Gouda cheese and put it on a small tray. Cut the Neufchâtel, butter, and margarine into a very fine dice and spread them on the tray with the Gouda. Cover the tray with plastic wrap and place in the freezer for at least 30 minutes.

2 Combine the mustard, salt, cake flour, and 1 cup of the all-purpose flour in the bowl of a stand mixer fitted with the paddle attachment. Set the mixer at medium-low speed and mix just to combine. Gradually add the frozen ingredients to the flour mixture. Once all of the frozen ingredients have been added, mix the rough dough for another minute. The dough will be very lumpy, with chunks of butter and cheese still visible.

3 Turn the rough dough out onto a large sheet of plastic wrap. Have ready the additional ⅓ cup all-purpose flour for your hands and for adding to the dough. Flour your hands, and pat and press the dry, crumbly dough into a 7 × 14-inch rectangle. Cover the dough tightly in the plastic wrap and refrigerate it overnight.

4 Prepare a work surface by sprinkling it with a little flour and 2 or 3 tablespoons of the grated Parmesan cheese. Roll the chilled pastry out into an 8 × 10-inch rectangle. Fold the dough from the top and the bottom into thirds (like a business letter). Rotate the dough 90 degrees so the top flap is to your right (like the cover of an unopened book). Roll the folded dough again into an 8 × 10-inch rectangle. Sprinkle some more of the Parmesan cheese on the pastry and then repeat the "business letter" fold. Rotate the folded dough to the "closed book" position with the top flap facing right.

Use the rolling pin and your hands to shape the dough into a thick rectangle. Wrap the dough in plastic wrap and refrigerate it for at least for 1 hour.

5 Place the rectangle of chilled dough on a work surface generously sprinkled with flour. With a heavily floured rolling pin, roll the dough into a 6 × 12-inch rectangle. Brush the surface of the dough with a pastry brush dipped in ice water. Fold both long sides of the rectangle to the center of the rectangle. Moisten the surface once again with the pastry brush and fold the dough in half lengthwise. The rectangle will now have four layers. Rewrap the dough in plastic wrap and place it in the freezer for 1 hour.

6 Meanwhile, preheat the oven to 450°F and place two racks close to the middle of the oven. Line two large baking sheets with parchment paper.

7 Sprinkle 3 or 4 tablespoons of the grated Parmesan cheese on a work surface. Use a serrated knife to cut the frozen pastry into 30 thin slices a little less than ¼ inch thick and lay them flat on the cheese-sprinkled work surface. Flatten the pastry slices one by one with the rolling pin until they are about 3 inches wide. Arrange the slices on the parchment-lined baking sheets approximately ½ inch apart.

8 Prepare an egg wash by combining the egg with the buttermilk and whisking until frothy. Brush the wash over the tops of the wafers, and sprinkle the wafers with any remaining Parmesan.

9 Bake the wafers on the center racks of the oven for 9 minutes. Switch and rotate the sheets and bake for another 9 minutes, or until the wafers are golden brown around the edges. Cool the baking sheets on racks for 5 minutes, then carefully transfer the wafers directly to the racks to cool completely. Store the cooled wafers in an airtight container until you are ready to assemble and deliver the gift.

wrapping it up

Since this is no ordinary cracker, no ordinary tin will do. Monogrammed coasters with magnetic backs will stay put on the tin top for decoration.

suggested supplies

blank pulp-paper, cork, or acrylic coasters (available at craft stores)

adhesive-backed magnetic rectangles (available at office-supply stores)

thin black felt

large paper cupcake liners, or shallower "muffin top" paper cupcake liners

1 large airtight tin, at least 3 or 4 inches deep

how to make magnetic monogrammed coasters

You can download or purchase copyright-free bordered monograms or design your own. Once you have chosen a design, you can create coasters from any number of materials, using your favorite mediums and techniques. Disposable pulp-paper coasters are perfect for stamping and embossing enthusiasts. Blank cork or acrylic coasters are suitable for paper crafting techniques like decoupage and collage. The adhesive-backed magnet rectangles can be applied directly to the backs of the coasters and covered with thin black felt.

Stack the Gouda spirals in paper cupcake liners and arrange them snugly in the tin. Decorate the tin with some of the magnetic-backed coasters and pack the rest of the coasters in the tin with the spiral wafers.

a glass of *port* and a very good *book*

Port, Stilton cheese, and walnuts were all integral parts of Edwardian dinner parties—for the gentlemen anyway. An embellished faux-book box filled with Stilton biscuits and ruby port–glazed walnut halves, along with a bottle of vintage port, makes a very distinguished gift for bibliophiles of either sex. These are English-style biscuits, which means they have a harder, almost cracker-like, texture.

FOR THE PORT-GLAZED WALNUTS:

10 ounces large walnut halves

¾ cup granulated sugar

¾ cup ruby port

2 fresh bay leaves

1 tablespoon unsalted butter, softened

⅛ teaspoon sea salt

½ teaspoon freshly ground black pepper

FOR THE STILTON BISCUITS:

2 cups sifted pastry flour

1 teaspoon sea salt

3 teaspoons baking powder

2 ounces crumbled Stilton cheese

¼ cup (½ stick) unsalted butter, cut in small bits, chilled

⅔ cup whole milk

overall prep time: 2½ to 3 hours

active prep time: 1½ hours

moderately easy

expensive

do not freeze

ships well

can be doubled

shelf life: 2 weeks in an airtight container for walnuts; 4 to 5 days in an airtight container for biscuits

makes: about 3 dozen stilton biscuits and 2½ cups glazed walnuts

1 To make the walnuts, preheat the oven to 350°F. Line an 11 × 17-inch baking sheet with parchment paper. Spread the walnut halves on the parchment in a single layer. Toast the walnuts in the oven for 10 minutes, or until they are lightly browned. Set the nuts aside to cool while you prepare the glaze, but leave the oven on.

recipe continues

2 Combine the sugar, port, and bay leaves in a heavy saucepan and stir until the sugar is dissolved. Bring the mixture to a simmer over medium heat and continue to simmer, stirring frequently, until the glaze is thick enough to coat the back of a spoon, about 8 minutes more. Add the browned walnuts and butter and continue to cook, stirring constantly, until the walnuts are thickly and evenly glazed and there is very little liquid remaining in the pan, about 5 minutes more.

3 Pour the glazed walnuts into a medium-mesh strainer. Discard the liquid and spread the glazed walnuts once again in a single layer on the parchment-lined baking sheet. Sprinkle the walnuts with salt and pepper. Bake the walnuts for 8 minutes. Stir the walnuts, rotate the pan, and bake for another 8 minutes, or until they are crisp and completely dry. Cool the baking sheet on a rack. Store the cooled nuts in an airtight container while you make the biscuits.

4 To make the biscuits, sift the flour, salt, and baking powder together into a large mixing bowl. Add the crumbled cheese and the butter. Using your fingertips or a pastry blender, blend the flour mixture into the butter and cheese until it is well blended, with a fine mealy texture. Gradually add the milk in three additions, blending each addition into the flour mixture with a fork or a pastry blender.

5 Turn the pastry out onto an unfloured work surface. Knead the dough, working quickly, until it holds together and can be patted into a thick rectangle. Wrap the dough tightly in plastic wrap and refrigerate it on a tray or baking sheet for at least 1 hour.

6 Preheat the oven to 425°F. Roll the chilled dough out on an 11 × 17-inch sheet of parchment paper until it is about ½ inch thick. Slide the dough and parchment paper onto a baking sheet. Cut the dough into plain or fluted 2-inch circles using a floured glass or a cookie cutter. Peel away the scraps of dough and refrigerate them.

7 Bake the biscuits on the center rack of the oven for 8 minutes. Rotate the pan and bake the biscuits for another 8 to 10 minutes, or until they firm up and are pale golden. Cool the pan briefly on a rack, then carefully transfer the biscuits directly onto the rack to cool completely. Knead the refrigerated scraps together and roll, cut, and bake them in the same way. Store the cooled biscuits in an airtight container until you are ready to assemble and deliver the gift.

wrapping it up

Book-shaped papier-mâché boxes are available at craft stores. Online resources offer a wide variety of styles and sizes as well (see Resources, page 290). Paint, stamps, decoupage, fabric, decorative paper, or stencils can be used to transform the boxes into whimsical or realistic "books," depending on your style and expertise, but note that products with a high water content can cause the papier-mâché to soften and warp. The suggested supplies below all have low moisture content.

suggested supplies

1 book-shaped papier-mâché box

acrylic craft paints, including primers

acrylic-based or low-moisture adhesives, such as super-tacky craft glue or spray adhesive

fabric or decorative paper

twill tape or thin ribbon

acrylic sealer in matte, satin, or glossy finish

parchment paper or tissue paper

glassine bag or waxed paper

how to prepare a book box for biscuits and nuts

Prime the book-shaped box inside and out with acrylic primer according to the manufacturer's directions. Paint the box inside and out with at least one coat of acrylic paint. Apply faux painting techniques, stamps, decals, decoupage, or fabric, according to your preferences, on the inside and outside of the box. Finish the decorated box with at least one coat of acrylic sealer, again following the manufacturer's guidelines. Allow the box to dry completely.

Line the dry book box with a sheet of parchment paper or tissue paper. Wrap stacks of the Stilton biscuits in glassine bags or waxed paper. Arrange the wrapped stacks of biscuits side by side in the box. Put the glazed walnuts in a small glassine bag and add them to the box.

the sweet life: three tiers of crème fraîche *fudge*

overall prep time: about 10½ hours per batch

active prep time: 2¼ hours

slightly challenging

expensive

do not freeze or ship

do not double

shelf life: 10 days in an airtight container

makes: 96 pieces

Some people do have everything, including a very large sweet tooth! Here's a gift that gives them multiple tiers of sweet temptation, in the form of three distinctly different flavors (and three different pastel colors) of crème fraîche citrus fudge, all presented in a stacked glass candy jar of grand proportions.

Note that to make all three flavors of fudge in one day (do the batches one after the other, not simultaneously), you will need three 8-inch square baking pans. Alternatively, you can spread the project out over three days and use the same pan each day.

2½ cups crème fraîche (page 46, or use store-bought)

6 tablespoons (¾ stick) unsalted butter

6 tablespoons corn syrup

¾ cup whole milk

6 cups granulated sugar

2 to 3 drops lemon oil, or more to taste

⅔ cup shelled pistachio nuts

finely grated zest of 1 lemon

1 to 2 drops yellow food coloring

2 to 3 drops lime oil, or more to taste

finely grated zest of 1 lime

⅔ cup toasted pine nuts

1 to 2 drops green food coloring

2 to 3 drops orange oil, or more to taste

finely grated zest of 1 orange

⅔ cup toasted macadamia nuts

1 to 2 drops orange food coloring

1 Prepare an 8-inch square baking pan by lining it with aluminum foil and coating the foil with nonstick cooking spray.

2 Combine ¼ cup of the crème fraîche, 2 tablespoons of the butter, 2 tablespoons of the corn syrup, ¼ cup of the milk, and 2 cups of the sugar in a large saucepan. Heat over medium-high heat, stirring constantly until the sugar dissolves. Attach a candy thermometer to the inside of the saucepan and slowly bring the mixture to a boil, stirring occasionally. Continue cooking, stirring occasionally, until the mixture registers 238°F on the candy thermometer (soft-ball stage).

3 Remove the pan from the heat immediately and stir in the lemon oil. Set the pan (with the thermometer) aside to cool; do not stir further.

4 Meanwhile, prepare the pistachio nuts by blanching them in boiling water for 3 to 4 minutes. Drain the nuts, fold them in a tea towel, and use the palms of your hands to roll them back and forth in the towel to remove the papery skins. Blot the skinned nuts completely dry and chop them coarsely.

5 When the candy thermometer registers 110°F, pour the fudge into the bowl of a stand mixer without scraping the bottom or sides of the pan. Beat the fudge at medium speed with the paddle attachment until the mixture loses all traces of glossy shine and turns thick and opaque, with a creamy texture. Stir the lemon zest and pistachios into the fudge. Stir in the food coloring. Pour the fudge into the prepared baking pan and set it aside on a baking rack to cool for 1 hour (or until the pan is completely cool to the touch). Gently cover the surface of the fudge with a square of wax paper or parchment and set the pan on a baking rack to cool for an additional 7 hours or overnight. If the room is warmer than 70° and the weather is humid, refrigerate the pan after covering the fudge.

6 While the lemon-pistachio fudge is cooling, make an 8-inch pan of lime–pine nut fudge by following steps 1 through 5, substituting lime oil for the lemon oil, lime zest for the lemon zest, toasted pine nuts for the pistachios, and green food coloring for the yellow food coloring.

7 Once the lime–pine nut fudge is set aside to cool, make an 8-inch pan of orange–macadamia nut fudge by following steps 1 through 5, substituting orange oil for the lemon oil, orange zest for the lemon zest, macadamia nuts for the pistachios, and orange food coloring for the yellow food coloring.

8 After all the fudge has cooled and set up, run a butter knife or small metal icing spatula around the edges of the pans, leaving the wax or parchment paper in place. Place three 18- to 20-inch lengths of plastic wrap on the work surface and smooth out all the wrinkles.

recipe continues

9 Invert a pan of fudge (with the wax paper or parchment covering) onto the center of one of the sheets of plastic wrap. Give the pan a sharp rap against the work surface to free the fudge from the pan. Repeat with remaining pans of fudge. If the pans do not release the fudge, saturate a tea towel with very hot water, wring it out completely, and hold it to the bottom of the inverted pan until the fudge drops out onto the plastic wrap. Repeat this process if necessary.

10 Wrap the unmolded fudge tightly in the plastic wrap and place on a baking sheet. Refrigerate the fudge for at least 1 hour before cutting it into rectangles approximately 1 × 2 inches in size. Wrap the pieces in plastic wrap and place them on a baking sheet in the refrigerator until you are ready to assemble the gift.

wrapping it up

A three-tiered glass container makes a very impressive display of the three fudges. You can find these containers in home-goods stores and online (see Resources, page 290). Line each tier with circles of tissue in deep colors of yellow, lime green, and orange, then carefully stack the fudges in the matching colors inside the appropriate tier. Depending on how the jar is constructed you may need to reinforce the stack with double-face tape, to hold the tiers tightly together for delivery; cover the tape with decorative ribbon. A bow of wired ribbon, no matter how large or fussy it is, would not be out of place atop a jar like this.

aromatic *fleur de sel* in a wooden *salt box*

If you don't think salt is a luxury item, you have never tasted, and certainly have never purchased, *fleur de sel*. *Fleur de sel* is hand-panned from the foamy salt blossoms that collect on top of French sea-salt pools. It has a rich, delicate flavor prized by chefs—and a very hefty price tag. Here I add aromatic herbs to make an exceptionally good seasoning salt for just about any savory dish. Then I package it in a wooden salt box with a magnetic finish for the ultimate seasoning in the ultimate user-friendly box.

overall prep time: less than 10 minutes

easy

expensive

do not freeze

ships well

can be doubled or tripled

shelf life: 6 months in wooden salt box

makes: about 3¼ cups

4 tablespoons dried rosemary leaves

6 tablespoons dried thyme leaves

4 tablespoons dried marjoram leaves

8 tablespoons freeze-dried parsley

2 teaspoons finely ground white peppercorns

2 cups *fleur de sel*

6 fresh bay leaves

1 Crumble the rosemary, thyme, marjoram, and parsley leaves between your fingers over a sheet of waxed paper. Then rub the herbs between your palms until you have a finely crushed and uniform mixture.

2 Mix the crumbled herbs and white pepper with the *fleur de sel* in a bowl. Add the bay leaves. Transfer the seasoned salt to a nonreactive airtight container until you are ready to assemble and deliver the gift.

recipe continues

wrapping it up

A classic salt box is made of wood and has a slanted flip-top lid. The wood keeps the salt dry, and the slanted lid is easy to open with one hand so that you can grab a pinch or scoop of the salt with the other. The slanted lid provides a nice space for holding a recipe or a reminder in place with small magnets.

Classic unfinished wooden salt boxes can be hard to find. A large craft or woodworking store may carry them. I also located several variations online, all of which work well and none of which are inexpensive (see Resources, page 290). Magnetic paint is a non-toxic, child-safe primer that transforms any surface into a magnetic one. The magnetic primer can be covered with one or two coats of latex paint in any medium to dark shade. Pure tung oil, with absolutely no additives or drying accelerants, is a safe and effective waterproof sealer for the inside of the salt box.

suggested supplies

1 wooden salt box

fine grit sandpaper

pure tung oil

magnetic paint primer

satin or semi-gloss latex paint

hot glue gun

2 or 3 small round magnets (available at craft and office supply stores)

beads, miniature wood turnings, buttons, or other small items to embellish the magnets

1 small wooden scoop (available at craft stores and online; see Resources, page 290)

1 large gift card

low-tack tape

ribbon

how to make a magnetic salt box

Lightly sand the box inside and out with the sandpaper and remove all the dust with a slightly damp cloth. Seal the inside of the salt box by applying pure tung oil according to manufacturer's directions. Allow the tung oil to dry completely, following the manufacturer's guidelines for recommended drying times and additional coats.

Apply at least 3 coats of magnetic primer to the exterior surfaces of the salt box, according to the manufacturer's directions, lightly sanding between coats.

Paint the primed and sanded box exterior with the latex paint, giving it 2 or 3 coats and lightly sanding between coats. Carefully and thoroughly remove all dust from the salt box, inside and out, with a slightly damp cloth. Allow the box to dry thoroughly while you decorate the magnets for the box.

Use a hot glue gun to attach buttons, beads, or small wood turnings to the magnets.

Fill the box with the seasoned *fleur de sel* and add the small wooden scoop.

Inscribe the large gift card (include the recipe for the seasoning salt on the reverse, so that the recipient can replenish the supply when the salt is gone). Use the magnets to hold the gift card in place on the top of the salt box. Use low-tack tape to hold the lid closed and cover it with a ribbon wrap and bow.

chalkboard *cheese* board with *quince paste*

There is a French expression that roughly translates to "A meal without cheese is like a pretty woman with one eye." A chalkboard cheese platter is ideal; a wooden cutting board with a chalkboard finish makes it possible write the name of each cheese served directly on the cheese board. Quince paste (called *membrillo* in Spain, where it is often served) is standard fare on all the best cheese boards from Manhattan to Madrid.

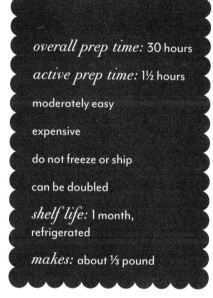

overall prep time: 30 hours

active prep time: 1½ hours

moderately easy

expensive

do not freeze or ship

can be doubled

shelf life: 1 month, refrigerated

makes: about ⅓ pound

4 pounds fresh quince, peeled, cored, and diced

1 fresh lemon

superfine sugar in a volume equal to the quince puree; see directions below

1 Put the diced quince in a large saucepan or small stockpot and cover with cold water. Use a swivel-bladed peeler to remove 2 or 3 strips of zest from the lemon, taking care to leave behind the white pith. Add the zest to the quince and water. Juice the lemon and set the juice aside. Bring the water to a boil over medium heat, reduce the heat to low, and simmer the quince, uncovered, for 45 minutes, stirring frequently to prevent the fruit from scorching. Add additional water a couple of tablespoons at time as needed to keep the quince from scorching.

2 Drain the quince. Puree the quince and zest in a food processor or blender until perfectly smooth.

recipe continues

3 Measure the quince puree. Combine it with an equal amount of superfine sugar in the saucepan; for example, 3½ cups of puree requires 3½ cups of sugar. Stir the puree until the sugar has dissolved, add 3 tablespoons of the reserved lemon juice, and very gently simmer the puree, stirring occasionally, over low heat for 1½ hours, or until the puree has thickened to the consistency of thin jelly and the color has changed from a cloudy pale orange to a translucent deep coral pink. Set the pan aside to cool briefly while preheating the oven to the lowest possible setting (125°F is ideal).

4 Butter an 8-inch square glass baking dish and line the bottom with buttered parchment paper. Pour the puree into the prepared pan and bake it on the middle rack of the oven for 2 hours, or until you can peel a corner of the quince paste away from the parchment paper liner. Set the pan aside to cool on a rack for 24 hours, loosely covered with a tea towel.

5 Lift the parchment and quince paste from the glass baking dish and cut it into 4 rectangles, about 2 × 8 inches each. Wrap each rectangle first in fresh parchment paper and then in clear cellophane. Refrigerate the quince paste until you are ready to assemble and deliver the gift.

wrapping it up

Plaid brand chalkboard paint is child safe and nontoxic. If you use a different brand for this project, carefully read the label first. Be sure to sand between each coat of paint for a flawless finish.

suggested supplies

1 hardwood cutting board, at least 11 × 14 inches

medium and fine grit sandpapers

tack cloth

low-adhesive painters' tape

1 container (8 ounces) water-based chalkboard paint, preferably Plaid brand (available at craft stores and online; see Resources, page 290)

clear cellophane

double face tape

chalk

an assortment of aged dry cheeses and creamy soft cheeses, each wrapped in parchment paper and labeled

1 cheese knife

1 small box chalk (optional)

paper cheese leaves to place under the cheese for serving, available at gourmet shops and some supermarkets (optional)

regular adhesive tape

1 length (about 2 yards) thin ribbon or raffia

how to make a "write right on it" cheese board

Lightly sand one side of the cutting board, first with medium grit and then with fine grit sandpaper.

Clean the sanded side of the board with the tack cloth and mask off the edges of the cutting board with the painters' tape. Apply at least 5 coats of chalkboard paint to the sanded side of the cutting board according to the manufacturers' directions. Sand between coats with fine grit sandpaper, and wipe the surface with the tack cloth to remove any dust before applying the next coat. Once the final coat of paint is completely dry, carefully remove the painters' tape and wash and dry the cheese board.

Wrapping the cheese board in cellophane is like wrapping a gift box "upside down." Cut a sheet of cellophane roughly twice the size of the cheese board, allowing for the cheese and other items that will be arranged on it and leaving generous margins. Smooth the cellophane out on the work surface and center a long strip of double face tape (no longer than one long side of the board) on each of the shorter sides of the cellophane. Center the cheese board on one taped edge so that about one-third of the board is sitting on cellophane; press the tape into the board to make sure the cellophane is firmly attached to the underside of the cheese board. Write a gift message on the cheese board. Arrange the quince paste, cheeses, and cheese knife on the board (if you like, add a box of chalk and some French paper cheese leaves). Carefully bring the cellophane sheet tightly over the cheese board, then carefully lift the board and press the second taped edge of the cellophane to the bottom of the board. Tuck both free ends of the cellophane under the cheese board and use the regular adhesive tape to attach these free ends to the underside of the cheese board. Center the wrapped cheese board on the thin ribbon or raffia. Bring the ribbon or raffia together over the top of the wrapped cheese board and tie it in a knot, followed by a simple bow. Trim the free ends of the bow as desired.

feel better

Making gifts of food for friends or family who find themselves under the weather or overwhelmed is not a new idea by any means. Such gifts nurture and comfort those who are in need of just that sort of attention and can also convey sentiments we might otherwise find awkward to express.

But while giving food to friends in need is common practice, wrapping the food gifts with effort and ingenuity isn't. Homemade soup is just homemade soup until it becomes part of a custom-made lap tray (page 249), and cookies are just cookies until their shape, and the container in which they are delivered, can make the recipient laugh out loud (page 265). In other words, the presentation can do every bit as much to lift spirits and brighten days as the food itself does. Whether the symptoms suggest a bad cold, a bad day, or a bad patch, I hope you will find something in this chapter to make your gift recipient feel better.

things to keep in mind

When preparing something for an ailing friend, it is very important to make sure that the food is "hassle free." An integral part of the gifts in this chapter is user-friendly design. When things aren't going well, the last thing a recipient needs is a list of complicated instructions for serving a dinner you delivered. You need to create meals simple enough that even the most stressed-out person can get it on the table. Stock an ailing friend's fridge or pantry with ready-to-eat items; nothing you give should require a lot of time or energy from the recipient.

Wrap the gifts with practicality in mind, but try to make them as cheerful and bright as possible. A witty presentation can go a long way toward boosting the spirits of someone who is down in the dumps or just plain sick. Bright colors surrounding tempting treats can be a small way of helping someone get through difficult times.

herbal tea sachets

Handmade herbal tea sachets are easy to create yourself, and the tea may make a common cold or flu easier to endure. You can find bulk herbal tea leaves and blossoms at tea and coffee stores, health-food stores, and online (see Resources, page 290). Each tea bag will hold 1 heaping tablespoon of leaves, petals, or blossoms. You can make sachets that contain a single ingredient or you can create combinations.

To get you started, here is a list of some common conditions and the tea ingredients that are thought to help cure or soothe them:

- Congestion: ginger, thyme, licorice, and hyssop
- Sore throat: comfrey and slippery elm
- Compromised immunity: elderberry, dried orange peel, dried lemon peel
- Sleeplessness: chamomile

overall prep time: 1 hour

easy

expensive

do not freeze

ships well

shelf life: 6 months in airtight container

makes: as many sachets as you like; each will brew about 8 ounces of tea

---

FOR EACH SACHET:

large embroidery needle

1 length (12 inches) cotton embroidery floss

1 heaping tablespoon selected varieties of herb leaves, petals, and blossoms (see suggestions above)

1 square (6 inches) double-ply cheesecloth

1 square (2 inches) or circle (2-inch diameter) card stock

---

1 Thread the embroidery needle with the length of the embroidery floss and set it aside. Place the herb or herbs on the double-ply square of cheesecloth; the herbs should be centered horizontally but slightly closer to you on the vertical axis.

recipe continues

2 Starting at the side closest to you, roll the tea up tightly, forming a fat "sushi roll" of tea. Bring the open ends of the roll together and twist them together tightly. Sew the twisted ends together with the embroidery floss, wrap the thread around the stitches twice, and then put the needle though the ends once more to secure the wound thread. Insert the needle through the edge of the card-stock square or circle and knot it tightly. Snip off the needle and trim away any ravels of cheesecloth.

3 Use a waterproof marking pen to write the name of the tea or tea blend on the card-stock label. If you wish, you can write the symptoms the tea may remedy on the reverse side of the label. Repeat to create as many sachets as you would like.

wrapping it up

A good cup of herbal tea should be brewed in a nice pot and sweetened with some honey.

suggested supplies

1 large new or vintage tea pot	**1 wire twist tie**
1 small jar honey	**ribbon**
1 large square cellophane	

how to fill a teapot with sachets

Fill a vintage or new teapot with the tea sachets and a small jar of honey. Center the filled pot on a large square of cellophane and gather the cellophane up around the teapot. Tightly twist the cellophane at the top of the teapot and secure it with the wire twist tie. Cover the twist tie with the ribbon and finish with a simple or flouncy bow.

eat your *vegetables*

This is an attractive and unusual combination of fresh vegetables and fruit, in the form of a layered salad in a jar, which will keep well for several days and makes a really thoughtful gift for someone who doesn't have the time or energy to prepare fresh, wholesome produce. Elephant garlic is far milder than regular garlic and stays very crisp. You can vary the ingredients according to individual tastes. Round slices of similarly sized items make the most attractive layers in the jar.

overall prep time: 30 minutes

easy

inexpensive

do not freeze or ship

can be doubled or tripled

shelf life: 2 to 3 days, refrigerated in a tightly sealed jar

makes: 1 quart

FOR THE LAYERED SALAD:

3 small ripe tomatoes, thickly sliced

2 small oranges, peeled and thickly sliced

1 large cucumber, peeled and thickly sliced

1 small yellow bell pepper, cored, seeded, and sliced into thick rings

1 elephant garlic clove, peeled and sliced paper thin

½ cup loosely packed fresh tarragon leaves

FOR THE DRESSING:

¼ cup freshly squeezed lemon juice

½ cup freshly squeezed orange juice

½ teaspoon sea salt

¼ teaspoon coarsely ground white pepper

¼ cup extra-virgin olive oil

1 To make the salad, in a wide-mouthed glass quart jar with a tight-fitting lid, alternate layers of sliced vegetables and oranges, interspersed with elephant garlic and tarragon leaves. Use a wooden spoon to tightly pack in each layer, so the jar has no gaps or spaces and is filled to the top.

recipe continues

2 To make the dressing, combine the lemon and orange juices with the salt and pepper in a small bowl and whisk until the salt is dissolved. Gradually add the olive oil, whisking constantly until the dressing is emulsified and slightly thickened.

3 Slowly pour the dressing into the jar, allowing each addition to trickle down through the layered salad before adding more. Cover the jar and store it in the refrigerator until you are ready to assemble and deliver the gift.

wrapping it up

The layered salad is perfectly delicious on its own, but some leafy lettuce looks good surrounding the salad, both in the jar and on the plate.

suggested supplies

1 small head of butter lettuce or Boston lettuce, washed and dried (see page 202 for instructions on cleaning whole heads of lettuce)

1 square (24 inches) cotton-mesh fish net, available at craft stores and party-supply stores

1 pair small wooden tongs

how to wrap a jar of layered salad

Wash the lettuce head and let it dry, keeping it intact. Spread out the cotton-mesh fish net flat on a work surface and put the lettuce in the center of the net. Gently open the leaves from the center of the head and spread them back so you can nestle the salad jar into the center. Once the jar is in place, rearrange the leaves so they surround the jar, or at least the lower part of it. Gather the net up around the lettuce and knot it into a hobo bundle. Lace the wooden tongs through the knot in the netting.

sunshine in a jar (with plenty of vitamin c)

You can prepare these orange slices in minutes for someone with the sniffles. I learned to make this dessert when I was a college student in London because my "bed sit"—the British term for a very small studio apartment—had no kitchen. The sugar and spices thicken the juice from the orange slices into a delicious syrup. This is yummy, sweet sunshine in a jar.

Try to find small to medium oranges whose diameter is no larger than the diameter of the quart jar you will use.

⅔ cup superfine sugar

1¼ teaspoons ground cinnamon

¼ teaspoon freshly grated nutmeg

3 to 4 oranges

1 long cinnamon stick (5 inches), or 2 shorter ones

juice of 1 lemon

overall prep time: 2 hours

active prep time: 10 to 15 minutes

easy

inexpensive

do not freeze or ship

can be doubled or tripled

shelf life: 3 to 4 days refrigerated in a tightly covered jar

makes: 1 quart

1 Combine the sugar, ground cinnamon, and nutmeg in a small bowl and set the mixture aside. Slice the tops and bottoms off the oranges. Using a flexible paring knife, cut away the orange peel, removing all the white pith with the peel. Slice the oranges crosswise ⅓ inch thick.

2 Starting with the widest slices, stack the orange slices in a 1-quart wide-mouthed glass jar with a tight-fitting lid, sprinkling each slice with a little of the sugar-and-spice mixture. When the jar is full, insert one or two cinnamon sticks through the center of the stacked oranges to hold them in place and infuse them with additional flavor.

recipe continues

3 Add the lemon juice and any remaining sugar-and-spice mixture to the jar. Refrigerate the jar for at least 2 hours, or until the sugar has dissolved and thickened the juice. Store the jar in the refrigerator until you are ready to assemble and deliver the gift.

wrapping it up

A paper bow made of scraps is a cute way to top the jar and use up that pile of odd bits of pretty paper and card stock you just can't bear to throw away.

suggested supplies

paper and card-stock scraps   **double-face tape**

how to make a paper bow jar topper

Cut the scraps into 1-inch wide strips. Make small loops with the strips, joining the ends of the loops together with a strip of double-face tape. Press the loops into place on the jar lid. Keep adding loops, varying their sizes, until the entire lid is covered and you achieve the bow look you like. You can also cover the lid rim with a paper strip or a ribbon, using the double-face tape to hold it in place.

first *ade*

Simple syrup infused with tummy-settling fresh ginger will be appreciated by anyone who needs to drink plenty of fluids, because it makes the fluids taste a lot more interesting. Your recipient can add First Ade to plain or sparkling water, fruit juices, hot or cold tea, and even warm milk.

overall prep time:
45 minutes

active prep time:
5 to 10 minutes

easy

inexpensive

do not freeze or ship

can be doubled or tripled

shelf life: 3 months refrigerated in an airtight container

makes: 1 quart

....

1¾ cups granulated sugar   3½ cups water   1 piece (4 to 5 inches long) fresh ginger

....

1 Combine the sugar and water in a saucepan. Stir briefly, and set the pan aside to let the sugar dissolve while you prepare the ginger.

2 Peel the ginger and shave the root into thin slices with a wide swivel-bladed peeler. Add the ginger slices to the saucepan, cover, and bring the pan to a boil over medium heat.

3 Once the mixture comes to a boil, uncover the saucepan and let the syrup boil for 2 minutes. Reduce the heat to medium-low and simmer the syrup, uncovered, for 5 minutes. Cover the pan and set it aside to cool completely.

4 When the syrup is cool, remove and discard the ginger, then pour the syrup through a cheesecloth-lined funnel into a 1-liter glass bottle with a tight-fitting lid. Cover the bottle and refrigerate it until you are ready to assemble and deliver the gift.

wrapping it up

You can buy fabric wine totes at home-goods, craft, and gourmet stores, or you can stitch one together easily with a folded rectangle of scrap fabric. In either case, there is usually room to tuck a small bouquet of fresh flowers next to the bottle of ginger syrup. Include a gift card with the serving suggestions that are given in the introduction to this recipe.

it's okay to *eat in bed*

It's okay, but it can be uncomfortable and a little messy. A thermos of creamy tomato soup and a bundle of rolled tarragon toasts fit very nicely in the side pockets of this plastic bed tray. Just for fun, cover the top of the tray with dry-erase vinyl. If someone is stuck in bed, he or she can jot down reminders for medication times or phone numbers (or even those all-important infomercial toll-free numbers and Web addresses) on the tray top. Be a real pal and stick around for a game of hangman on the tray top after you have cleared away the soup and toast.

These crisp rolled herb toasts are one of the best things you can make from packaged sandwich bread, I think. And the instant coffee granules in the soup recipe neutralize the acidity of the canned tomatoes.

overall prep time: 2 hours

active prep time: 1 hour

easy

inexpensive

do not freeze or ship

can be doubled or tripled

shelf life: 2 days in an airtight container at room temperature for toasts; 3 days refrigerated for soup

makes: 12 toast rolls and about 8 cups of soup

FOR THE ROLLED TARRAGON TOASTS:

3 tablespoons dried tarragon

generous grating of fresh nutmeg

¼ tablespoon sea salt

7 tablespoons unsalted butter, melted

12 thin slices white or whole-wheat (but not seeded) sandwich bread

FOR THE CREAMY TOMATO SOUP:

5 tablespoons unsalted butter

1 cup finely chopped yellow onions

3 cups peeled, diced canned tomatoes

1 tablespoon fresh tarragon or 1 teaspoon dried tarragon leaves

3 tablespoons all-purpose flour

2 cups chicken or vegetable stock

pinch of instant coffee granules (optional)

½ teaspoon granulated sugar

½ cup crème fraîche or heavy cream

recipe continues

1 To make the tarragon toasts, preheat the oven to 275°F. In a small saucepan, stir the tarragon, nutmeg, and sea salt together. Keep the mixture warm over very low heat.

2 Use a heavy rolling pin to flatten the slices of bread; make them very thin, then trim the crusts. Brush the herbed butter on both sides of the slices. Roll the buttered slices tightly from one corner to opposite corner, forming tight diagonal rolls, and arrange them side by side on a small baking sheet lined with parchment paper.

3 Bake the rolls in the center of the oven for 30 to 35 minutes, or until they are a deep golden color and firm to the touch. Turn off the oven, prop open the oven door with a wooden spoon, and allow the rolled toasts and the oven to cool completely. Store the cooled rolled toasts in an airtight container while you make the soup, and until you are ready to assemble and deliver the gift.

4 To make the soup, melt the butter over medium-low heat in a heavy-bottomed stockpot. Add the onions and cook them until they are transparent and limp but not browned, about 10 minutes. Reduce the heat to low, add the tomatoes and tarragon, and cook for 5 minutes more.

5 In a small bowl whisk the flour into ½ cup of the stock until smooth. Pour this into the tomato base, whisking constantly. Add the remaining stock to the soup, cover the pot, and cook over low heat, stirring occasionally, for 30 minutes. Turn off the heat and allow the soup to cool slightly.

6 Puree the soup in a food processor or blender in batches. Return the pureed soup to the cooking pot and stir in the coffee granules. Stir in the sugar and cream. Gently reheat the soup, but do not allow it to boil, before you pour it into the thermos carafe in which you will deliver it.

wrapping it up

Craft stores carry brightly colored molded-plastic lap trays with generous side pockets. They're very inexpensive and are perfect for bedbound meals. Transforming the tray takes about 30 minutes.

how to improve a plastic bed tray

Measure the dimensions of the flat center part of the tray-top surface and cut a sheet of dry-erase paper to fit it. Carefully peel away the protective backing from the leading edge of the paper, align it with the tray top, and, working slowly and carefully, gradually peel and stick the paper to the surface. Use a bone folder or craft squeegee to eliminate bubbles and wrinkles from the dry-erase paper liner.

Starting at the lower righthand corner of the tray top, attach a border of trim over the raw (cut) edge of the applied surface with the low-temp glue gun. Leave an 8-inch length of trim free at the finish end of the border. (The felt pocket for the pens will be attached to the end of this.)

To make a pocket for the dry-erase markers, pin the free end of the border trim along the edge of one long side of a felt rectangle, and pin the second rectangle of felt over this. Using the embroidery floss and needle, sew the two long sides and one short side together, making sure to catch the pinned border trim in your stitches, so that the felt pocket is now attached to the tray.

Put the soup into the thermos and pack the toast rolls in the wax-paper sandwich bag. Tuck the soup, toasts, and the eraser pocket of markers in the side pockets of the bed tray. You can write a get-well message on the dry-erase surface, if you like.

Feel Better
Soon!

Honey
Candy

cuter than a *bee's knees*

Pasteli, a Greek honey-and-sesame-seed chewy candy, is a healthy energy booster. The miniature bee skep container will boost spirits, too. Many allergy sufferers believe that consuming local organic honey alleviates their worst symptoms.

....

1 teaspoon unsalted butter, softened   1⅓ cups organic honey   3 cups white sesame seeds

....

1 Lightly coat an 11 × 20-inch sheet of parchment paper with the butter. Place the parchment paper on a heat-resistant surface, such as a marble slab or counter or a plastic cutting board, and have ready a second 11 × 20-inch sheet of parchment paper. Bring the honey slowly to a boil in medium saucepan over medium-low heat. Stir in the sesame seeds and attach a candy thermometer to the inside of the pan. Continue to cook the mixture, stirring frequently, until the thermometer reaches 270°F (firm ball stage).

2 Slowly pour the boiling honey mixture onto the parchment paper; do not scrape the bottom or sides of the pot. Cover the top of the hot candy with the second sheet of parchment paper. Use a wide dough scraper to spread and level the pasteli between the two sheets of parchment paper. Allow the candy to cool completely.

3 Oil the blades of heavy-duty kitchen shears and cut the candy-filled parchment paper into squares or rectangular bars. Store the pasteli in an airtight container until you have made the bee skep and are ready to assemble and deliver the gift.

recipe continues

overall prep time: 2 hours

active prep time: 30 minutes

easy

expensive

do not freeze

ships well if pasteli are individually wrapped and packed in an airtight tin

can be doubled

shelf life: 4 to 5 weeks in an airtight container

makes: a little more than 1 pound

wrapping it up

I collect bee skeps, which are garden ornaments in the shape of beehives. Their form and materials appeal to me, as does the fact that they symbolize energy and industry. Small skeps are hard to find. But it is easy to make one using a skein of rope and a plastic flower pot. You will have an 8-inch-tall skep when you are done.

suggested supplies

1 terra cotta–colored plastic flower pot (8 inches), and a matching plant saucer 10 inches in diameter

low-temp glue gun

1 styrofoam ball, about 3 inches in diameter, cut in half

1 skein (22 to 30 feet long) thin sisal or hemp rope

1 wide-mouthed glass jar that will fit inside the finished skep

1 sheet pale-yellow or honey-colored tissue paper

1 square (14 inches) clear cellophane

1 wire twist tie

honey-colored ribbon

how to make a bee skep

Invert the flower pot on a work surface and use the low-temp glue gun to attach one Styrofoam hemisphere, flat side down, to the outside bottom of the flower pot. The inverted pot will now have a bell-like shape, which will be covered with the rope to make the bee skep. Use a large screwdriver to poke a hole through the Styrofoam, aligned with the center hole of the inverted pot.

Insert one end of the rope through the Styrofoam and the flower-pot hole. Double knot the rope inside the pot and pull the rope on the outside of the pot to tighten and secure the knot inside the pot. Make a 2-inch loop at the top of the inverted pot, and start tightly coiling the rope around the loop, gluing each coil in place as you continue around the pot all the way to the opening of the flower pot. Closely trim the end of the rope and glue it to the inner edge of the opening, to keep it from unraveling. Starting at the bottom outside edge of the plant saucer, use the same technique of gluing the rope in a tight coil around the saucer, from bottom to top of the outside edges. Fill the glass jar with the pasteli. Center the yellow tissue paper over the plant saucer and place the jar in the center of the tissue-covered saucer. Gently crush the tissue around the jar and place the skep over the top, pushing it into the saucer. Center the filled skep and saucer on the cellophane and gather the cellophane up and around the skep. Tightly twist the cellophane over the top of the skep and secure it with a wire twist tie. Cover the twist tie with the honey-colored ribbon and finish with a pretty bow.

everything is going to be ginger *peachy*—and *crisp*

The mere aroma of this homey crisp will brighten someone's day. The quilted "casserole cozy" is a clever gift wrap that you may want to make again and again for all sorts of hot food gifts. Note that the cozy must be made before you bake the crisp, if you plan to deliver it hot from the oven.

FOR THE PEACH-GINGER FILLING:

2 tablespoons (¼ stick) unsalted butter, softened

6 large, firm peaches, peeled, pitted, and thickly sliced

3 tablespoons granulated sugar

1 tablespoon freshly squeezed lemon juice

1 tablespoon grated lemon zest

1½ tablespoons finely chopped preserved ginger

1 tablespoon syrup from the bottle of preserved ginger

FOR THE CRUMB TOPPING:

5 tablespoons (⅝ stick) cold unsalted butter, cut into very small cubes

¾ cup crushed gingersnap cookies

¼ cup pastry flour

heaping ¼ teaspoon ground ginger

¼ teaspoon ground cinnamon

¼ teaspoon ground mace

several generous gratings fresh nutmeg

⅓ cup firmly packed dark brown sugar

2 tablespoons granulated sugar

recipe continues

overall prep time: 1 hour

active prep time: 20 to 30 minutes

easy

inexpensive

unbaked crisp can be wrapped in foil and frozen (thaw completely before baking); do not freeze baked crisp

do not ship

do not double

shelf life: 24 hours loosely covered

makes: 1 crisp

1 Coat the bottom and sides of a shallow 8-cup baking dish with the softened butter. To make the peach-ginger filling, toss the peach slices with the sugar, lemon juice and zest, preserved ginger, and ginger syrup in a bowl. Spread this mixture evenly over the bottom of the buttered baking dish. Set the dish aside and preheat the oven to 350°F.

2 To make the crumb topping, combine all of the topping ingredients in a shallow bowl. Rub the butter and dry ingredients between your fingertips until you have a homogeneous crumbly mixture. Sprinkle the topping over the prepared peaches, gently pressing it in.

3 Bake the crisp in the lower third of the oven for 35 minutes, or until it is a deep golden brown.

4 You can slip the piping-hot crisp directly into the cozy and deliver it right away, but if that's not possible, place it on a rack to cool. The cooled crisp can be set aside for up to 6 hours. Before assembling and delivering the crisp, reheat it according to the following directions: Place a baking sheet on the middle rack of the oven and preheat the oven to 350°F. Lay a large sheet of foil over the top of the crisp and place the crisp on the baking sheet. Heat the crisp for 30 to 40 minutes, or until the filling is hot and bubbly.

wrapping it up

I have made dozens of adorable quilted sleeves like this over the years, for delivering gifts from the oven. They are simple, inexpensive, and practical, involving little more than sewing placemats together into a sleeve with a large opening and then adding fun embellishments of your choosing. Quilted placemats can be picked up for a song at linen outlet stores and import shops. They are available in the same shapes (squares, rectangles, and ovals) and sizes as typical casseroles and baking dishes, and they come in wonderful colors and great-looking prints. Most are reversible as well. The quilted cozy will keep food warm and protected in transit, and it can be used as a trivet under the hot dish. I warn you: It is easy to get carried away making these, because it is so much fun to mix and match them with buttons, fabric frog closures, grommets, ribbons, twill tapes, gimps, and cords.

suggested supplies

2 attractive full-size quilted placemats

cotton 2-ply embroidery floss in a matching or contrasting color

sharp tapestry needle or embroidery needle

buttons, ties, fabric frogs, snaps, grommets, ties, or other similar items, for closures

parchment paper

how to make a quilted cozy sleeve for a baking dish

Pin the 2 placemats together on 3 sides, leaving a wide enough opening to slide in the baking dish you will be giving. Sew the pinned portion of placemats together with embroidery floss, barely catching the outermost edges of the fabric. Use a simple whip stitch or blanket stitch; if you have a talent for needlework, you can do something more decorative and complicated to sew the edges together, like running vines or French knots.

Just about anything you like or have on hand can be used for closures. I usually sew a couple of fabric-covered buttons on one side and simple ties in the same fabric on the opposite side, so that I can wrap and tie adjustable bows around the buttons. Grommets laced with ribbon or fabric ties, fabric frog closures, large snaps, or even Velcro can be used for the closures. Just be sure that whatever you use leaves enough room for the baking dish when you close the cozy around it. Cover the peach crisp with a sheet of parchment paper before sliding it into the cozy.

life should be a bowl of *cherries*

I don't think there is a more delicious way to say "Cheer up, I know things are going to get better for you" than with a pretty little bowl filled with these bite-size cherry-and-almond pastries.

overall prep time: 1 hour

active prep time: 20 minutes

slightly challenging

moderately expensive

raw dough freezes well; do not freeze finished pastries

do not ship

can be doubled or tripled

shelf life: 2 days in an airtight container at room temperature

makes: 50

1 tube (7 ounces) almond paste, cut in very small pieces

½ cup (1 stick) unsalted butter, cool but not cold

2 cups confectioners' sugar

½ teaspoon baking powder

1 teaspoon vanilla extract

3 large egg whites

1⅔ cups cake flour

50 maraschino cherries with stems

sugar crystals or "sparkling" sugar

1 Combine the almond paste and butter in the bowl of a stand mixer and beat them at medium-high speed until they form a smooth paste. Continue to beat as you gradually add 1⅓ cups of the confectioners' sugar along with the baking powder. Add the vanilla, then add the egg whites one at a time, continuing to beat at medium-high speed. Gradually add the flour, and beat the dough until the flour has been thoroughly incorporated. Cover the dough and refrigerate it for at least 45 minutes, or until it is firm to the touch.

2 Preheat the oven to 350°F. Drain the cherries and set them on a tray lined with paper towels. Roll the chilled dough into 1-inch balls and set them on a tray. Place the remaining ⅔ cup of confectioners' sugar in a shallow pie plate or a deep dish. Roll the dough balls, 4 or 5 at a time, in the sugar until they are completely coated.

Press each sugar-coated ball into a mini paper cupcake liner and set it in a compartment of a mini-muffin pan. Make a deep depression in the center of each dough ball with your finger and press a cherry into the depression. Sprinkle each pastry (including the cherry) with sugar crystals.

3 Bake the pastries on the center racks of the oven for 5 minutes. Switch and rotate the pans and bake the pastries for another 6 minutes, or until they are pale golden. Cool the muffin pans on baking racks until the pastries are completely cooled. Store them in a single layer in airtight containers until you are ready to assemble and deliver the gift.

wrapping it up

The pastries look especially pretty in a blue and white container or bowl, but any attractive bowl will work. Inexpensive blue-and-white Japanese or Chinese bowls can be found at import stores and ethnic markets. Tag sales and resale shops usually abound in good-looking bowls as well.

suggested supplies

1 attractive medium-size serving bowl

several sheets of pale-blue or pale-pink tissue paper

1 large sheet clear cellophane

1 wire twist tie

1 length (18 to 24 inches) ½- to ¾-inch-wide red ribbon

how to fill a bowl with cherries

Line the bowl with several sheets of the tissue paper and gently press the tissue to conform to the shape of bowl. Pile the cherry pastries high in the bowl. Fluff and arrange the tissue so it cradles and frames the pastries. Center the bowl on the cellophane and gather it tightly over the bowl. Twist the cellophane tightly over the bowl and secure it with the wire twist tie. Center the ribbon over the twist tie and wrap the ribbon around the wire twist tie twice. Tightly knot the ribbon twice. Tie a simple bow, and then tie a second bow over the first, gather all four loops, and knot them at the base of the bow. Trim the free ends of the bow so they do not extend past the loops. Trim the top of the tightly gathered cellophane.

mixed berry *ice pops*

Blackberries and strawberries give these fruit-puree ice pops an amazingly vibrant purple color plus a big dose of vitamin C and antioxidants. Instead of the typical craft sticks, use disposable bamboo spoons for the ice-pop handles, which come in handy if the ice pops start to get slushy while being consumed. If you like, you can substitute any frozen berry combination for the blackberries and strawberries used here.

overall prep time: 8 to 10 hours

active prep time: 15 minutes

easy

inexpensive

do not ship

can be doubled or tripled

shelf life: 1 week, tightly covered with plastic wrap and frozen

makes: 8

1 cup granulated sugar

1 cup water

3 cups hulled strawberries

3 cups blackberries

1 tablespoon freshly squeezed lime juice

8 plastic cups, 5 ounces each

8 small disposable bamboo spoons (available at some supermarkets and at party stores)

1 Combine the sugar and water in a saucepan and stir until the sugar is dissolved. Cover the pan and bring to a boil over medium heat. Boil the syrup for 1 minute, remove the cover, and boil for another 5 minutes. Pour the syrup into a heatproof pitcher or measuring cup to cool at least to lukewarm.

2 Combine half the berries and half the syrup in a blender or food processor and puree the mixture until it is smooth. Transfer the puree to a large pitcher. Repeat with the remaining berries and syrup. Stir in the lime juice.

3 Arrange the eight plastic cups on a tray and divide the berry mixture among the cups. Freeze the cups for 1 hour, or until the mixture is firm enough to hold the bamboo spoons upright. Insert the spoon, bowl end first, into the semi-frozen pops. Freeze the pops until they are firm, at least overnight. Store the pops in the freezer until you are ready to assemble and deliver the gift.

recipe continues

wrapping it up

Wrap the ice pops individually, which makes each one look like a special present and keeps them fresher. The brightly colored paper or silicone cupcake liners provide nice drip catchers for each ice pop.

suggested supplies

8 small paper or silicone cupcake liners

8 squares (8 inches each) cellophane, plus 1 larger additional sheet for over-wrapping the container of ice pops

9 wire twist ties

raffia or paper ribbon

1 leak-proof container, such as a cachepot, a tin or galvanized metal pail, or a bright plastic bucket, large enough to hold the 8 ice pops in a single layer over a bed of ice

ice cubes

how to wrap drip-proof ice pops

Punch a small hole in the center of each cupcake liner and turn the liners upside down over the bamboo spoon handles. Push them all the way down and over the cups.

Center each ice-pop cup on a square of cellophane, gather the cellophane tightly around the spoon handle, and secure the cellophane with a wire twist tie. Cover the twist tie with raffia or paper ribbon, and finish with a simple bow. Refreeze the pops until delivery time.

When it is time to deliver the gift, add some ice cubes to the gift container you have chosen and nestle each frozen pop in the bed of ice. Place the container on a large square of cellophane and gather the cellophane over the top of the container. Twist the cellophane tightly around the container to hold everything in place and secure it with the remaining wire twist tie. Cover the twist tie with additional paper ribbon or raffia.

The pops will stay solidly frozen for 35 to 40 minutes at normal room temperature. For hot weather or long delivery distances, pop them in an insulated tote or cooler.

go *fish*

When a family under stress needs an opportunity to regroup, you can come to the rescue quickly with dinner. This fresh fish dinner in an oven-ready parchment wrapper can be prepared in less than an hour, and you can find everything you need, including the cookie sheet, at the local supermarket.

1 new baking sheet or jellyroll pan (11 × 17 inches)

1 large Yukon Gold potato, peeled and very thinly sliced

2 or 3 small zucchini, trimmed of their stems and cut into quarters lengthwise

¼ cup extra-virgin olive oil

sea salt to taste

freshly ground white pepper to taste

1¾ pounds fresh fish fillets, such as haddock, cod, tilapia, or lemon sole, no thicker than 1 inch at any point

1 medium yellow bell pepper, seeded and diced

3 sprigs fresh thyme or 2 teaspoons dried thyme or basil

2 garlic cloves, finely minced

3 shallots, peeled and chopped

2 medium tomatoes, peeled, seeded, and diced

⅓ cup pitted black oil-cured olives, coarsely chopped

¼ cup capers

overall prep time:
30 minutes

easy

moderately expensive

do not freeze or ship

do not double

shelf life: fish should be purchased, prepared, cooked, and eaten on the same day

makes: 4 generous servings

1 On a 9 × 15-inch sheet of parchment paper, draw a very simple fish shape. Your fish drawing should almost touch the edges of the paper on all four sides; it will be a very wide fish with a short, thick tail. (For a sample fish drawing, see my website, DinahsGourmetGifts.com.) Place this traced sheet of parchment paper on top of another 9 × 15-inch sheet of parchment, and cut through both sheets just inside the pencil lines. You should now have 2 large fish-shaped pieces of parchment.

recipe continues

2   Place 1 parchment cut-out on the baking sheet.
    Arrange the potato slices in a slightly overlapping
    pattern on the parchment, leaving a 2½-inch border of
    paper all the way around. Arrange half the zucchini in
    a cross-hatch pattern over the potatoes, again leaving a
    2½-inch border. Drizzle the layered vegetables with 2
    tablespoons of the olive oil and a pinch of sea salt and
    white pepper.

3   Cover the vegetables with the fish fillets. The fillets can
    overlap one another at their thinnest point in order
    to form an evenly thick layer of the fillets. Season the
    fillets with sea salt and white pepper. Spread the bell
    pepper over the fillets and strew the fresh herb sprigs
    or sprinkle the dried herbs over the fish. Cross-hatch
    the remaining zucchini spears over the whole and
    judiciously add a little more sea salt and white pepper.

4   Combine the garlic and shallots with the diced
    tomatoes, olives, and capers in a small bowl and stir
    in the remaining 2 tablespoons of olive oil. Spoon the
    tomato mixture over the vegetables and fish.

5   Cover the fish dinner with the second parchment
    fish cut-out and tightly fold the edges of the bottom
    parchment up and over the edges of the top parchment
    sheet at a 30 to 40 degree angle going all the way
    around the fish, to form a fish-shaped leak-proof
    pouch or papillote. Tie a short length of kitchen twine
    around the narrowest point of the papillote, just before
    the "tail," to give it added dimension. Refrigerate
    the baking sheet and papillote until you are ready to
    deliver the gift.

wrapping it up

The fish dinner is already "wrapped" in its papillote.
Simply attach a white tag to the twine on the fish "tail"
with these cooking instructions written on it: "Place the
baking sheet on the middle rack of a 350°F oven for 35
minutes. Allow the fish to rest 5 minutes, then carefully cut
open the top of the pouch to allow the steam to escape.
Serve hot."

an exceptional coconut *pound cake*

Most coconut cakes fall short of full, natural coconut flavor, and many pound cakes lack the perfect fine-crumb texture and moist consistency of yesteryear's rich recipes. This large cake receives very high marks in both categories, I believe. It is sure to be admired and deeply appreciated.

....

2 tablespoons (¼ stick) unsalted butter, softened

2 tablespoons all-purpose flour

¾ cup (1½ sticks) unsalted butter, cool but not cold

¾ cup sour cream

3 cups granulated sugar

8 large eggs

4 cups sifted cake flour

1 teaspoon salt

1 tablespoon baking powder

½ teaspoon baking soda

½ cup sweetened coconut milk

1 teaspoon vanilla extract

1 teaspoon coconut liqueur

1 cup shredded unsweetened coconut, preferably thawed frozen coconut (look for it in the frozen ethnic foods section of a large supermarket)

....

overall prep time: 2 hours

active prep time: 45 minutes

easy

moderately expensive

freezes and ships well

can be doubled

shelf life: 3 to 4 days in an airtight container

makes: 1 cake

1 Prepare a 10-inch springform tube pan by coating the sides and bottom with the softened butter and then lining the bottom with parchment paper. Butter the parchment paper as well. Coat the pan with the all-purpose flour and tap out the excess. Set the pan aside.

2 Position an oven rack on the second-to-lowest level and remove the other racks from the oven. Preheat the oven to 325°F. Combine the ¾ cup butter with the sour cream in the bowl of a stand mixer and beat at low speed. Slowly add the sugar, then increase the speed to medium and beat for 3 minutes. Reduce the mixer speed to low and add the eggs one at a time, beating well after each addition.

recipe continues

3 Resift the cake flour with the salt, baking powder, and baking soda into a bowl. Combine the coconut milk, vanilla, and coconut liqueur in a large liquid measure or a small pitcher. Alternately add the cake-flour mixture and the coconut-milk mixture in two additions each to the mixer bowl, beating very briefly after each addition. Fold the shredded coconut into the batter. Scoop the batter into the prepared tube pan and use a thin icing spatula to distribute and level the batter evenly in the pan.

4 Bake the cake for 1 hour and 10 minutes, or until a skewer inserted into the thickest part of the cake comes away clean. Cool the cake on a rack for 10 minutes. Run a thin-bladed spatula around the edge of the cake and gently unclamp and remove the side of the pan. Use the spatula to loosen the cake from the tube and bottom of the pan. Invert the cake on a rack or plate and remove the tube and bottom of the pan. Put a 10-inch round cake board over the cake and invert the cake onto the cake board. Wrap the cake and board tightly in plastic wrap, bringing the edges of the wrap to the bottom of the cake board. Store at room temperature until you are ready to assemble and deliver the gift.

wrapping it up

There are times when you might want to wrap a gift of food discreetly and simply. Tightly wrapping the cake in cellophane keeps it fresh and makes it easy to deliver. The wrap will keep the pound cake fresh until it is served.

suggested supplies

1 round cake board, 10 inches in diameter

double-face tape

clear cellophane

raffia or paper ribbon

how to wrap a cake simply

Make two lines of double-face tape around the edge of the cake board and set it aside, taped side up. Tightly cover the plastic-wrapped cake, along with the cake board it rests upon, with cellophane. Keep the cellophane covering tight enough so that there are no wrinkles in it and the cake is held snugly in place by using more double-face tape to secure the excess cellophane to the bottom of the cake board. Press the wrapped cake and its board firmly onto the cake board with the taped edges, sandwiching the cellophane wrapping tightly between the two cake boards. Set the wrapped cake on a length of raffia or paper ribbon and tie it over the top of the cake, finishing with a simple slipknot.

chocolate *poodles*

This is a seriously good chocolate butter cookie in the shape of a silly poodle. If you know someone with the blues or blahs, give them a batch of chocolate poodles decked out in pink frills ASAP.

You will need a poodle-shaped cookie cutter for this recipe. They are surprisingly easy to find at your local craft or kitchen store, and there are literally dozens of places online to find them (see Resources, page 290).

3 cups cake flour

½ cup Dutch-processed cocoa powder

¼ teaspoon sea salt

1 teaspoon instant espresso powder

1¼ cups (2½ sticks) unsalted butter, softened but cool

1½ cups confectioners' sugar

1 large egg, lightly beaten

overall prep time: 9 hours

active prep time: 1 hour

slightly challenging

inexpensive

unbaked cookie dough freezes well; do not freeze finished cookies

ships well

can be doubled

shelf life: 1 week in an airtight container

makes: 3 to 4 dozen cookies

1 Whisk together the flour, cocoa, salt, and espresso powder in a large bowl. Using a hand mixer or a wooden spoon, cream the butter with the sugar for 2 minutes, or until it is well blended. Add the egg and beat for 2 minutes more. Gradually beat the flour mixture into the butter mixture until you have a stiff and evenly colored dark brown dough.

2 Divide the dough in half and sandwich each half between two 11 × 17-inch sheets of parchment paper. Roll each half of the dough into a 9 × 16-inch rectangle. Slide the parchment-covered sheets of dough onto a tray or baking sheet and refrigerate them for at least 8 hours or overnight.

3 Preheat the oven to 400°F. Slide each sheet of chilled dough onto a baking sheet and peel off the top sheets of parchment paper. Use a poodle-shaped cookie cutter to cut the cookies, spacing them 1 inch apart. Peel away the scraps and refrigerate them.

recipe continues

4 Bake the cookies on the middle racks of the oven for 4 minutes. Rotate and switch the baking sheets and bake the cookies for another 4 minutes. Be sure to adjust the baking times according to the size of your poodle cutter; smaller cookies will bake more rapidly than large ones. Combine the refrigerated scraps of dough, and roll, cut, and bake them using the same procedures.

5 Set the baking sheets on racks and allow the cookies to cool completely before removing them from the parchment. Store the cookies in an airtight container until you are ready to assemble and deliver the gift.

wrapping it up

It is pretty hard to go too far over the top when gift-wrapping chocolate poodles. The poodle cookie jar can be decorated with or without restraint. After all, it is your poodle and you can dress it up however you like—rhinestones for a collar, perhaps, or a leash of silver cord—and most definitely a pink bow in the topnotch.

suggested supplies

1 poodle image to trace, or an appropriately sized tracing of the poodle cookie cutter

1 large wide-mouth glass or heavy clear plastic jar with a lid

1 sheet tracing paper or plain white paper

painter's tape

glass marking pen (available at craft stores)

craft paint suitable for glass or plastic

super-tacky craft glue

1 tiny pink bow, and other embellishments as desired

pink fabric

pink cord or thin pink ribbon

pink tissue paper

how to make a poodle cookie jar

You will need a large, simple image of a poodle to serve as a pattern. You can either trace a simple poodle image on the tracing paper or trace around your cookie cutter onto a sheet of printer paper. Use your printer to copy the image up or down in size as needed to fit your jar.

Slide the paper pattern inside the jar and tape it in place with painter's tape. With the paper pattern as a guide, carefully trace around the poodle image with the glass marking pen and then fill in the poodle with craft paint, following the manufacturer's directions. To get a bold image you will need to do at least two coats.

Using the super-tacky craft glue, which dries clear, attach the tiny pink bow to the poodle's topknot, and other embellishments of your choosing, to the poodle when it is dry. Trace around the jar lid and cut a pink fabric (or tissue paper) circle to cover the jar top; use the craft glue to attach it. Cover the edge of the jar lid with the pink cord or ribbon, using a glue gun or the super-tacky craft glue to attach it. Cover the ends of ribbon where they meet on the lid with a small bow. Remove the tracing paper from the jar and line it with pink tissue paper, then fill with the cookies.

special
delivery

Everyone should have a childhood memory of opening a "care package" from home. When I went away to summer camp for the first time, I discovered my mother was an absolute virtuoso in the art of making creative—and seriously overloaded—care packages, and she would remain so all through my years of boarding school and college. The containers and wrappings she came up with were always as much fun as what was inside.

Gifts this much fun shouldn't be reserved for campers and college students; there are plenty of sophisticated treats for adults that can be wrapped with ingenuity and shipped with great success. There are many recipes throughout this book that ship well, but these are especially well suited for going the distance.

things to keep in mind

Know all the shipping and mailing requirements ahead of time. Be aware of the costs of fast shipping, and the time you need to allow if you choose a cheaper method. Make sure the gifts are packed carefully in boxes that meet postal or commercial shipping regulations. Take advantage of convenient shipping options like flat-rate boxes and "click-and-ship" computerized shipping quotes and pick-up orders.

Embellish your gifts with flat rather than dimensional embellishments, which may get crushed in transit. Use the smallest shipping box possible and tightly pack tissue or shredded paper around the gift to keep it stable.

Surprise packages are undeniably special. But while none of the recipes in this chapter are highly perishable, they shouldn't sit on the front porch for a week, either. Consider giving the recipient a "heads up" that something is on its way.

blond *biscotti*

overall prep time: 2 hours

active prep time: 1 hour

easy

moderately expensive

do not freeze

ships well

can be doubled

shelf life: 2 weeks in an airtight container

makes: 3 dozen

Biscotti are built for travel. Since they are twice baked, they won't break or crumble in shipment and they stay fresh and crisp for a long time. These are particularly good biscotti that are also fairly simple to make. They are not too sweet, with lots of ginger and toasted pine nuts.

5 cups unbleached all-purpose flour

1 cup granulated sugar

1 teaspoon baking soda

2 tablespoons ground dried orange peel

1 teaspoon ground ginger

¼ teaspoon ground cinnamon

⅔ cup pine nuts, briefly toasted in a dry sauté pan over medium heat

¼ cup finely diced crystallized ginger

6 tablespoons (¾ stick) unsalted butter, melted

2 eggs, slightly beaten

⅔ cup water

2 tablespoons turbinado sugar

1 Arrange your oven racks near the middle of the oven and preheat the oven to 325°F. Combine the flour, sugar, baking soda, orange peel, ground ginger, cinnamon, pine nuts, and crystallized ginger in a large mixing bowl or the bowl of a stand mixer.

2 Combine the melted butter, eggs, and water, and slowly pour the liquid into the dry ingredients, beating either with a wooden spoon or with the paddle attachment on the stand mixer set at low speed. As soon as the dough is evenly blended and forms a mass, turn it out onto a clean work surface and knead it lightly for 3 or 4 minutes.

3 Divide the dough in half, and roll and pat each portion into a 1-inch-thick rectangle measuring 3 × 8 inches. Place both portions of the shaped dough side by side on a parchment-lined baking sheet. Sprinkle 1 tablespoon of the turbinado sugar over the surface of each rectangle and gently press the sugar into the dough.

4   Bake the biscotti dough for 20 minutes. Rotate the pan and bake for another 25 minutes. Set the baking sheet on a rack to cool for 10 minutes; do not turn off the oven. Meanwhile, line 2 large baking sheets with parchment paper.

5   Use a serrated knife to cut the partially cooled dough diagonally into ¼-inch-wide slices. Lay the slices, cut side down, on the two prepared baking sheets and return them to the middle racks of the oven. Bake for 10 minutes. Remove the baking sheets from the oven and use an offset spatula to turn each cookie over in place. Rotate and switch the pans and place them back in the oven. Bake the biscotti for another 10 to 15 minutes, until they are firm and a light golden brown.

6   Set the baking sheets on racks to cool for 5 minutes, then transfer the biscotti directly to the racks for another 45 minutes, or until they are completely cool and dry. Store the cooled biscotti in an airtight container until ready to assemble and ship the gift.

wrapping it up

Biscotti are one of the easiest baked goods to ship. Here, you pack each wrapped bundle in a drawstring pouch made of tissue paper and run up on a sewing machine, using brightly colored thread (if you can find button twist or heavy duty thread, that works best). These pouches are also ideal for wrapping canned goods like jellies and chutneys, loose candy, giant cookies, and popcorn balls.

suggested supplies for each pouch

glassine or wax paper	**4 sheets colored tissue paper**
colored twine	**2 lengths (about 8 inches each) thin, silky ribbon**

how to sew a tissue gift pouch

Stack the biscotti in groups of 6 and wrap each stack in glassine or wax paper. Tie the top closed with colored twine. Evenly stack the tissue paper sheets and fold the stack in half. The folded side will be the bottom of the pouch. Measure and cut the folded tissue 4 inches taller and 3 inches wider than the finished size of the pouch you want. Fold the top of the tissue sheets down 4 inches on both sides to form casings for the drawstrings and press the creases with a warm iron. Position a length of ribbon inside of the crease and directly against it.

With a sewing machine, sew the casings closed 2 inches from the top of the bag, leaving a 2-inch hem of tissue extending below the stitches. Use a medium zigzag stitch, and take care not to catch the ribbon in the stitches. Starting just below the top casing and 1½ inches from the edge, sew the sides of the pouch together with the same stitch. Fill each pouch with a packet of wrapped biscotti and gently tighten the drawstrings to close the tissue pouch over them. Join the ribbons at each end with bows.

an impressive
chocolate chiffon *cake*

Extra-virgin olive oil, also known as EVOO, helps to give this cake a very rich and complex chocolate flavor and a fine, moist texture. The taste and looks of this chocolate chiffon cake are equally impressive, and it ships perfectly.

You will need an electric mixer for this recipe. If you have both a handheld and a stand mixer you can beat the batter with the handheld mixer and use the stand mixer for the egg whites. Otherwise, wash your mixer and/or the beaters very carefully before beating the egg whites.

overall prep time: 1½ hours

active prep time: 30 minutes

slightly challenging

moderately expensive

do not freeze

ships well

do not double

shelf life: 5 to 7 days in an airtight container

makes: 1 cake

⅔ cup sweet amber Marsala wine

1 teaspoon vanilla extract

4 tablespoons water

½ cup plus 2 tablespoons cocoa powder

1¾ cups cake flour

1¾ cups granulated sugar

1½ teaspoons baking soda

7 large eggs, separated

½ cup high-quality extra-virgin olive oil

½ teaspoon fine sea salt

¼ teaspoon cream of tartar

Combine the Marsala, vanilla, and water in a small saucepan and quickly bring the liquid to a boil over high heat. Sift the cocoa powder into a small mixing bowl. Whisk the boiling liquid into the cocoa powder until the cocoa has dissolved completely. Set the bowl aside until the cocoa mixture has cooled to room temperature.

recipe continues

2 Remove all but the lowest rack from the oven and preheat the oven to 325°F. Combine the cake flour, sugar, and baking soda in a large mixing bowl and whisk them together. Stir the egg yolks and olive oil into the cooled cocoa mixture and add it to the flour mixture. Beat the mixture at medium speed until it forms a smooth, thick batter. Set it aside.

3 Place the egg whites in a large mixing bowl or the bowl of a stand mixer and beat them at low speed for 1 minute, or until they are frothy. Add the salt and the cream of tartar and beat the egg whites at low speed for another minute. Gradually increase the beater speed to high and beat the whites until they form stiff, firm peaks, 6 to 8 minutes.

4 Add a large scoop of the egg whites to the cocoa batter and gently fold the egg whites through the batter to lighten it. Pour the lightened chocolate batter over the rest of the egg whites and, using a spatula, gently fold the two together until the batter is no longer streaked with white. Scoop the batter into an ungreased 10-inch tube pan and use the spatula to level the batter in the pan. Run a table knife or icing spatula through the batter in the pan several times to settle the batter and eliminate any air pockets.

5 Bake the cake on the lowest rack of the oven for 65 minutes. Place a cake rack over the top of the cake pan and invert the cake over the rack to cool upside down for 5 minutes. Turn the cake right side up and use an icing spatula to loosen the cake from the sides of the pan. Fit the center hole of the cake pan over a wine bottle and gently push the sides of the cake pan down and away from the cake. Invert the cake on a round cardboard cake board and loosen and remove the tube and bottom portion of the pan. With the help of a long serrated knife, you can level the cake so that it sits flat on the cake board. Using a gentle sawing motion with the knife, cut a thin slice from the bottom of the cake just above the cake board. Invert the cake onto a work surface, remove the cake board, discard the thin slice you have made, and replace the cake board. Turn the cake over again, so it's resting on the board. Store the cake in an airtight container until you are ready to assemble and ship the gift.

wrapping it up

A great-looking hatbox makes gift wrapping and shipping this cake fun. A few simple packing techniques guarantee the cake will ship well, keeping all the impressive looks and taste intact. You can embellish the hatbox using any number of craft techniques. Paper punches and adhesive-backed linen tape (bookbinding tape) can give the box streamlined good looks.

suggested supplies

1 round cake board, 10 inches in diameter	paper punches
2 to 3 tablespoons melted chocolate	bone folder or burnishing tool
1 sheet (8½ × 11 inches) printer-weight card stock	8 to 10 sheets tissue paper
wooden spoon	ribbon or cord
plastic wrap	cellophane
transparent tape	1 wire twist tie
1 pasteboard hatbox (9 × 11 inches is ideal)	1 shipping box large enough to hold the hatbox, at least 12 inches square
adhesive-backed linen tape (linen bookbinding tape), available at craft stores	packing tape

how to ship a cake in a pretty box

Smear the cake board with the melted chocolate and quickly transfer the cake from its board to the chocolate-smeared board. (Discard the old board.) Set this aside for a few minutes until the chocolate sets and the cake adheres firmly to the cake board.

Roll the sheet of card stock around the handle of a wooden spoon (this is the best way to roll the card stock tightly and smoothly, without causing cracks or wrinkles). Insert the card-stock roll into the center hole of the cake, remove the spoon, and allow the card stock to unfurl, filling the cavity of the cake and supporting its interior. Wrap the cake tightly in plastic wrap, sealing the wrap with transparent tape on the bottom of the cake round. Measure the circumference of the hatbox and the hatbox lid. Cut two strips of bookbinding tape 1 inch longer than the circumference of the hatbox. Cut a third strip 1 inch longer than the circumference of the lid. Use the paper punches to make a pattern all along the strips of tape and then carefully adhere them to the bottom edge of the hatbox, the midsection of the hatbox, and the edge of the hatbox lid. Use a bone folder or burnishing tool to press the tape firmly to the box.

Put the cake in the decorated box and surround it with crumpled sheets of tissue paper. Keep adding tissue until the cake is fully surrounded with tissue and unable to shift in the hatbox. Put the lid on the box and tie it firmly in place with the ribbon or cord. Center the hatbox on one or two sheets of cellophane and gather the cellophane tightly up and over the box. Twist the cellophane tightly at the top and secure it with the wire twist tie. Cover the twist tie with more ribbon or cord, finishing with a slipknot or simple bow. Put the wrapped hatbox in the shipping box, surrounding it with more tissue to prevent the hat box from shifting in the shipping box. Seal the shipping box tightly with packing tape.

baharat caravan *bells*

overall prep time: 3 to 4 hours

active prep time: 1 hour

slightly challenging

expensive

do not freeze

ships well

can be doubled

shelf life: 1 to 2 weeks in an airtight container

makes: 48

Baharat is a spice mixture used in Turkish and Arabic cuisines. In Moroccan cooking, it is a blend of cardamom, coriander, ginger, cloves, cinnamon, pepper, nutmeg, and rose petals. The flavor is exotic and sweet. These nut pastries are encased in foil cupcake liners and strung onto paper ribbon, which makes them resemble the long tasseled ropes with bells that were worn by caravan camels. You will need a food processor and a stand mixer to make these marvelous pastries.

1 cup blanched whole or slivered almonds

1 cup blanched pistachio nuts

1½ cups plus 3 tablespoons all-purpose flour

2½ teaspoons *baharat* spice blend, available at Middle Eastern markets and online (see Resources, page 290)

6 green cardamom pods

1 tablespoon mace blades or 1 teaspoon ground mace

1 cup (2 sticks) unsalted butter, softened but cool

2 teaspoons vanilla extract

grated zest of 1 orange

1½ cups firmly packed light brown sugar

2 large eggs, lightly beaten

½ cup semolina flour

½ teaspoon baking powder

⅔ cup chopped dates

⅔ cup shredded sweetened coconut

3 egg whites

1 tablespoon honey

1 tablespoon hot water

1 In the work bowl of a food processor fitted with the stainless-steel chopping blade, combine the almonds, pistachios, the 3 tablespoons of flour, baharat blend, cardamom pods, and mace. Finely chop the mixture using quick on/off pulses until the nuts resemble a very coarse and lumpy cornmeal. Set the mixture aside.

2 Combine the butter, vanilla, orange zest, and brown sugar in the bowl of a stand mixer. Using the paddle attachment, cream the butter mixture at medium speed for 1 minute. Increase the speed to medium-high and beat the mixture for another

2 minutes. Add the beaten eggs to the butter and sugar mixture, increase the mixer speed to high, and beat for 2 or 3 minutes, until well blended.

3 Combine 1 cup of the reserved chopped nut mixture, the 1½ cups of all-purpose flour, semolina flour, and baking powder in a bowl and blend them with a wire whisk. Set the mixer to low speed and gradually add these dry ingredients to the butter mixture until thoroughly incorporated. Add the dates and coconut, and continue to beat the dough on low speed just until they are evenly distributed through the dough. Turn the dough out onto a large sheet of plastic wrap and tightly wrap it around the dough. Refrigerate for 1 hour or until very firm.

4 Meanwhile, line two large baking sheets with parchment paper. Whisk the egg whites, honey, and hot water together in a pie pan or rimmed dish. Pour the remaining chopped nut mixture into a separate pie pan or shallow bowl.

5 Preheat the oven to 325°F and arrange two racks near the middle of the oven. Roll a heaping tablespoon of the chilled dough between the palms of your hands into a walnut-sized ball and place it on one of the lined baking sheets. Repeat with the remaining dough. Roll the pastry balls, four or five at a time, in the egg-wash mixture and then in the chopped nuts. Space the pastries 1 inch apart on the prepared baking sheets.

6 Bake the pastries for 9 minutes, switch and rotate the pans, and bake for another 5 to 8 minutes, or until they are set and the bottoms are lightly browned. Remove the pans from the oven and immediately pierce the center of each pastry with a wooden skewer (to make holes for stringing the pastries). Cool the pans on racks for 1 hour, then store the pastries in an airtight container until ready to assemble and ship the gift.

wrapping it up

The pastries are strung onto paper ribbon or colored twine between foil or paper cupcake liners, and then they are wrapped in colored tissue for shipping.

suggested supplies

48 foil or paper cupcake liners

upholstery or trussing needle

colored twine or paper ribbon

colored tissue paper or cellophane

1 small shipping box

how to string caravan bells

Stack the pastries in pairs between pairs of cupcake liners. Thread an upholstery or trussing needle with the twine and string the pastries and cupcake liners onto the twine. Knot both ends of the twine to hold the pastries in place and roll the finished string of pastries tightly in tissue or cellophane. Place the wrapped pastries in a small shipping box and surround them with crumpled tissue paper.

big and soft
rum raisin *cookies*

overall prep time:
45 minutes

active prep time:
20 minutes

easy

inexpensive

freezes well

ships well

can be doubled

shelf life: 10 days wrapped
and stored in an airtight
container

makes: 3 dozen

In creating these super—and super-sized—cookies, I tried several combinations of spirits and dried fruits, and I loved them all. Large, soft cookies are ideal for shipping: They won't break, and, in this case, the rum-soaked raisins keep the cookies moist in transit. For a tasty variation, try substituting golden raisins and a good-quality Spanish sherry, or chopped dates and Cognac, for the dark raisins and dark rum.

1⅓ cups dark raisins

½ cup dark rum

1 tablespoon vanilla extract

½ teaspoon ground mace

1 teaspoon grated nutmeg

½ cup (1 stick) unsalted butter, softened but cool

½ cup tightly packed dark brown sugar

½ cup tightly packed light brown sugar

1 large egg

2¼ cups all-purpose flour

½ teaspoon baking powder

½ teaspoon baking soda

⅓ cup turbinado sugar

1 Combine the raisins, rum, vanilla, mace, and ½ teaspoon of the nutmeg in a small pan. Bring the mixture to a boil over medium heat, cover the pan, and simmer for 3 minutes. Set the pan aside to cool.

2 Combine the butter and the brown sugars in a bowl and cream them with a mixer on medium-high speed for 3 minutes. Add the egg and beat for another minute. Add the raisins and their liquid to the mixture. Beat the dough just long enough to distribute the raisins evenly.

3 Preheat the oven to 375°F and line two cookie sheets with parchment paper. Whisk the flour, baking powder, and baking soda together in a bowl. With the mixer set

at low speed, gradually add the dry ingredients to the creamed butter mixture until the flour is incorporated.

4 Place large scoops (a heaping ¼ cup each) of dough 2 inches apart on the prepared cookie sheets. Sprinkle each cookie with ¼ teaspoon of turbinado sugar, followed by a pinch of the remaining nutmeg.

5 Bake the cookies on the middle racks of the oven for 6 minutes. Switch and rotate the pans and bake for another 6 to 8 minutes, or until the cookies are set and the bottoms are lightly browned. Set the cookie sheets on baking racks to cool; do not remove the cookies until they have cooled completely. Store them in an airtight container until you are ready to assemble and ship the gift.

wrapping it up

Repurposed cylindrical food containers like oatmeal and raisin cartons make excellent gift boxes for shipping cookies, cupcakes, and candied nuts. They are nearly airtight, fairly solid, and lightweight. Put each cookie in an extra-large paper cupcake liner or a shallow "muffin top" cupcake liner before adding to the finished cartons. An oatmeal container will hold about a dozen of these large cookies.

suggested supplies for each dozen cookies

1 round raisin or oatmeal box

brown or white craft paper

double-face tape

1 gift card

waxed string or cotton twine

12 extra-large paper cupcake liners or shallow "muffin top" cupcake liners

how to wrap a raisin or oatmeal box

Measure the height and circumference of the round box you are using and cut a rectangle of craft paper 2 inches higher than the box and 3 to 4 inches longer than the circumference of the box. Apply two lines of double face tape to the outside of the box, a third inside the bottom rim, and a fourth around the inside carton lip. Center the box on one short side of the paper rectangle and tightly roll it one complete turn in the craft paper. You will have a 1-inch border of paper at the top and bottom of the carton and 3 to 4 inches free on the side. Make several small cuts in the craft paper around the top and bottom borders and fold the paper over the top of the carton and under the bottom rim, pressing it into the tape. Take the free end of the paper and fold the corners toward the center, forming a point. Roll this paper tightly around the box, secure it with some double-face tape, and slip the gift card just under the tip of the paper point. Wind a length of waxed string or cotton twine around the carton several times to hold the pointed flap tightly over the gift card, and finish with a slipknot or simple bow. Cut a round of craft paper to cover the carton's plastic top. Stack the cookies in their paper baking cups in the box and seal it tightly.

lulu's tin-can
lemon-lime cake

overall prep time:
35 minutes

active prep time:
10 minutes

easy

inexpensive

can be frozen

ships well

shelf life: 3 days at room
temperature tightly wrapped

makes: 1 cake

A 48-ounce (6-cup) can is a great leak-proof container for baking and shipping this heavily glazed citrus cake. The cake arrives fresh, moist, and uncrushed just about anywhere you send it.

1 lemon

1 lime

½ cup granulated sugar

½ cup (1 stick) unsalted butter, chilled and cut into 8 slices

2 large eggs

1 scant cup all-purpose flour (1 cup less about 1 tablespoon)

1 teaspoon baking powder

½ teaspoon baking soda

1 tablespoon unsalted butter, softened

1 can (48 ounces), cleaned and dried

½ cup confectioners' sugar

1 Using a sharp swivel-bladed peeler, remove the zest from the lemon and lime, leaving any white pith behind. Juice the lemon and lime, combine the two juices, and set aside.

2 Combine the lemon and lime zests and the sugar in the bowl of a food processor fitted with the steel chopping blade. Process the zests and sugar for about 20 seconds, or until is the mixture has a coarse, mealy texture. Add the chilled butter slices and process until the butter softens and the mixture is fluffy and smooth, about 2 minutes. Pause to scrape down the sides of the work bowl and add the eggs one at a time through the feed tube, processing for about 15 seconds after each addition. In a small bowl, combine the flour, baking powder, and baking soda. Add the flour mixture to the batter and process with 15 long pulses of the machine.

3 Preheat the oven to 350°F and place an oven rack on the next-to-lowest level. Cut an 11 × 15-inch strip of parchment paper and butter one side with the softened

butter. Liberally coat the interior of the 48-ounce can with nonstick cooking spray. Line the can with the buttered parchment paper (buttered side in), which will form a 4-inch collar above the top of the can. Carefully spoon the batter into the prepared can, or use a pastry bag with a plain 1-inch tip to pipe the batter into the can (the latter approach helps you avoid smearing the parchment collar). Run a long-handled spatula through the batter to eliminate gaps or air bubbles. Tap the can on the counter to further settle the batter and eliminate air pockets.

4 Bake the cake for 1 hour. Insert a wooden skewer through the center of the cake. If it comes away clean, the cake is done. If not, bake for another 10 minutes and test again. Set the can directly on a rack to cool.

5 To make the glaze, combine 1/3 cup of the reserved lemon-lime juice and the confectioners' sugar. Whisk the mixture until it is smooth. Poke several holes in the top of the hot cake with a wooden skewer and ladle the glaze over the cake, a couple of tablespoonfuls at a time, until all the glaze has been absorbed. Set the glazed cake back on the rack to cool completely. Wipe the cooled can with a damp cloth to remove any buttery fingerprints or smudges of batter, and dry it before wrapping the cake. Trim away any parts of the parchment collar that are browned and brittle, making the collar flush with the top of the cake. Wrap the entire canned cake in plastic wrap and set aside at room temperature until you are ready to assemble and deliver the gift.

wrapping it up

The can provides protective packaging for the cake. Additional wrapping paper and ribbon dress it up in style.

suggested supplies

1 square (5 inches) plastic wrap

1 square (about 6 inches) parchment paper

double-face tape

1 rectangle (7 × 15 inches) wrapping paper, craft paper, or fabric

ribbon, punched-paper strips, or stickers, for embellishing the can (optional)

1 large square cellophane

1 wire twist tie

ribbon

how to decorate a tea-cake can

If the cake has been stored wrapped in plastic wrap, remove the plastic wrap. Lay the 5-inch square of plastic wrap directly onto the surface of the cake and press it into place. Lay the parchment square over the plastic wrap. Using double-face tape, tape it down onto the outside of the can at the corners. Cover the can with the rectangle of paper or fabric, attaching it with double-face tape. Embellish the can with ribbon, punched-paper strips, or stickers, if you choose. Center the cake in its can on the square of cellophane, gather the cellophane tightly up around the cake, and secure it with a twist tie. Cover the twist tie with ribbon, finishing it with a bow.

maui *macadamia* munch

Think of this as trail mix for couch potatoes with expensive tastes. Maui munch is buttery, sweet, and chock full of tropical delicacies like macadamia nuts and dried banana chips. No matter how much you make, it will disappear far too quickly.

3 tablespoons unsalted butter, softened

4 cups roughly chopped macadamia nuts

4 cups dried banana chips

2 cups flaked coconut, preferably unsweetened

1 cup (2 sticks) unsalted butter, cut in cubes

2 cups firmly packed light brown sugar

½ cup light corn syrup

½ teaspoon cream of tartar

½ teaspoon baking soda

1   Using the softened butter, generously butter two large sheet pans at least 10 × 15 inches in size. Evenly distribute the macadamia nuts, banana chips, and coconut over the entire surface of the buttered pans.

2   Combine the cubed butter, brown sugar, corn syrup, and cream of tartar in a large, heavy saucepan and stir until the sugar has dissolved. Attach a candy thermometer to the inside of the pan and cook the mixture over medium heat, without stirring, until the candy thermometer registers 300° to 310°F (hard crack stage).

3   Remove the pan from the heat and quickly stir in the baking soda until the hot syrup is light and foamy. Immediately pour the sugar mixture over the nut mixture on the buttered baking sheets. Use a buttered wooden spoon to press the nut mixture into the hot syrup, making it as flat as possible.

4   Cool the pans completely, then break the mixture into bite-size pieces. Store the macadamia munch in an airtight container until you are ready to assemble and ship the gift.

wrapping it up

This paper rendition of a Hawaiian shirt won't wrinkle, crease, or crumple when packed for travel.

suggested supplies

1 sheet (8 × 10 inches) card stock

rubber stamps and ink pad

1 heavy-duty clear plastic jar (½ gallon size) with an airtight lid

paper leis, available at craft and party stores

tissue paper in bright tropical colors

1 shipping box, slightly larger than the plastic jar

packing tape

how to make a hawaiian shirt

Make a line drawing of a short-sleeve shirt freehand, or find a simple shirt image in a child's coloring book or paper doll book to copy. Use your printer or a copy machine to scale the shirt image onto the card stock to fit the inside of the plastic jar. Rubber-stamp large-scale design motifs in wild colors onto the "shirt," and use a colored marker to delineate the collar and front placket of the shirt. (Visit my website, DinahsGourmetGifts.com, for an example of a simple shirt drawing.) You can use the back of the "shirt" as a gift card. Insert the shirt image into the jar, colored side out, and smooth it against the inside of the jar. Fill the jar with macadamia munch and tightly cover the jar. Place the jar in the shipping box and surround it with enough paper leis and crumpled tissue paper to prevent the jar from shifting in the box. Seal the box tightly with packing tape.

poster-sized
peach leather

A really big sheet of peach fruit leather all rolled up and mailed in a shipping tube is a great long-distance gift for families with children. The grownups in charge will appreciate that this treat is made from fresh fruit and a good deal healthier than most sweet snacks.

overall prep time: 6 hours

active prep time:
45 minutes

moderately easy

inexpensive

can be frozen

ships well

do not double

shelf life: 1 month at room temperature tightly wrapped; 1 year in freezer tightly wrapped

makes: just under 1 pound

3 pounds ripe peaches, to yield 8 cups of peeled and diced fruit

1 cup superfine sugar

1 tablespoon peach or apricot jam

1. Bring a large kettle of water to a boil; have ready a large bowl of ice and water. Peel the peaches by blanching a few at a time in the boiling water for 60 seconds. Using a slotted spoon, transfer the peaches to the bowl of ice and water. The peels should slip off easily after 5 minutes in the iced water. Halve and pit the peeled peaches and dice them over a large bowl to collect all the juices. Measure the diced fruit and all the juice; you need 8 firmly packed cups of diced fruit and juice.

2. Combine the diced peaches and the sugar in a large, heavy stockpot and stir to distribute the sugar. Set the stockpot over medium-low heat and slowly bring the peaches to a boil. Cook, stirring constantly and gently, for 8 to 10 minutes. Remove from the heat, stir in the jam, and transfer the mixture to a shallow dish to cool for 10 minutes.

recipe continues

3 Preheat the oven to 170°F and prop the oven door slightly ajar with a wooden spoon. Pour the slightly cooled peaches into a blender or the work bowl of a food processor fitted with the steel chopping blade. Puree the peaches until they are completely smooth. Line a 12 × 15-inch sheet pan with heavy-duty plastic wrap. Pour the peach puree into the prepared sheet pan and tilt the pan back and forth to spread the puree into a thin, even layer over the surface of the pan.

4 Dry the peach puree on the center rack of the oven for 2 hours. Rotate the pan and continue drying for 3 more hours, or until the leather peels easily away from a corner of the plastic wrap. Set the pan on a rack to cool.

5 Spread a 12 × 17-inch sheet of plastic wrap out smoothly on a work surface. Loosen the edges of plastic wrap from the sides of the pan and invert the pan over the fresh plastic wrap on the work surface. Discard the plastic wrap used for cooking and drying the fruit leather, and replace it with a fresh sheet of plastic wrap. Tightly seal and fold the edges of the plastic wrap over the fruit leather, roll it up, and store it an airtight container until you are ready to assemble and ship the gift.

wrapping it up

Opaque smooth-surface markers can be used to write a gift message directly on the plastic wrap covering the fruit leather. Here, you roll the fruit leather up in a poster, a wall calendar, or in plain card stock and tape the ends to hold it tightly around the fruit leather.

suggested supplies

1 poster, wall calendar, or large sheet of plain card stock	**2 wire twist ties**
	wired ribbon
1 large sheet colored cellophane, colored tissue paper, or thin wrapping paper	**1 shipping tube with plastic cap**

how to wrap a roll of fruit leather

Place the poster, calendar, or sheet of card stock on top of the plastic-wrapped fruit leather and roll up tightly. Center the roll on the sheet of cellophane, tissue paper, or wrapping paper and roll it up tightly. Twist both ends of the outer wrapper tightly and secure them with the wire twist ties. Cover the wires with ribbon and finish each end with a tightly knotted bow. Slip the gift-wrapped peach leather inside the shipping tube and seal it tightly with the plastic cap provided. Cover both ends of the sealed shipping tube with masking tape to keep the package airtight for shipping.

fiesta by mail

Tequila-plumped raisins and spicy hot-roasted pepitas in stand-up burlap bags with wooden scoops can be sent anywhere—north or south of the border. The pepitas, which are spiced-up pumpkin seeds, are just about perfect with cold beer or frozen margaritas, and the raisins and pepitas are especially nice together.

overall prep time: 4½ hours

active prep time: 35 to 40 minutes

easy

inexpensive

do not freeze

ships well

can be doubled or tripled

shelf life: 2 weeks in an airtight container for raisins; 3 weeks in an airtight container for pepitas

makes: 3 cups drunken raisins and 2 cups seasoned pepitas

FOR THE PEPITAS:

1 lime

½ teaspoon ground cayenne, or to taste

¼ teaspoon sea salt

1 tablespoon olive oil

3 to 5 small dried red chile peppers

2 cups roasted and salted pepitas

FOR THE DRUNKEN RAISINS:

6 tablespoons gold tequila

1½ cups golden raisins

1½ cups dark raisins

2 tablespoons peanut oil

1 tablespoon Grand Marnier

1 tablespoon freshly squeezed lime juice

1 tablespoon grated lime zest

2 teaspoons sea salt

1. To make the pepitas, preheat the oven to 140°F and prop the oven door slightly ajar with a wooden spoon. Juice the lime, reserving the reamed peel, and combine 2 tablespoons of the lime juice with the cayenne, sea salt, and olive oil in a medium bowl. Using a mortar and pestle or the back of a heavy wooden spoon, crush the dried chile peppers and add them to the bowl along with the roasted pepitas.

2. Toss the pepitas with the seasonings until they are evenly coated, then spread them out on a baking sheet lined with parchment paper. Dry the pepitas in the oven for 4 hours, rotating the pan every hour. Meanwhile, use your fingers to remove the fibers and any traces of fruit from the lime peel, then slice the peel into very thin julienne strips. Set aside until the pepitas come out of the oven.

recipe continues

3 While the pepitas continue drying, make the drunken raisins. Combine the tequila and raisins in a sauté pan and bring them to a simmer over low heat. Drain the raisins, reserving the tequila, and blot them dry. Add the peanut oil to the same sauté pan and increase the heat to medium. When the oil is hot (but not smoking), add the raisins. Swirl the pan to coat the raisins in oil and heat them through. Carefully add the reserved tequila, the Grand Marnier, and the lime juice. Cook the raisins until all the liquid in the pan has evaporated, about 10 minutes.

4 Turn the raisins out onto a baking sheet lined with paper towels. Let the raisins cool and dry for at least 2 hours. Toss the raisins with the lime zest and salt until they are evenly coated. Store the raisins in an airtight container until you are ready to assemble and ship the gift.

5 Add the reserved lime-peel strips to the warm pepitas as soon as they come out of the oven and toss them among the pepitas to combine well. Set the pan on a baking rack to cool. Store the cooled pepitas in an airtight container until you are ready to assemble and ship the gift.

wrapping it up

Since these little burlap bags stand upright, they are suitable for serving the raisins and pepitas as well as shipping them, especially if you attach a small wooden scoop to each bag. The pepitas and the raisins should be packed in plastic bags and sealed tightly before enclosing them in the burlap bags.

suggested supplies

2 rectangles (about 9 × 18 inches each) burlap	**2 rectangles (about 3 × 4 inches each) cardboard**
polyester thread	**2 plastic bags**
tapestry needle	**2 small wooden scoops**
thin hemp cord or waxed string	**card stock or adhesive-backed labels**

how to make a burlap snack sack

Use a polyester thread and a very short stitch when stitching burlap by hand or with a machine.

For each bag, topstitch the short ends of a burlap rectangle so they will not unravel. Fold the rectangle in half so that the topstitched ends meet at the top and the folded end is at the bottom. Pin both long sides of the rectangle together. Sew a double seam down each of the pinned sides 1 inch from the fabric's edge. Remove the pins and unravel the burlap up to the stitched lines. Stand the bag up and flatten the bottom until it is about 2 inches wide. This will cause the outside edges to form triangular extensions on either side of the bottom.

Measure and mark a point 1½ inches from the apex of the triangular extensions along the center seam. Stitch across the bases of the triangles at this point to form gussets. Fold the gussets down under the bag along the seams you have just sewn, so that the tips of each gusset point toward one another and almost meet at the center of the bag's bottom. Use a large tapestry needle threaded with the hemp cord to join the two gusset points with three or four tight stitches. Push a cardboard rectangle into the bottom of the gusseted bag, to provide definition and stability to the base. Repeat to make a second bag. Pack the pepitas and raisins into the plastic bags and place them in the burlap bags. Stitch the burlap bags and plastic bags closed together with the hemp cord. Wind the handles of the scoops with the cord and stitch a scoop to each burlap bag. You can make labels of card stock and sew them to the bags, or apply adhesive-backed labels to each bag instead.

resources

This section contains my recommendations for the best online and brick-and-mortar sources of containers, craft supplies, ingredients, and tools for your homemade gifts.

BAKING SUPPLIES, CONTAINERS, AND TOOLS

THE BAKER'S KITCHEN
thebakerskitchen.net
419-381-9693

Excellent source for cake boards, doilies, plain bakery boxes, cellophane cookie and candy bags, and cupcake liners in every conceivable size, shape, and color.

COPPERGIFTS.COM
620-421-0654

My favorite source for cookie cutters, with a great variety in both tin and copper.

KEREKES BAKEWARE
bakedeco.com
800-525-5556

Cake boxes, cake boards, baking cups, and every sort of baking mold or pan you might want.

KING ARTHUR FLOUR
kingarthurflour.com
800-827-6836

A wide range of baking supplies.

BASKET CONTAINERS
(including creels and trugs)

ARTISTIC GIFT BASKETS
artisticgiftbaskets.com
866-360-GIFT

This is the only website I have found that has a decorative small version of a fishing creel basket.

BARBER'S BASKETS
barbersbaskets.com
541-888-4066

Quality trugs at reasonable prices.

COOKWARE CONTAINERS
(including porcelain ramekins, terrines, pâté molds, and casseroles)

CHEFS
chefscatalog.com
800-338-3232

An excellent resource for hard-to-find cooking gadgets and tools as well as reasonably priced casseroles, terrines, and molds that can be easily converted into unique containers for gifts.

CREATIVE COOKWARE
creativecookware.com
866-291-9199

A great source for affordable ceramic and porcelain casseroles and terrines, including hard-to-find heavy French tinned terrines and pans.

SUR LA TABLE
surlatable.com
800-243-0852

A terrific assortment of good-quality porcelain containers, terrines, casseroles, and bowls.

CRAFT SUPPLIES AND TOOLS

(including papers, embellishments, trims, paper punches, and stamping tools)

A.C. MOORE ARTS AND CRAFTS

acmoore.com
888-226-6673

East Coast chain of craft stores with a wide variety of supplies in stores and online.

CREATE FOR LESS

createforless.com
866-333-4463

One of the most comprehensive and affordable online sources for all types of craft tools and materials, including unique and affordable paper punches.

DRY NATURE DESIGNS

drynature.com
212-695-8911

The definitive source for dried leaves, flowers, barks, and woods, including birch-bark sheets.

FUN SCRAPPIN

fun-scrappin.com
909-338-9394

Affordable papers in wonderful patterns, including realistic wood patterns, and a wide selection of affordable labels.

HOBBY LOBBY

hobbylobby.com
405-745-6053

A nationwide chain of craft stores, with a comprehensive online store as well.

MICHAELS

michaels.com
800-642-4235

A nationwide chain of craft stores, with a comprehensive online store as well.

STAMPENDOUS

stampendous.com
800-869-0474

A great resource for all your stamping needs, with low prices.

TINSEL TRADING COMPANY

tinseltrading.com
212-730-1030

Fabulous embellishments, ribbons, tassels, beaded leaves, and flowers, at good prices.

TROY SCHOOL AND OFFICE PRODUCTS

troydryerase.com
888-853-7279

Self-adhesive dry-erase paper and other innovative paper products.

WOODWORKS LTD.

craftparts.com
800-722-0311

This website will open up a world of possibilities for making any gift more upscale. I use this site for very nice wooden spoons, dippers, spreaders, and scoops, as well as embellishments like lids, plugs, balls, and knobs.

INGREDIENTS

AMAZON.COM

I never cease to be amazed at the scope of this site: I have yet to search for an ingredient or tool that cannot be purchased through Amazon. It is also a wonderful place to acquaint yourself with all the resources available to the cook and the crafter.

BEANILLA

beanilla.com
888-261-3384

Beanilla offers a huge selection of vanilla beans at varying prices. You can also locate hard-to-find vanilla products like vanilla powder and paste here.

FRIEDA'S INC.

friedas.com
800-241-1771

One of the leading sources for unusual or hard-to-find ingredients. Some of their products are found in major supermarkets, but the website offers the full product line and a directory of their retailers nationwide.

HAMPTON FARMS

hamptonfarms.com
757-654-1400

You can buy raw, blanched, red-skinned peanuts online at this website, or check the list of retail locations nationwide that offer Hampton Farms products.

MOUNTAIN ROSE HERBS

mountainroseherbs.com
800-879-3337

Every conceivable ingredient for making herb teas and an equally impressive variety of tea-making gadgets, tools, and containers. You will find paper tea bags with heat-seal closures and comprehensive advice and instructions for making your own tea blends.

SPICES INC.

spicesinc.com
888-762-8642

A user-friendly and informative website that offers an impressive array of herbs, spices, and seasoning blends, including a large selection of hard-to-find Asian and Middle Eastern blends.

SWEDEN'S BEST

swedensbest.com
877-864-8503

An online store for Swedish and Norwegian products, including pearl sugar.

GLASS CONTAINERS

(including canning jars, jelly jars, infusing bottles, beverage servers, elaborate apothecary jars, stacked or terraced jars, ice buckets, and spice jars)

CLASSIC HOSTESS

classichostess.com
888-280-6539

The largest selection of beverage servers and drink dispensers available online. Also has top-quality and unique cake stands, cupcake servers, and candy containers.

FILLMORE CONTAINER

fillmorecontainer.com
866-345-5527

One of the few places I have found that sells the perfectly plain canning jars with plain white enameled lids that I prefer for all my canning gifts.

FREUND CONTAINER AND SUPPLY

freundcontainer.com
877-637-3863

A one-stop website for glass, plastic, and tin jars and bottles in every shape and size.

INFUSIONJARS.COM

501-639-8639

If you plan to make and give infused wines, flavored vodkas, or fortified wines you should check out this website for its useful information and its large variety of jars, bottles, and beverage servers.

MY WONDER JAR

mywonderjar.com
954-937-4746

The definitive source for the best priced and best quality Kilner jars (glass jars with wire bale clamp lids).

METAL CONTAINERS

(including woven wire baskets and bottle totes, seamless tin boxes, cookie tins, and multiple sizes of galvanized tubs, pails, and bins)

COOKIETINS.COM

e-cookietins.com
832-518-2800

The tins are of excellent quality, the shapes and colors are endless, the prices are very low, and the service is excellent.

THE LUCKY CLOVER TRADING CO.

luckyclovertrading.com
800-338-5825

Wire baskets and a variety of trays, including leatherette trays that are fabulous and unbelievably inexpensive. Check out their packing supplies and gift-basket accessories as well.

MISCELLANEOUS CONTAINERS

If you prefer brick-and-mortar shopping to Web surfing, any of the six national chain stores listed below is a great place to find a wide variety of containers for food gifts. Check their websites for the location nearest you.

BED BATH AND BEYOND
bedbathandbeyond.com

THE CONTAINER STORE
containerstore.com

HOME GOODS
homegoods.com

IKEA
ikea.com

PIER 1 IMPORTS
pier1.com

WORLD MARKET
worldmarket.com

Other Sources

BEAUCOUP
beau-coup.com
877-988-2328

Specializes in favor-sized or individual containers, which include everything from miniature bamboo steamers to gumball machines. You can also order custom stamps and personalized labels from this site. If you dream up a theme, rest assured they have containers to match.

CRAFTAMERICA.COM
800-407-5090

The largest selection of chip-wood boxes and tin boxes and buckets, this is a one-stop shop for just about every sort of container at exceptionally reasonable prices.

ECONOMY HANDICRAFTS
economyhandicrafts.com
800-216-1601

An excellent source for crafting materials and small bulk quantities of unfinished and unique containers at deeply discounted prices.

FACTORY DIRECT CRAFT
factorydirectcraft.com
800-252-5223

A great bargain resource for every sort of unfinished container in wood, tin, and pasteboard.

ORIGIN CRAFTS
origincrafts.com
914-329-8446

Purveyors of unique containers and luxury serviceware, like crystal beverage servers and stacked or terraced containers. The prices are not prohibitive for the quality and choices offered.

SAVEONCRAFTS
save-on-crafts.com
831-768-8428

An extraordinarily comprehensive website, including distinctive items like birch bark–covered flower pots and cupcake and cake stands. Beautiful beverage servers and tiered apothecary jars are on this site at terrific prices, along with great-looking plain glass bottles for flavored vodka, homemade beverages, and flavored oils and vinegars.

SKS
sks-bottle.com
518-880-6980

A huge selection of glass, plastic, and metal jars and bottles, plus lots of lids, caps, and closures.

NOTIONS, SUPPLIES, AND SPECIALTY FABRICS

HANCOCK FABRICS
hancockfabrics.com
877-322-7427

A chain of fabric stores, with a comprehensive online store as well, with a full range of sewing notions and harder-to-find fabrics like canvas and ripstop.

JO-ANN FABRIC AND CRAFT STORES

joann.com
888-739-4120

A nationwide chain of fabric stores, with a comprehensive online store as well, with a full range of sewing notions and harder-to-find fabrics like burlap and tulle.

PAPER CONTAINERS

(including bakery boxes, candy boxes, to-go boxes, ice-cream cartons, and tea bags)

BAKINGBOXES.COM

800-681-1074

This website specializes in coordinated boxes, tissue papers, stickers, and ribbons in your choice of colors. Everything can be monogrammed, in a wide variety of fonts and styles.

CPS CONTAINER AND PACKAGING SUPPLY

containerandpackaging.com
800-473-4144

While catering to the commercial food industry, this site allows individuals access to a wide variety of great looking, functional food containers at wholesale prices if you can meet the minimum order requirements.

GARNISH

thinkgarnish.com
508-832-4431

Simple and chic containers, labels, and packaging materials. I especially like their plain adhesive labels, cardboard take-out containers, and waxed tissue paper.

PACKAGING SUPERSOURCE

usbox.com
973-481-2000

Comprehensive and affordable website for straightforward packaging, including take-out containers, tubes, tins, tubs, and labels, plus crates and mailers.

PAPER MART

papermart.com
800-745-8800

Paper will always be the most economical choice for gift-wrapping food gifts, but this website makes paper packaging look anything but economical. I depend on this website for many of my standard supplies, especially when I am mailing food gifts.

THE WEBSTAURANT STORE

webstaurantstore.com
717-392-7472

Huge inventory of restaurant supply items at wholesale prices, but available to individuals. A good source for classic white-paper ice-cream containers in several sizes, and bamboo disposable spoons and forks in bulk.

PLASTIC CONTAINERS

(including Bento boxes, acrylic boxes, ice buckets, and hot and cold beverage containers)

LAPTOP LUNCHES

laptoplunches.com
831-457-0301

A wide range of items for traveling food, including Bento boxes, ice packs, cold or hot drink containers, and insulated totes.

ORGANIZE.COM

800-600-9817

You can find a lot reasonably priced containers in the craft, cleaning, kitchen, storage, and laundry sections of this website that are highly adaptable and affordable alternatives for food gifts, such as large acrylic cookie jars and 4 x 5-inch acrylic storage boxes.

UNFINISHED WOOD CONTAINERS

(including boxes, tubs, salt boxes, bentwood lidded boxes, chipboard containers, berry boxes, disposable baking baskets, trays, and spice boxes)

FANTE'S KITCHEN WARES SHOP

fantes.com
800-443-2683

Large selection of covered salt boxes.

HOTCRAFT

hotcraft.com
800-828-0359

Supplies for painting anything and everything, plus an impressive array of baskets, wooden bowls, chargers, boxes, and both tin and galvanized-metal containers.

KITCHEN KAPERS

kitchenkapers.com
800-455-5567

Small wooden salt and herb boxes.

REPLITIQUES

replitiques.com
717-938-3503

One of the only online sources for traditional hanging wooden salt boxes.

TECHNOBAKE

technobake.com
866-856-2979

The largest assortment of Panibois and baking baskets available online. Reasonable prices, especially if you buy larger quantities.

TEXAS BASKET COMPANY

texasbasket.com
800-657-2200

The best source for simple market-stand berry boxes and other small market baskets.

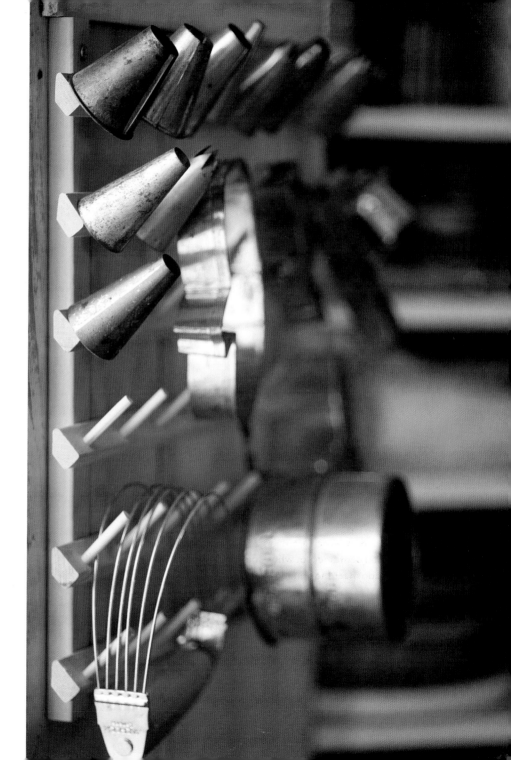

TURN OF THE CENTURY WOOD PRODUCTS

turnofthecentury-in.com

765-436-2647

Some of the loveliest and finest unfinished turned-wood boxes, bowls, and baskets.

VIKING WOODCRAFTS

vikingwoodcrafts.com

800-328-0116

A cost-conscious alternative. Features a very large assortment of unfinished solid wood boxes and containers with hinged lids.

WEBSITES WITH IMAGES AND TEMPLATES FOR DOWNLOADING

THE GRAPHICS FAIRY

graphicsfairy.blogspot.com

An addictive blog with new vintage graphics posted daily for downloading, an archive of thousands of images, craft tutorials, and inspirational ideas.

MIRKWOOD DESIGNS

ruthannzaroff.com

This website offers a wonderful assortment of box templates that you can download free of charge.

acknowledgments

EVERY BOOK IS A COLLABORATIVE EFFORT ON SOME LEVEL. It is in great measure the skills, talent, and generosity of others that made this book a reality.

Rosemary Stimola is an amazing person, loyal friend, and literary agent extraordinaire. Her unflagging faith in me and in this project influenced every aspect of the book. Alison Shaw's remarkable talent shines through every image, and I feel the book is as much hers as mine. I value her friendship as well as her extraordinary ability. Thelma Agopian has selflessly cast herself in a supporting role throughout my culinary career, though she is the finer cook. She worked tirelessly to help me create and test the recipes that form the core of this book. Over a span exceeding 30 years, Thelma has taught me the best things I know of food and friendship. A long time ago I brought out Vinton McCabe's inner cook, he brought out my inner writer, and a special bond was formed in the process. Vinton ushered my first articles into print, and he has been an invaluable sounding board for this project. Charlie Layman gives the term "technical support" new meaning. He always made sure I had the tools I needed and taught me how to use them. Despite his very busy schedule, he and his associate Karla Ross personally oversaw every detail of my proposal and manuscript. My dear friend Dee Dee Clarke was a daily source of support and encouragement and her husband, Sam, was my favorite "taster." John Richards responded to the urgent calls precipitated by my technical ineptitude, fixing every glitch and finding every lost document in record-breaking time.

I am grateful to have had an editor of Daniel Rosenberg's caliber for my project. Jane Dornbusch is surely the most extraordinary of copyeditors. Virginia Downes's art direction has beautifully enhanced both Alison's work and my own. The skill and experience of these talented individuals made the book immeasurably better.

I want to thank Bailiwick Antiques of Middleburg, Virginia; The Ashley Inn of Paris, Virginia; and Mr. and Mrs. William Clinton of Scuffleburg, Virginia, for giving Alison and me free rein and unlimited access to their wonderful properties for photo shoots.

I cannot thank any of these people sufficiently for their help, but I hope that the final product justifies their faith in me and their efforts on my behalf.

measurement equivalents

Please note that all conversions are approximate.

LIQUID CONVERSIONS

U.S.	IMPERIAL	METRIC
1 tsp	—	5 ml
1 tbs	½ fl oz	15 ml
2 tbs	1 fl oz	30 ml
3 tbs	1½ fl oz	45 ml
¼ cup	2 fl oz	60 ml
⅓ cup	2½ fl oz	75 ml
⅓ cup + 1 tbs	3 fl oz	90 ml
⅓ cup + 2 tbs	3½ fl oz	100 ml
½ cup	4 fl oz	120 ml
⅔ cup	5 fl oz	150 ml
¾ cup	6 fl oz	180 ml
¾ cup + 2 tbs	7 fl oz	200 ml
1 cup	8 fl oz	240 ml
1 cup + 2 tbs	9 fl oz	275 ml
1¼ cups	10 fl oz	300 ml
1⅓ cups	11 fl oz	325 ml
1½ cups	12 fl oz	350 ml
1⅔ cups	13 fl oz	375 ml
1¾ cups	14 fl oz	400 ml
1¾ cups + 2 tbs	15 fl oz	450 ml
2 cups (1 pint)	16 fl oz	475 ml
2½ cups	20 fl oz	600 ml
3 cups	24 fl oz	720 ml
4 cups (1 quart)	32 fl oz	945 ml

(1,000 ml is 1 liter)

WEIGHT CONVERSIONS

U.S./U.K.	METRIC
½ oz	14 g
1 oz	28 g
1½ oz	43 g
2 oz	57 g
2½ oz	71 g
3 oz	85 g
3½ oz	100 g
4 oz	113 g
5 oz	142 g
6 oz	170 g
7 oz	200 g
8 oz	227 g
9 oz	255 g
10 oz	284 g
11 oz	312 g
12 oz	340 g
13 oz	368 g
14 oz	400 g
15 oz	425 g
1 lb	454 g

OVEN TEMPERATURE CONVERSIONS

°F	GAS MARK	°C
250	½	120
275	1	140
300	2	150
325	3	165
350	4	180
375	5	190
400	6	200
425	7	220
450	8	230
475	9	240
500	10	260
550	Broil	290

index

Note: Page references in *italics* indicate photographs. See page 304 for Index of Craft/Wrapping Projects.

index of craft/wrapping projects

Note: Page references in *italics* indicate
photographs. See page 299 for index of
recipes and ingredients.